SHADOW OF THE DICTATORS

AD 1925-1950

THE WORLD AT WAR
EUROPE

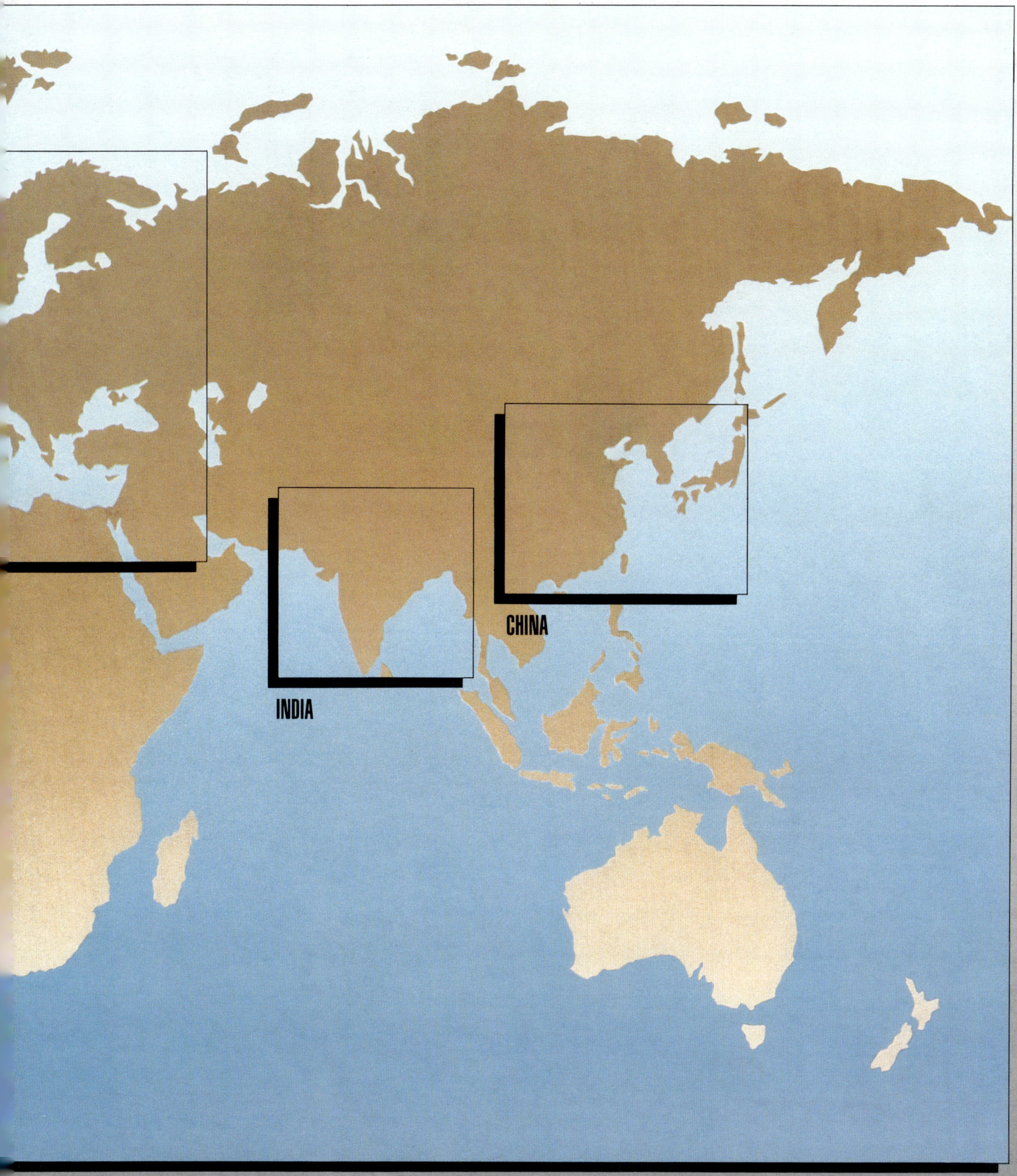
CHINA
INDIA

TIME
LIFE
BOOKS

This volume is one in the Time-Life series
HISTORY OF THE WORLD

SHADOW OF THE DICTATORS

AD 1925-1950

BY THE EDITORS OF TIME-LIFE BOOKS

TIME-LIFE BOOKS, AMSTERDAM

TIME-LIFE BOOKS

EUROPEAN EDITOR: Ellen Phillips
Design Director: Ed Skyner
Director of Editorial Resources: Samantha Hill
Chief Sub-Editor: Ilse Gray

TIME-LIFE HISTORY OF THE WORLD

SERIES EDITOR: Tony Allan

Editorial Staff for *Shadow of the Dictators*
Editor: Windsor Chorlton
Designer: Lynne Brown
Writers: Douglas Amrine, Chris Middleton
Researchers: Paul Dowswell, Caroline Lucas, Caroline Smith
Sub-Editors: Frances Dixon, Christine Noble
Design Assistant: Rachel Gibson
Editorial Assistant: Molly Sutherland

Picture Department
Picture Administrator: Amanda Hindley
Picture Coordinator: Zoë Spencer

Editorial Production
Chief: Maureen Kelly
Production Assistant: Samantha Hill
Editorial Department: Theresa John, Debra Lelliott

Second European English language printing 1992.

ISBN 0 7054 0990 2
TIME-LIFE is a trademark of Time Warner Inc. U.S.A.

CONSULTANTS

General:
GEOFFREY PARKER, Professor of History, University of Illinois, Urbana-Champaign, Illinois.

CHRISTOPHER BAYLY, Reader in Modern Indian History, St. Catharine's College, Cambridge University.

Europe:
DENIS MACK SMITH, former Senior Research Fellow of All Souls College, Oxford University.

The World at War:
H. P. WILLMOTT, Senior Lecturer, Department of War Studies, Royal Military Academy, Sandhurst.

India:
CHRISTOPHER BAYLY, Reader in Modern Indian History, St. Catharine's College, Cambridge University.

China:
DENIS TWITCHETT, Gorden Wu Professor of Chinese Studies, Princeton University, Princeton, New Jersey.

SPECIAL CONTRIBUTORS: James Chambers, Ron Coates, Alan Lothian, John Man (text); Stephen Rogers (research).

Correspondents: Elisabeth Kraemer-Singh (Bonn); Christina Lieberman (New York); Maria Vincenza Aloisi (Paris); Ann Natanson (Rome). Valuable assistance was also provided by: Betty H. Weatherley, Robert H. Wooldridge Jr. (Alexandria, Virginia); Jane Walker (Madrid); Felix Rosenthal (Moscow); Robert Nickelsberg, Anita Pratap (New Delhi); Elizabeth Brown (New York); Michal Donath (Prague); Ann Wise (Rome); Dick Berry (Tokyo); Traudl Lessing (Vienna).

30 29 28 27 26 25 24 23 22 21 20 19 18 17 16 15 14 13 12 11 10 9 8 7 6

CONTENTS

THE GREAT DEPRESSION

"The fundamental business of the country is on a sound and prosperous basis," insisted U.S. president Herbert Hoover, speaking in the wake of "Black Thursday", October 24, 1929, when panic gripped New York's Wall Street. The stock market had crashed, as 13 million shares were sold in a single day's trading, and millions of American investors suddenly found themselves destitute.

On the face of it, there was reason for Hoover's optimism. America had enjoyed a decade of unparalleled prosperity, with four years of surging "bull" markets pushing the *New York Times* stock index from 110 points at the beginning of 1924 to 338 points in January 1929. Thousands of ordinary Americans had grown rich by investing in the country's thriving new industries. Although the events of Black Thursday were worrying, there seemed no good reason why the future should not be every bit as prosperous. Wall Street had shaken off the effects of serious crashes in 1893 and 1907, and had overcome a severe setback in the early 1920s.

This time, however, there would be no quick recovery. For, despite Hoover's reassurances, economic problems had been gathering over the years. Prices for grain exports, a major source of America's wealth, had been falling for more than a year, driven down by competition from Europe. At home there were signs that American workers, flush from years of wage rises, had bought just about all the consumer goods they wanted. Yet, despite low demand, industry was still expanding.

The stock market, too, had been spoilt by success. Thousands were buying "on the margin" – borrowing heavily to acquire stock, certain that they could repay their loans from the handsome profits they expected to make on resale. With money pouring in, the market went from strength to strength, buoyed up by its own self-confidence. But a moment had to come when the market could no longer float on euphoria alone.

The first signs of impending trouble became apparent more than a month before Black Thursday. From the first week of September, the market began to falter, rising and falling unpredictably, unnerving a public familiar only with unbroken boom. By the middle of the next month it was obvious that the market, while still uncertain, was on a gradual downward trajectory, and, from October 21, the fall steepened. On Black Thursday, anxiety turned to blind panic as investors sold as fast as they could.

That weekend, a chorus of eminent bankers, economists and industrialists echoed Hoover's statement of confidence, but their soothing words, and intervention by the big banks to support prices, checked the momentum of the crash only momentarily. Within days, the banks too were joining in the selling. Many slid into bankruptcy, dragging with them some of America's greatest corporations.

The collapse of financial confidence was to affect all Americans. Millions of workers lost their jobs during the following months. Hoover had no answers to the problem. Although his government eventually intervened to help tottering businesses, which usually only prolonged their agony, he was against state welfare payments, believing that they would destroy self-reliance. So the urban unemployed went hungry, unable to pay for food, while farmers across the country were left with livestock and crops they could neither sell nor afford to maintain.

And so the slump continued until, by 1933, more than 13 million Americans were unemployed, the ranks of the urban poor swollen by a massive influx of jobless agricultural workers. In the cities, armies of homeless lived on the streets, reduced to begging and sleeping rough under old newspapers – "Hoover blankets".

The effects of the Crash were soon felt beyond the borders of the U.S. The outside world had benefited from the years of American prosperity; Europe's industrial nations, especially Britain and Germany, as well as Japan, had found a ready market in the booming United States. But the reduction in American demand soon took its toll on exports, and Hoover's subsequent attempts to shield the home economy by setting up virtually impregnable tariff barriers worsened the situation, plunging the rest of the world into a nightmare spiral of unemployment, poverty and hunger. Protectionism rebounded on the United States, however, for the impoverished foreign countries could no longer afford to buy American goods.

One of the few industrialized nations that escaped the Depression was Stalin's isolationist U.S.S.R., although Soviet citizens, who were caught up in the economic turmoil of the first Five-Year Plan, faced privations that were worse than any experienced in the West. Elsewhere, political extremism – desperate remedies for desperate ills – flourished in all its forms. America was racked by industrial strife, and communism found increased support, although insensitive and dogmatic interference from distant Moscow prevented any real consolidation.

Communism and the Left gained ground in Europe, too, but in Germany they were soon overshadowed by Nazism, Adolf Hitler's ultraright nationalist movement. Reparations payments, which had been imposed on Germany by the victors of World War I, became an increasingly heavy burden as the world depression grew worse. Hitler, for years a little-heeded prophet of doom, came in from the wilderness, his direst predictions all apparently coming true. On the other side of the world, Japan, too, was veering to the right, its military enraged at the straits to which liberalism and foreign trade had brought the country.

Towards the end of the 1930s, the huge public spending programme of President Franklin Roosevelt's "New Deal" began to take effect, bringing the promise of renewed growth in the United States and of recovery for the world economy. The measures came too late, however, to redeem the deteriorating political situation. By then the world was already sliding inexorably towards war.

Only a few newspapers made the Wall Street Crash a front-page story. Newspapers in the leading financial centres, New York and London, were unruffled – or strove to give that impression. But London's *Daily Mail*, in its continental edition, made the crisis headline news, and in the U.S. *The Philadelphia Inquirer* reported the panic while attempting to present an optimistic gloss. The hoped-for upswing failed to materialize, however, as a sobering follow-up story from *The Evening Gazette* – printed in Worcester, Massachusetts, the following Monday – indicates.

Unable to afford proper lodgings, homeless men in Berlin slump in exhausted sleep over a rope provided by a flophouse landlord.

Cattle gather round a feeding trough on a prairie state farm devastated by drought.

A street scene in a Tokyo slum conveys the despair felt by Japan's rural immigrants.

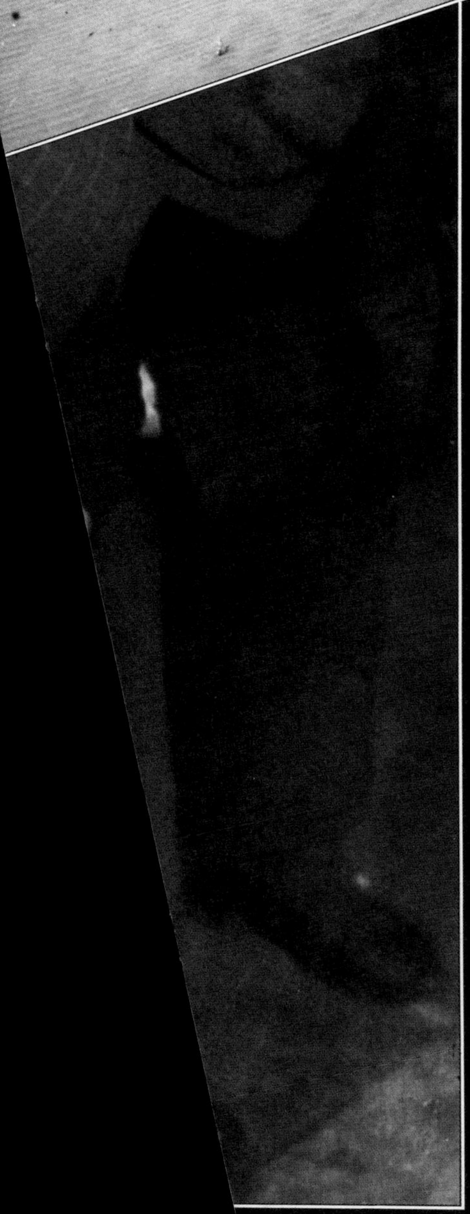

A MOUNTING TIDE OF MISERY

As the Depression deepened in the 1930s, it brought hunger and misery to town and country alike across the globe. In the American Midwest, the severe economic problems were compounded by natural disaster in mid-decade, when freak winds following a scorching drought carried off the over-cultivated topsoil, turning nine million acres of the Great Plains into the "Dust Bowl", and badly damaging a further 80 million acres. All over the world, ever-increasing numbers of people joined the drift away from the rural areas, in the search for some form of employment in the big cities. Unlike the barren countryside, the cities offered at least the hope of opportunity, however illusory this proved to be. But the mass-migration, which continued throughout the Depression years, placed an intolerable burden on communities that were already teeming with the urban destitute.

THE VOICE OF PROTEST

Inevitably, the hardships of the Depression years produced unrest and led to social conflict. With traditional politics apparently discredited, radical ideologies began to appeal as never before to the many desperate people who had little to lose and everything to fight for. Some parts of America became an industrial battleground as workers campaigned in support of trade unions, which were resisted fiercely and often violently by the employers, sometimes with the support of authorities. In France, a union of all the leftist parties into one "Popular Front" produced the country's first ever socialist government. In Britain, where some cities and towns in the industrialized north of the country suffered more than 75 per cent unemployment, the jobless staged hunger marches to bring their plight to national attention. But radicalism was not the monopoly of the Left. In many democratic countries, the rhetoric of right-wing extremism found widespread support.

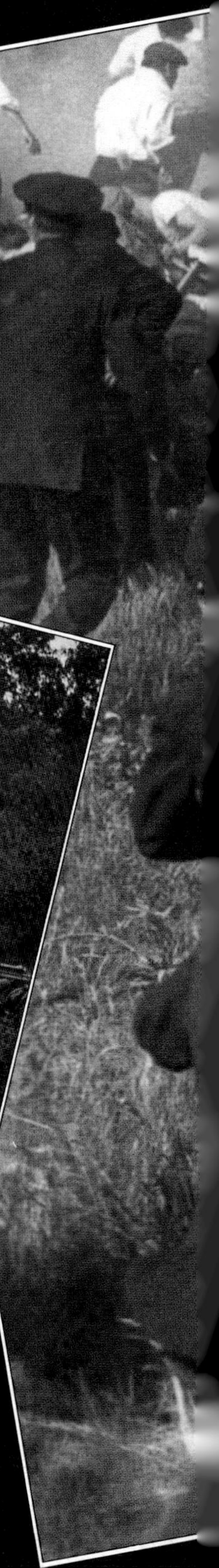

Unemployed shipyard workers from Jarrow, in northeast England, march on London in 1936 to present a petition on behalf of their town.

Police fight a running battle with pickets demonstrating for trade union representation at a Chicago steel company on May 30, 1937. Five workers were killed in the clash.

STORM CLOUDS OVER EUROPE

1

On June 14, 1934, Adolf Hitler flew to the Italian city of Venice on his first foreign visit as German chancellor. He was worried about a proposed alliance between France and the Soviet Union, and he hoped to counter it by establishing a working partnership with his fellow dictator, Italy's Benito Mussolini, who was then at the height of his reputation.

On the face of it, the two leaders appeared to have much in common. From inauspicious beginnings, both men had risen to the supreme leadership of nations embittered by the terms of the Treaty of Versailles, which had been drawn up by the victors of the First World War. Germany, branded the aggressor, had been saddled with the heavy burden of paying reparations to its enemies, while Italy, although one of those enemies, had not received all the lands that she had been promised by her allies. Both leaders, addressing their fellow countrymen in highly emotional terms that swayed millions, had won massive popular support by promising to restore national pride, prosperity and military power. For both Hitler and Mussolini, organized violence was an essential means to these ends. Virulently anti-communist and yet contemptuous of all forms of parliamentary democracy, they saw themselves as omniscient, the embodiment of the state, in which the rights of the individual were as nothing.

These very parallels made it unlikely that the two men could form any sort of relationship based on trust. Hitler, who had been in power for little more than a year, had long admired Mussolini and the methods by which he had come to absolute rule in Italy 12 years previously; but he was still smarting under the rebuffs that had been administered by Mussolini during the Nazi leader's years in the political wilderness. Only five years earlier, when Hitler had requested an autographed picture of "this great man south of the Alps", the Italian dictator had snubbed him in typically bombastic fashion, instructing one of his aides to: "Please thank the above-mentioned gentleman for his sentiment and tell him in whatever form you consider best that the Duce (Leader) does not think fit to accede to the request." Now that the two dictators were meeting ostensibly on equal terms, Mussolini still regarded his guest as an upstart – and a dangerous one at that, who was fomenting intrigue in Austria, a country that the Duce had promised to defend against "Prussian barbarism".

In any case, the visit was an utter disaster from the start. Hitler had requested a low-key meeting, but when he stepped out of his plane, dressed in a shabby overcoat and a blue serge suit, he was confronted by the world's press and greeted by Mussolini attired in full Fascist uniform, complete with jackboots, black shirt and a liberal garnish of gold braid. Mussolini's other attempts to upstage his visitor went embarrassingly awry; the military parades were sloppy, and the ceremonial

Adolf Hitler, Germany's Fuhrer or Leader, addresses his followers at a 1935 rally of his ruling Nazi party in Nuremberg. Like his fellow dictator, Italy's Benito Mussolini, Hitler used such massive rituals as a way of manipulating the emotions of his followers to almost hypnotic effect. The awesome setting and the swelling roars of the half-million-strong crowd were calculated to reduce the participants to a single entity bewitched by the Fuhrer's simplistic promises to resist communism, restore the nation's prosperity, and make Germany once again a great military power. At rallies such as these, so the Nazi propaganda chief Joseph Goebbels boasted, the individual was transformed from "a little worm into part of a large dragon".

concert degenerated into farce when the music was punctuated by organized shouts of "Duce, Duce". Nor was Hitler impressed by the Italian navy when he saw sailors' washing flying from the masts.

In their discussions, it was Hitler who dominated the conversation, delivering lengthy harangues on subjects that ranged from his plans to start a European war by attacking France, to the congenital weakness of the British and the need to establish a pro-Nazi government in Austria. Visibly bored by Hitler's monologue during their final meeting together, held on a golf course, Mussolini later dismissed the German leader as a man without intelligence or dynamism, "a gramophone with just seven tunes", as he described him.

Either Mussolini had seriously misjudged Hitler, or else his petulant denigration was the bluster of a man who felt himself to be in the presence of a demonic ruthlessness he could never emulate. For though the two would indeed prove to have a community of interest, Hitler would soon come to dominate the relationship. As his nightmarish plans unfolded through the 1930s, and then as Nazi armies stormed

By September 1, 1939, the day on which Germany's invasion of Poland triggered World War II, Hitler and Mussolini had created in central Europe an unstable "Axis" whose only rationale was further conquest. Germany's territory *(shaded red)* by now included the Rhineland, a demilitarized zone that Hitler had reoccupied in 1936; and Austria, which had been annexed in March 1938. Then, seven months later, Germany also swallowed up the Sudetenland, Czechoslovakia's German-speaking border area; and in March 1939, German troops occupied the neighbouring western provinces of Bohemia and Moravia, and established a puppet regime in Slovakia. Italy's sole acquisition in Europe was Albania *(yellow)*, seized in 1937 as a springboard for an intended invasion of Greece.

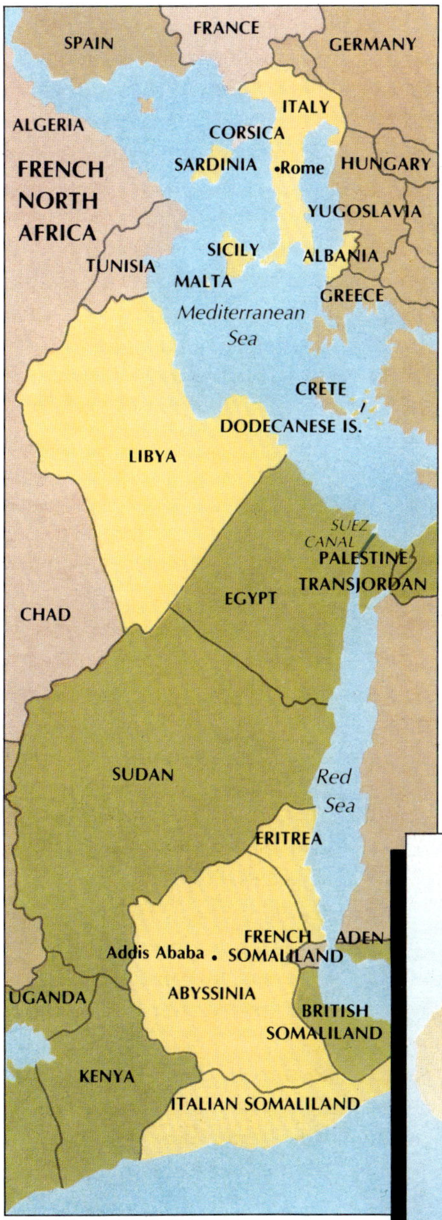

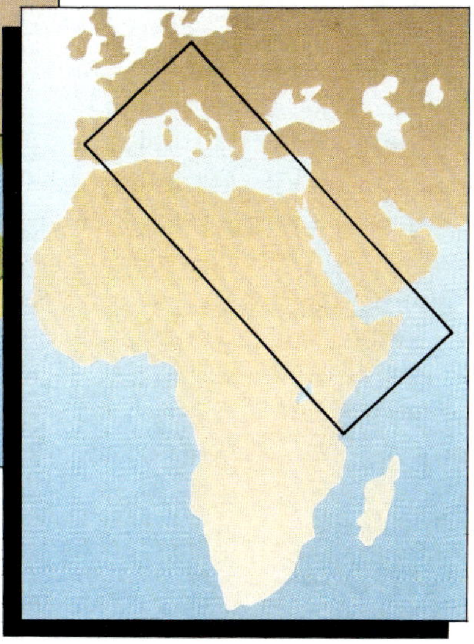

Unlike Hitler, Italy's ruler Benito Mussolini sought to increase his nation's territory by colonial adventures outside of Europe. When he came to power in 1922, Italy already possessed Eritrea, Italian Somaliland and Libya. Mussolini, however, felt that in comparison with the larger holdings of Britain *(shaded green)*, and France *(pink)*, the Italian possessions were no more than a "collection of deserts". Determined to enlarge them, in 1935 he invaded Ethiopia, a country he had previously championed when it applied to join the League of Nations in 1928.

across western Europe during the first two years of World War II, Mussolini would find himself reduced to a mere vassal, his own attempts at creating an Italian empire leading to crushing failure and a humiliating reliance on the man he had once called a "mad little clown".

Being second best was something Mussolini had always sought to escape. He was born in 1883 to a devout Catholic schoolmistress and a hard-drinking blacksmith, an uneducated socialist who dabbled in anarchism and who kept discipline with a thick leather strap. Benito – named after the Mexican revolutionary Benito Juarez – shared his father's brutality; he was once suspended from school for stabbing a fellow pupil, and on another occasion he knifed one of his many girlfriends.

Before the First World War, Mussolini lived a Bohemian existence, writing poetry, dallying with left-wing politics and preaching violent revolution. He had no fixed views, but adopted poses that suited the occasion, at one time claiming to be a Marxist, at another to have written a treatise on the history of Christianity. Abandoning a job as a temporary teacher in German-speaking northern Italy, he went to Switzerland, where he drifted between jobs and was sometimes reduced to begging and stealing food. On several occasions he was arrested for vagrancy and for political agitation. The Swiss eventually expelled him, handing him over to the Italian police, who marked him as an "impulsive and violent" young man.

In 1909 he began a career as a journalist, editing small socialist papers in Austria, where he was convicted five times for his ferocious libels. Back in Italy after only seven months, he continued his newspaper career, arguing strongly for international working-class solidarity and against Italian nationalism. "The national flag," he wrote, "is for us a rag to plant on a dunghill."

Driven by a desire for recognition and by an unfocused rage, he was forever experimenting with different roles, now unkempt and vulgar to appear as a champion of the proletariat, now dressed in modish patent-leather shoes and a silk-lapelled coat for some social occasion. In his commitment to violence as a political weapon, however, he was unwavering.

Sentenced to five months' imprisonment for antipatriotic agitation in 1911 – he opposed Italy's expansion into Libya – he emerged as a minor celebrity and was invited to edit the Socialist party's daily newspaper *Avanti!* When World War I broke out, he condemned it as a capitalist plot, but then came to support Italy's intervention, hoping the conflict would provoke a revolutionary "blood bath". Turning against the Socialists, he started his own newspaper, *Il Popolo d'Italia* (Italian People), subsidized by industrialists who stood to gain from war – the very people he had previously castigated. At the end of 1914, he took over a pro-intervention pressure group which called itself a *fascio*, a name inspired by the bundle of rods with an axe borne before ancient Roman magistrates as a badge of authority. When Italy entered the war in 1915, Mussolini was conscripted, serving for 17 months and reaching the rank of sergeant before he was injured.

After the war, he found a political base among the many ex-servicemen who were disgruntled both by the failure of the Allies to grant Italy all she demanded at Versailles, and by the inflation, unemployment and political paralysis that gripped the country. Sure that the parliamentary regime was doomed, Mussolini called a meeting in a Milan hall to formalize the fight against the nation's woes and launch the movement that would become the Fascist party. The assembly, held on March 23, 1919, was attended by a mixed bag of anarchists, communists, trade unionists, republicans, Catholics and anticlerics. Not wishing to exclude any potential followers, he tried to appeal to them all. He was, he said, "an adventurer for all roads". Over the next few months, he recruited a private army of ex-servicemen and students whose methods would soon become familiar: destroying the printing presses of rival movements, beating up opponents and humiliating them by forcing castor oil, "Fascist medicine", down their throats.

In the 1919 elections, the Fascists won not a single parliamentary seat, but from then on their rise was rapid. To give the party a strong identity, Mussolini opted for a more right-wing image, using his paper to emphasize his "electric", "explosive" dynamism. Within a year, he had 320,000 members from all sections of society, and enjoyed increased backing from employers who saw in him a possible national leader who would restore stability and growth. In the next elections, in May 1921, the Fascists received a helping hand from the dominant Liberal party, whose leader, the grand old man of Italian politics, Giovanni Giolitti, offered to include the Fascists in a coalition. With Giolitti's backing – and the help of strong-arm squads – 35 Fascists, including Mussolini, found themselves in Parliament, along with a dozen other diverse political parties, none of whom commanded a majority.

But Mussolini was not willing to share power. By declaring himself against democracy, he made it impossible for the coalition to hold together. Giolitti resigned, and for a while local Fascist groups, sharing little but a love of violence and their black-shirt uniforms, became laws unto themselves. Many stockpiled bombs and firearms. To retain control, Mussolini tightened organization, grouping the squads into cohorts and legions under a hierarchy of commanders, with himself as the Duce. His aim was simple: to prove that democratic government could not defend law and order. In many areas, Fascist *squadristi* unleashed such violence that civil war seemed to threaten. Antifascists claimed that between 1920 and 1922, 3,000 opponents of Fascism were killed. The army, the police and the magistrates, all seeing in the Fascists a force for strong rule and an end to uncertainty, turned a blind eye. In February 1922, a new government under a feeble liberal, Luigi Facta, was formed, but it lacked the courage and foresight to challenge Mussolini's brutal tactics.

Acknowledging the adulation of a crowd in Venice's Piazza San Marco, in 1934, Fascist leader Benito Mussolini adopts a typically aggressive and histrionic pose. A journalist before he came to power in 1922, Mussolini pioneered oratorical techniques and a use of propaganda and state pageantry that were to be assiduously copied by Hitler.

Events now played right into the Duce's hands. The unions declared a general strike, ostensibly to force the government to restore peace. They accomplished precisely the opposite. Mussolini set his Fascists to break the strike, thus being able to pose as the defender of law and order. Insurrection spread. Fascists seized control of half a dozen town councils, but still the government took no action. Mussolini, while maintaining contact with most factions in Parliament, suggesting to all that he might collaborate with them, held back until, on October 24, in Naples, he judged the time had come to make his bid for power. "Either we are allowed to govern," he shouted at a cheering crowd of supporters, "or we will seize power by marching on Rome." He was greeted by ecstatic shouts of "To Rome! To Rome!"

Mussolini waited in Milan to see how events turned out, while some 30,000 Fascists assembled outside the capital and others occupied telephone exchanges and government offices in various parts of the country. This was a challenge even Facta could not ignore: on October 28, he declared a state of emergency. Overnight, the army retook the occupied buildings, meeting little resistance. The Fascists camped around Rome were cold, wet and hungry, and were ready to head for home.

Then came an astonishing reversal. King Vittorio Emanuele, a small, timid man, refused to ratify Facta's decree. Perhaps he doubted Facta's ability to resolve the crisis; perhaps he felt the Fascists would provide a popular, effective government. In any event, it was an extraordinary breach of convention by the constitutional monarch. Facta, his authority fatally undermined, had to resign.

With a cameraman on hand to record his efforts, Mussolini makes a show of gathering in the harvest on a farm in the Pontine Marshes, near Rome, in 1936. This display of manly vigour was part of a drive to publicize Mussolini's campaigns to create more agricultural land by draining the malarial wetlands, thereby increasing wheat production. Both goals were achieved, helping to make Italy almost self-sufficient in grain. But the years of plenty were few, for good harvests depended on imported foreign fertilizer, and yields slumped when war cut off the supply.

The King's decision was a turning point: it conferred respectability on the Fascists and made Mussolini's cooperation crucial to the formation of the next government. Antonio Salandra, Facta's would-be successor, attempting to form an administration, begged Mussolini to come to Rome. He refused. He would stay where he was, he said, unless allowed to form his own government. Salandra gave in. A day later, on October 29, Mussolini received a telegram from the King inviting him to be the next prime minister.

That evening, Mussolini caught the night-sleeper to Rome. Only later did his Black Shirts arrive, also by train, to find Rome celebrating the end of the anarchy that they had instigated. In Fascist mythology, the events of those five days, known as the March on Rome, assumed heroic status. Government-sponsored history books soon told children stirring but utterly fanciful tales of Mussolini arriving in Rome on horseback, of an armed revolt involving 300,000 Fascists, of 3,000 Fascists martyred, and of Mussolini seizing power from an unwilling king.

With a total of only 32 Fascist deputies in his administration, Mussolini was still a long way from wielding the absolute authority that he sought. He at once demanded emergency powers which would enable him to rule by decree for a year, and Parliament meekly acquiesced. A year after taking office, the law was changed yet again. By a huge majority – the opposition was now too cowed to offer further resistance – Parliament agreed that any party obtaining at least 25 per cent of the parliamentary vote would have an absolute majority. The only party that could win such a share was the Fascists. Thus a largely non-Fascist parliament effectively voted to end parliamentary government.

Freed from the threat of civil war, the country responded as if by magic to Mussolini's show of strength and energy. Strikes ended. Production picked up. By 1924, confident that he now enjoyed the massive support of the Italian people, Mussolini ordered new elections. In a campaign that was designed to increase the Fascists' electoral attractiveness, he opposed Freemasonry in order to appeal to Catholics, halved death duties to win over the middle classes, promised imperial expansion to please the nationalists, and privatized national industries to gain support from capitalists. To retain the loyalty of his *squadristi*, Mussolini gave them official status and wages, while students who were wounded in the Fascist cause were rewarded with university degrees without the necessity of passing an

examination. That spring, Fascist candidates polled an astonishing 65 per cent of the vote in the elections, winning more than two thirds of the parliamentary seats, the greatest electoral victory in Italian history.

Undoubtedly, the result genuinely reflected public opinion, but the size of the majority struck at least one deputy, a moderate Socialist named Giacomo Matteotti, as fraudulent. When Parliament reassembled, he accused the Fascists of electoral fraud, presenting convincing evidence to support his claims. A few days later, Matteotti's mutilated body was found outside Rome. No-one doubted that Mussolini had connived at, if not actually ordered, the murder. In the outcry that followed, most of the non-Fascist opposition withdrew from Parliament.

But once again, Mussolini's enemies only succeeded in providing him with another opportunity to extend his power. On January 3, 1925, he boldly claimed responsibility for Matteotti's murder, and challenged anyone to impeach him. No-one took up the challenge.

Mussolini's undeviating aim had been to seize absolute power, but he had given little thought to how he would wield it, and from the start his rule was as much show as substance. He claimed that government was "97-cents-worth of mere public clamour and three-cents-worth of solid achievement", and he once remarked that to govern Italy, "you needed only two things: policemen, and bands playing in the streets". A few weeks after assuming office in 1922, he had insisted on taking part in a congress in Switzerland so that he could display himself in public surrounded by a phalanx of Black Shirts. Although he had nothing to contribute to the congress — which was held to ratify a treaty between Greece and Turkey — he held 11 press conferences. At one of them, the author Ernest Hemingway, then a foreign correspondent, found Mussolini frowning ostentatiously at a weighty tome as the journalists were admitted to his presence. It was, Hemingway noticed, a French-English dictionary held upside down.

Manning an M-shaped triumphal arch, soldiers and children of the Fascist Youth Organization prepare to honour their Duce, or Leader, as he passes through the province of Aosta in 1939. The arch was a typical example of *ducismo*, as Mussolini termed the cult of personality which he manufactured around himself. School teachers were ordered to instruct their pupils to learn from his example, stressing his courage and intellectual brilliance which, his Fascist acolytes maintained, made him a figure greater than Dante and Michelangelo, comparable with, if not superior to, Aristotle and Napoleon.

But once he was installed as dictator, Mussolini realized that his regime needed at least the semblance of a positive programme if it was to maintain its impetus. His plan was to extend Fascism into as many facets of Italian society as possible. Predominantly, this was to be achieved by establishing a score of huge corporations that combined the roles of trade unions and employers' federations. In addition, each major institution also had a parallel Fascist organization: Fascist militia were attached to the army; Fascist tribunals worked alongside the law courts; Fascist secretaries oversaw provincial administrators. Ostensibly, the purpose of this massive upheaval was to create prosperity and self-sufficency. In fact, the moves had a twofold political purpose: to exercise control over the entire workforce, and to provide jobs for the immense Fascist hierarchy.

For a while there were some notable successes. Huge sums of money were poured into a succession of economic "battles" — for food, for agricultural land, for higher population. Several hundred thousand acres of marshland were reclaimed, wheat production raised by 30 per cent, roads built and — in a catch phrase used by English-speakers at the time to summarize the positive results of Fascism — the trains were made to run on time.

Such feats were little more than window-dressing, however. The increase in home-grown wheat, for example, allowed grain imports to be cut, but Italians paid 50 per cent more for their wheat than Americans paid for theirs. The corporations were overstaffed by armies of Fascist bureaucrats who supplemented their low

Sentenced to Landsberg Prison after his failure in 1923 to seize power in Bavaria, Adolf Hitler *(far left)* faces the camera with fellow-Nazi conspirators, including Rudolf Hess *(second from right)*, his secretary and future deputy. Reflecting official sympathy with Nazi aims, the prison authorities granted the inmates remarkable liberties. In this picture – taken by one of their many visitors, Hess's future wife – they face the camera confidently, well fed and snappily dressed in the Bavarian style. Their confidence was well placed: within a year they had all been released, and Hitler was rebuilding his political career.

salaries by creaming off a percentage of the businesses they controlled, and by selling their influence to the highest bidder. Corruption was endemic.

Steadily, Fascism intruded into the everyday life of ordinary Italians. People were urged to date events from the *anno primo* of 1922, and encouraged to use the "hygienic" Fascist salute instead of shaking hands. Children from the age of four were expected to join Fascist youth clubs. Roadside hoardings displayed Mussolini aphorisms such as "Mussolini is always right", and "Better to be a lion for a day than a sheep for 100 years".

That such a system not only survived but was also generally popular was due in large part to the personality of the Duce as he presented himself to the public. He used his histrionic talents – he had a fine baritone voice and an actor's way with expression and gesture – to project an image of wisdom, industry and urgent activity. His 20-by-13-metre marble office in the Palazzo Venezia was designed to awe visitors, and he habitually left the light burning late, suggesting to admirers outside that he was working into the night, when in fact he was asleep. Carefully edited photographs and press releases gave the impression that he was a gifted violinist, an expert pilot, daring horseman, penetrating intellectual – "pardon my learned references" was one of his favoured asides – and a devil-may-care free spirit. Foreign journalists could be expelled for mentioning that he wore glasses or had an ulcer. He himself claimed that he was greater than Napoleon and that, like Napoleon, he was more than capable of leading in both peace and war.

This play-acting, much of it absurd, could not disguise Mussolini's inadequacies as an administrator. He surrounded himself with yes-men who would never contradict him or point out his errors: to do so, he said, would only divert "me from what I know to be the right path, whereas my animal instincts are always right". Disdainful of anyone else's political abilities, he found it impossible to delegate responsibilities, personally holding eight government offices in 1926; among other roles, he was prime minister, foreign minister, interior minister, and minister for all three armed services. Consequently, he was unable to concentrate on any one area of policy for long. He would contradict himself to avoid acknowledging failure. "The ideals of democracy are exploded," he wrote on one occasion, and on another, "Fascism is the purest kind of democracy".

As the economy failed to measure up to his initial promises, he adjusted his message. Instead of boasting about his commitment to prosperity, he began to preach on the restorative virtues of adversity. "Fortunately," he said dismissively, when informed that food production had fallen, "the Italian people are not accustomed to eat much." As the benefits of corporatism continued to elude the country, he found another catchword, "autarchy", self-sufficiency, which he repeated like an incantation: henceforth, Italy was to be self-sufficient not only in food, but also in industrial products. However, he also initiated a major rearmament programme that would inevitably make Italy – deficient in the raw materials of war – more dependent on imports. He needed weapons for a campaign of imperial expansion in Africa: 1935, he stressed, was to be the year when he would be ready to go to war.

Although Hitler was the newcomer when he met Mussolini in 1934, he was already seen by millions of Germans as the embodiment of Germanic culture. But he was not German by birth. Born in 1889, he grew up near Linz in Austria. His father, a customs official for the Habsburg empire that linked Austria and Hungary, died when he was 13. Left to his fond, simple-minded mother, he became solitary and rebellious, showing interest in little but drawing. At 18 he went to Vienna, and failed to win admission to the Academy of Fine Arts. His mother died of breast cancer, and he was reduced to living in dosshouses, eking out a meagre allowance by painting advertisements and postcards. These were unhappy years, and also formative ones. Lazy, moody, at odds with society, he had one consuming passion: talking politics. He was an intense admirer of German culture, for Germany, a young and strong nation, offered a far brighter future than the Austro-Hungarian empire, undermined as it was by the nationalist demands of its

Dictated by Hitler during his time in prison, *Mein Kampf* – "My Struggle" – was a manifesto in which he set out his racist theories and dreams of empire. After he came to power, six million copies were sold or distributed free; all newlyweds, for example, received one from their local government. Copies were often kept in presentation boxes, such as the one shown here, which is carved with the lightning flashes of the SS, the *Schutzstaffel*, Hitlers elite personal bodyguard.

subject peoples. He was particularly resentful of Vienna's Jews, believing that they threatened the fabric of German culture. His narrow, powerful mind, stimulated by an anti-Semitism that was endemic in Vienna's gutter press, conceived a catch-all explanation of the sickness — as he saw it — of the modern world: all true ideals, all good government, had been undermined by a worldwide Jewish conspiracy, operating through social democracy, Marxism and Christianity. Avidly skimming books by the hundred, he absorbed those ideas that confirmed his prejudices. Acquaintances later recalled him as a brooding, wild-eyed figure, bursting out of dark moods into violent, bitter diatribes.

In 1913 Hitler moved to Munich, a city he loved, and when the First World War broke out he enlisted in the German infantry, serving as a dispatch runner in Flanders throughout most of the conflict. Never rising above the rank of corporal, he proved himself a brave soldier, winning the Iron Cross, First Class — a rare distinction for a combatant of his rank. Invalided to Germany after falling victim to a gas attack in October 1918, he was shocked to the core of his being by Germany's sudden capitulation the following month.

In a sequence of studio photographs taken in 1925, Hitler strikes dramatic attitudes intended to increase the impact of his oratory. It was practice well spent. His public speeches, delivered with dramatic gestures and rising intensity, induced in his audiences a sort of hysteria that overwhelmed the critical faculties of most of his listeners.

He returned to Munich through a country in ruins. Germany's postwar republican government, named after Weimar, the town in which the national assembly first met, was in disarray. While left-wingers hoped for revolution, millions of others — especially disaffected veterans like Hitler — could not accept the armistice, claiming that Germany had been "stabbed in the back" by its own republican politicians, abetted by socialist agitators, by Jews, and by war profiteers. The peace treaty signed at Versailles in 1919 was seen as another betrayal. Only some new movement, backed by the army, could hope to restore German national pride.

Bavaria in particular, the largest of Germany's constituent states, was near revolt. Independent until 1866, with their own monarch until the previous year, Bavaria's

Catholic people disliked Protestant Berlin. There were many who would have preferred a south German union with Catholic Austria, which had emerged as an independent country after the dismantling of the Austro-Hungarian empire in 1918.

Hitler was given work in the army's political department, and was assigned to investigate a small right-wing group, the German Workers' party. It interested him, for its few dozen members turned out to be fervently patriotic, reflecting opinions that were current in the Bavarian police and army, and anxious to gain working-class support. Hitler accepted an invitation to join the party's committee, and was placed in charge of propaganda.

In his new role, Hitler demonstrated two exceptional gifts: he could organize others, and as a speaker he was able to sense and express the mood of an audience, articulating their own hopes and fears and thus personifying their raw

emotions. "He could play like a virtuoso on the well-tempered piano of lower-middle-class hearts," said one of his later associates. When he appeared in public, his customary moroseness dropped away, his pale-blue eyes took fire, and he acquired a compelling and utterly self-assured passion.

He quickly dominated the party and began to rebuild it, changing its name to one taken over from a minor Austrian group, the National German Workers' party – Nazi for short. From the same source, he adopted as the party symbol an ancient cross motif known as the swastika. He insisted on a ritual greeting, *"Heil!"*, which means "Hail!", but which also evokes concepts of wholeness, salvation and health. Most important of all, he formed a private army of thugs, known as the Storm Section – the *Sturmabteilung*, or SA – which he used to intimidate political opponents. It was led by a local army officer, Captain Ernst Röhm, a scar-faced tough who persuaded his ex-commander to divert secret army funds for the purchase of a virulently racist local newspaper, the *Völkischer Beobachter* or

National Observer. Under the editorship of Alfred Rosenberg, this publication became a vehicle for Hitler's ultra-nationalist views.

Conditions soon favoured the burgeoning party. Reparations payments to the victors of World War I were proving such a burden that the German economy collapsed. To enforce payments, in January 1923 France occupied Germany's industrial heartland, the Ruhr. The government responded by backing a general strike, financing it by printing more money. Confidence in the currency began to slip, and within months rampant inflation, the worst in German history, set in. In November, the exchange rate peaked at 4,000,000,000,000 marks to the dollar. Savings were worthless, property unsaleable, labour had no rewards. The very foundations of the state seemed about to vanish.

In these chaotic circumstances, many in Bavaria were ready to back an army revolt against the republic. Hitler had already discussed the possibility with several people, including the eminent World War I commander General Erich Ludendorff, who was living in retirement in Munich. For the moment, however, sympathetic military leaders urged restraint on the plotters. The time was not yet ripe: there were signs that the republican government could, after all, surmount the crisis. But Hitler was not to be deterred. He determined to seize the initiative, take over the army, police and government, and use Bavaria as a springboard to national power.

On November 8, 1923, a group of government officials, military leaders and civil servants gathered in a large Munich beer hall, the Bürgerbräukeller, to hear the Bavarian state commissioner deliver a lecture on the moral justification of dictatorship. Twenty minutes into the meeting, 25 armed SA men burst in — the signal for Hitler, who had been waiting by a pillar, to fire a shot into the ceiling and yell that the national revolution had begun. After bundling the senior officials into a back room, he returned to the hall and announced that he was setting up a national government with the help of Ludendorff. The General knew nothing of the plan but, when hastily informed, agreed to back the Nazis. He went to the hall, where Hitler, after a brief impassioned speech that roused his hostages to cheers, let the officials go.

He had totally miscalculated. Next morning, when he and Ludendorff led a march of over 2,000 men through the streets towards the Bavarian war ministry, believing the city would fall to him, the police barred their way. Shots rang out. Sixteen Nazis fell dead; the rest fled, to be arrested later. Ludendorff was released, but Hitler and several others were jailed.

In March 1933, Hitler defers to President Paul von Hindenburg at a ceremony in Berlin in honour of the dead of World War I. Hitler had been appointed chancellor two months previously, after unsuccessfully challenging the popular Hindenburg for the presidency. The 85-year-old former field marshal had a constitutional right to veto Nazi legislation, but Hitler used the threat of communist subversion to push through his party's programme by decree. When Hindenburg died in August of 1934, Hitler simply assumed his office and thereafter ruled supreme.

This badge identified its owner as a member of the National Socialist German Workers' – or Nazi – party. The party symbol, later adopted as the national emblem of the Third Reich, was the swastika, or *Hakenkreuz*, "crooked cross". A good luck charm in ancient Asian cultures, the swastika was used by early Christians as a distorted form of cross to disguise their religious affiliations. Hitler borrowed it, together with the party name, from a tiny Austrian nationalist party which he joined after World War I.

He put his year in prison to good use, reading voraciously and dictating his thoughts to his closest associate and fellow prisoner, Rudolf Hess. The result of this collaboration was the book that would eventually become the Nazi bible, *Mein Kampf* (My Struggle). In this turgid work Hitler expressed the thoughts, aims and methods that were to became the heart of Nazism.

In the past, he argued, successful cultures – such as the classical world and medieval Europe – had been weakened by an effeminate Jewish-Christian ethic. The same destructive ethic, compounded by insipid leadership, had enfeebled postwar Europe. The culture that would revitalize it was Germanic, or "Aryan" as Hitler termed it. The Germans had acted as "culture-bearers" before, after the fall of Rome, and would do so again, not under any milksop democracy but under a single messianic figure of iron will. Such a man could change the entire course of history; indeed, Mussolini, "that unparalleled statesman", had demonstrated how with the March on Rome.

Hitler himself, of course, was the new messiah – a unique combination of politician, philosopher and military strategist. Working through the Nazi party, he would unite all German-speakers into a new empire that would dominate lesser races, in particular the Slavs, and seize new lands to the east – as German crusaders had done in the 13th century. Germany "must again set itself on the march along the road of the Teutonic knights of old, to obtain by the German sword sod for the German plough and daily bread for the nation". In Russia, Germany would find the *Lebensraum*, the "living space", that its people needed. Russia was Germany's natural enemy, more so now than ever, for it was in the hands of a rival ideology, Marxism, behind which – according to Hitler – stood the Jew, the incarnation of all evil. The real battle would be with Russia and the "half beast, half giant" Stalin; it would be an apocalyptic struggle that would decide the fate of Europe for centuries to come. Russia was to be utterly crushed, its cities levelled, its people enslaved. In this new empire, the Jewish "problem" would find its "final solution" in the total eradication of Jewish culture.

Compared to the grand scheme of expansion to the east, war with the West, though possibly unavoidable, was a small matter. Liberal democracy was so debilitated it would collapse of its own accord. France would be defeated – and in this, Italy would prove an ally. Britain, which was itself a Germanic nation, would offer no opposition and would come to an understanding.

To achieve these ambitions, Hitler would direct the German people by means of propaganda. "To be a leader," he said, "means to move masses." This could never be done by rational means, but only by using the spoken word to create emotions of hysterical intensity. The leader must recycle a crowd's emotions, feeding the people with their own feelings, reinforced by utter self-confidence. There must be no hesitation, weakness or concession. The leader must lie, if that served his purpose, and make the lies big, "because in the big lie there is always a certain force of credibility".

This oratorical technique would be backed by two other elements: paraphernalia and ritual that would create a sense of power greater than the individual, and brute force to ensure that no opposing voices would be heard.

It was a vision devoid of humanity, spirituality or creativity; it was a barbaric vision, and deliberately so, for it was through barbarism, Hitler firmly believed, that the dynamic, healthy new culture would replace the degenerate old one.

Dr. Joseph Goebbels, who orchestrated Hitler's campaign for office during the 1920s, gives the camera a baleful glance during a 1933 visit to the League of Nations' Geneva headquarters. An academic turned journalist, Goebbels built up support for the Nazis in Berlin by means that included, on his own admission, "slanderous agitation and all the vile cunning of the gutter press". He was largely responsible for creating the myth of Hitler's infallibility and was rewarded in 1935 with control of the ministry of information and propaganda. In that capacity he also exercised strict supervision of the press, radio, cinema, theatre and literature.

"We are barbarians!" he proclaimed proudly. "We want to be barbarians! It is an honourable title. We shall rejuvenate the world!"

It was a vision conceived against all the odds. When Hitler was released in December 1924, he was apparently finished as a political force. Yet within nine years, he was ready to re-create his nation, and Europe, in his own terrible image.

His methods would not be those that had failed him in Munich. He would not again challenge authority directly. He would establish his own political organization and work his way to power legally. "Democracy," he declared, "must be destroyed by the weapons of democracy."

For a while, conditions did not favour him. For one thing, he was still on parole, and banned from making public speeches. For another, the economy revived. After the horrors of the 1923 inflation, a new currency restored stability. Reparation payments were reduced, and France evacuated the Ruhr. International confidence was further restored by the election as president of Field Marshal Paul von Hindenburg, the last chief of the general staff, who had with Ludendorff effectively controlled military and civilian policy during the last two years of the war. Generous dollar loans poured in from America.

All Hitler could achieve in these years was a slow growth in party membership, up to 178,000 in 1929, and the establishment of a national organization. The Nazis won their first seats in the Reichstag (Berlin's parliament building) in 1928; among the 12 successful candidates were the swaggering former Luftwaffe pilot Hermann Göring, whose contacts with industrialists would prove important to Nazi finances, and the brilliant propagandist, Joseph Goebbels.

Not until 1929 did the tide turn in Hitler's favour. When the American stock market crashed, U.S. banks called in their loans. Dole queues grew longer, businesses closed, properties were repossessed, public works ended. In 1930 unemployment rose to four million. A second plan for reparations rescheduled payments at a lower level, but for a forbidding 60 years.

In the 1930 elections, the Nazis broke through, winning 107 seats and six million votes, second only to the Social Democrats. With the party's leader now a figure of national importance, Nazi membership rose to 800,000. The next elections, which were held in 1932, were for the presidency, when Hitler challenged the venerable Hindenburg, now 84. Hitler lost but, as luck would have it, Hindenburg failed by 0.4 per cent to achieve the overall majority required by law. A second campaign followed, which allowed Goebbels to mastermind an unprecedented publicity campaign: Hitler covered the country by plane, speaking in 20 towns in a week. Hindenburg won again, but Hitler increased his vote and was in a strong position for the forthcoming parliamentary elections.

With unemployment now around six million, Hitler's extremist views and simplistic solutions appealed to almost all sections of German society. Again he toured the country by air, covering 50 cities in the second half of July. In each, SA troops paraded though the streets, breaking up rival meetings and beating up opponents. This time the Nazis won the most seats, 230 out of 608 – still not an absolute majority, but enough to make Hitler the most powerful figure in German politics. The chancellor, the aristocratic Franz von Papen, offered him the vice-chancellorship.

But Hitler, as Mussolini had done in 1922, determined to play for higher stakes. Spurning von Papen's offer, he demanded the post of chancellor itself. Von Papen and Hindenburg turned him down flat. Fortunately for Hitler, there then followed months of political deadlock, until finally Hindenburg, fearing civil war, backed down and offered Hitler the position he wanted. But there were conditions attached: Hitler would have to accept von Papen as his vice-chancellor and appoint no more than three Nazis to the cabinet.

One of these was Göring, who as Prussian minister of the interior at once began a drastic purge of the Prussian administration, replacing hundreds of officials with Nazis and establishing an auxiliary Nazi police force of 50,000 – the Gestapo.

Still not satisfied, Hitler demanded yet another election. Events now played dramatically into his hands. On February 27, 1933, Hitler was dining with Goebbels when news reached them that the Reichstag was on fire. A young Dutch Communist, Marinus van der Lubbe, was arrested shortly before Göring – by apparent coincidence – arrived at the scene of the crime. Hitler seized his opportunity. Claiming that the fire was a signal for a leftist uprising, he insisted on an emergency

Members of the Nazi Labour Corps drill with shovels soon after Hitler came to power. The corps had a dual purpose. It trained potential soldiers at a time when the official German army was limited to a strength of 100,000 by the terms of the Treaty of Versailles, drawn up by the victors of World War I. It also provided a cheap labour force for industry and public works programmes, and was instrumental in lowering unemployment, which dropped from some six million in 1933 to less than three million the following year.

decree suspending civil rights. Göring's Gestapo arrested 4,000 Communists. Van der Lubbe was tried, found guilty and executed.

At the next elections, in early March, the Nazis increased their seats to 288, polling 43.9 per cent of the votes. Despite the near-monopoly of propaganda they now enjoyed and the intimidating tactics of the SA, this was still not a majority. But it hardly mattered. Hitler demanded the right under a so-called Enabling Act to rule by decree for four years. In a parliamentary chamber dominated by a huge swastika and ranks of SA troops, the frightened deputies granted him dictatorial powers by a large majority. (They had good reason to be frightened: of the 94 dissenters, 24 were subsequently murdered.)

As the Nazi revolution got under way, there remained one further possible source of opposition: the street-brawling storm-troopers who had bludgeoned Hitler's opponents into silence. The two million SA outnumbered the army many times over, and their coarse, outspoken boss, Ernst Röhm, was eager to take over the army completely. But Hitler was already thinking of conquests outside Germany, and for that he needed the regular army more than a mob of sadistic hooligans. To deal with Röhm, he called upon his own newly formed bodyguard, the *Schutzstaffel* (Protection Squad) or SS, a small elite later to become an army in its own right.

On the night of June 29 to 30, 1934 – the "Night of the Long Knives" – the SS arrested Röhm and many others of Hitler's rivals and opponents, inside and outside the Nazi party. No-one knows how many were killed: 82, according to Nazi sources; over 400, according to more objective estimates. "So! Now I have taken a bath and feel clean as a newborn babe again," Hitler told his private secretary.

Five weeks later, the ailing Hindenburg died and, in a move pre-arranged with the grateful leaders of the army, Hitler had the chancellorship merged with the presidency, which carried with it supreme command of the armed forces. Designating himself Fuhrer (Leader) of the German people, Hitler demanded that all officers and men swear an oath of "unconditional obedience", not to the state or to any of its offices, but to him personally. Finally, to rubber-stamp his actions, he held a plebiscite: 90 per cent of the population approved. "Thus I have conquered the German people," he boasted.

There was now nothing to prevent Hitler starting on the course he had mapped out for the creation of a greater Germany under his sole authority. A process of "coordination" legalized his efforts, bringing all organized life under the control of the Nazi party. Local parliaments, administrations and police forces were all given Nazi leaders. All political parties save the Nazis were outlawed. A new People's Court held trials for treason – a crime defined by the court itself. SA gangs were immune from prosecution. A new Labour Front replaced trade

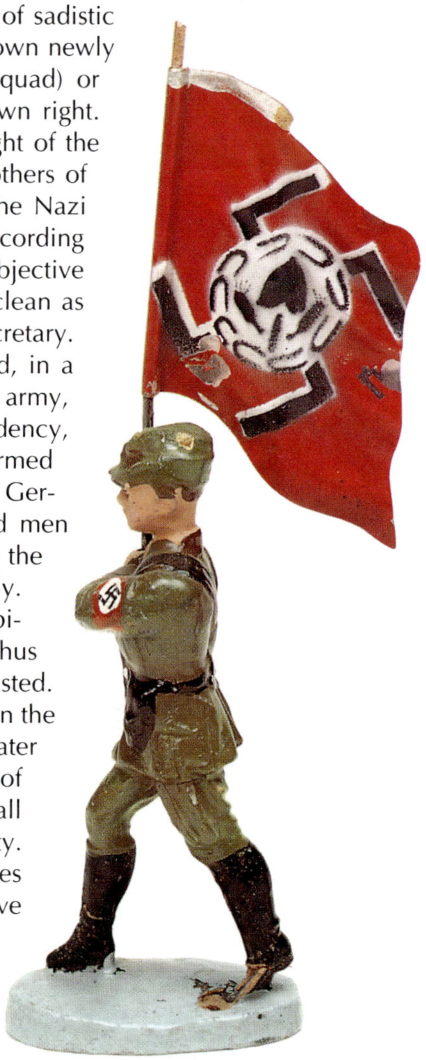

These six-centimetre-high toy soldiers, produced by the million in the 1930s, helped to spread the cult of Nazi militarism among children of the Third Reich. The models represent Hitler himself, with an arm that rotates to give the Nazi salute, and four standard-bearers. From left to right, they show members of the Labour Front, the only legal trade union; the Air Sports Club, which trained military pilots in contravention of the ban on a German air force that was imposed after World War I; the League of German Girls, a Nazi youth organization; and its male equivalent, the Hitler Youth.

unions. The first concentration camps were set up. In 1935, by the infamous Nuremberg Laws, Jews were barred from businesses and professions, and forbidden to marry German "nationals". Teachers were required to join the Nazi Teachers League, and all children from the age of six were co-opted into the Hitler Youth. The Protestant church came under state control, and an agreement with the Vatican forbade Catholic clergy from engaging in active politics.

For a while the Nazi revolution seemed to provide precisely what had been promised. Hitler knew nothing of economics, but he knew what the German people wanted: work and pride in their country. In some areas, Nazi measures did strengthen the economy. Strikes were forbidden, and labour schemes – principally in the armaments, agricultural and building industries – helped to reduce unemployment from six million to 1.7 million by 1935. In general, however, Germany's economic revival owed more to the country's clever financial administrators and industrial managers than to Nazi initiatives. Under the guidance of Hjalmar Schacht, president of the Reichsbank and economics minister, foreign debts were again rescheduled, export subsidies were granted to boost foreign trade, and barter

agreements were reached in order to give access to vitally needed raw materials. As a consequence, production per head rose 64 per cent in the first six years of Hitler's rule. Domestic production of oil, plastics, fibres and synthetic rubber rose as much as tenfold in the late 1930s.

The majority of Germany's new-found prosperity was diverted into rebuilding the nation's military strength. Hitler had made his priorites quite clear within a few weeks of becoming chancellor: "Every publicly supported project for creating employment must be judged by one criterion alone: is it or is it not requisite for the restoration of the German nation's fighting capability?" Under the terms of the Treaty of Versailles, Germany was allowed an army of no more than 100,000, only a token navy and no air force at all. This limitation Hitler had always declared to be iniquitous. Now he demanded equality of status. Perhaps, he suggested, other countries should disarm down to Germany's level. When that suggestion was rejected, he withdrew from the League of Nations, the international organization set up by the Treaty of Versailles to preserve world peace. At first secretly, and then openly, Hitler oversaw a massive programme of rearmament which was designed to make Germany capable of waging an aggressive war by 1940. In 1936 he announced his intention to multiply arms expenditure sixfold, from almost six billion marks to over 32 billion in 1939.

On November 5, 1937, Hitler revealed in a secret conference with his military chiefs his long-term ambitions in Europe. The need for *Lebensraum* was paramount, and so it was vital that in the period between 1938 and 1943 Austria and Czechoslovakia be taken over by Germany, Poland be overrun, and finally that Russia be invaded and conquered.

When Hitler met Mussolini in 1934, he was already thinking about his first foreign adventure, the annexation of Austria. Since his rise to power, Vienna's Nazi party had been preparing for Germany to forge an indissoluble union – Anschluss – with the country of his birth. In July 1934, a group of party members dressed as Austrian soldiers shot dead the Austrian chancellor, Engelbert Dollfuss, a dictatorial character who hated Nazis and Communists alike. But the Austrian army and government failed to back the plotters. They were arrested, and Mussolini, who was guarantor of Austria's independence, dispatched 50,000 troops to guard the country's borders. Hitler was shocked: he thought that he had won the Duce's compliance in Venice the previous month. For the moment, he pulled back from any further action, disclaiming any connection with the murder, and set about weaning Mussolini from his commitment to Austria.

The next two years were frustrating ones for Hitler. It was not until 1936, by which time his army had grown to more than half a million, that he achieved his first coup in foreign policy. On March 7, columns of goose-stepping infantrymen marched into Cologne and other major cities between the Rhine and the French border. Under the Treaty of Versailles, the whole Rhineland was a buffer zone, out of bounds to German soldiers. Hitler had in effect torn up the treaty. German crowds roared their delight, and in a subsequent plebiscite – now an established tactic to display his popularity – the people of the Rhineland approved his action by an overwhelming 98.8 per cent.

France and Britain protested, but did nothing: no-one was willing to believe that Hitler was actively preparing for war. Most statesmen preferred to think that he was merely undoing the worst humiliations of Versailles – humiliations that many had regarded as unfair in the first place. If France had sent in her own troops, Hitler's token force would have had to withdraw, but no-one had the stomach to wage war against Hitler for marching into German territory. As the London *Times* remarked, Hitler had done nothing more than go "into his own back garden".

Mussolini, meanwhile, had looked further afield. As Italy's economy faltered in the 1930s, he sought to extend the country's possessions in Africa, where Italy's colonial holdings – Eritrea, Italian Somaliland and Libya – were, in the Duce's words, mere "crumbs from the sumptuous booty of others". On Somaliland's border lay a likely victim, Ethiopia, which was, he declared, a treasure house of gold, platinum, oil, coal and agricultural wealth. In October 1935, 300,000 Italian troops equipped with artillery, bombers and mustard gas invaded Ethiopia. Their ragged, poorly armed opponents proved easy victims. Among the combatants was Mussolini's son, Vittorio, a pilot, who wrote that every Italian boy should try his hand at warfare some day because it was the most thrilling of sports. He found it particularly "diverting" to bomb Galla tribesmen and see the group "bursting out like a rose after I had landed a bomb in the middle of them". On May 5, 1936, Italian tanks rolled unopposed into Addis Ababa: the emperor, Haile Selassie, together with his family and hundreds of retainers, had fled to exile in Britain.

Other countries expressed shock, but did not intervene. The League of Nations proved woefully inadequate at imposing international constraints. It branded Mussolini an aggressor and imposed economic sanctions. From the start, however, these trade restrictions were a dead letter, for no-one wanted to drive Mussolini into starting a European war either on his own or – far worse – in alliance with Germany, the other threat to international peace. As a result, the sanctions were never meant to be punitive. They did not include such essential commodities as coal, steel and oil; they did not even involve forbidding Italy to use the Suez Canal, the main conduit of Italian overseas imports.

In any case, the result of the sanctions was precisely the opposite of what had been intended. Angered by criticism from France and Britain, which had hitherto enjoyed reasonably amicable relations with Italy, Mussolini spoke bitterly of European governments preferring "a horde of barbarian negroes" over the "mother of civilization". Moreover, he began to see in Hitler a possible ally. In late 1936, after both countries had sent military support for the Nationalists in the Spanish Civil War, a bitter conflict between communist-backed Republicans and the right-wing forces of General Francisco Franco, Mussolini spoke for the first time of a Rome-Berlin "Axis". The following year he made a state visit to Germany, where Hitler laid on an SS parade, military manoeuvres, and a Berlin rally of one million people, all roaring support for the two leaders. After that, Mussolini's doubts about Hitler vanished, as did his commitment to Austria's independence. "Austria," he said not long afterwards, "is German state number two."

At last Hitler was free to settle the unfinished business with his country of birth. On February 12, 1938, he invited the Austrian chancellor, Kurt von Schuschnigg, to his mountain retreat at Berchtesgaden, southeast of Munich. There he subjected him to a two-hour tirade, demanding that a team of named Nazis be included in the Austrian government and that all arrested Nazis be released. He then produced an ultimatum: Schuschnigg must sign a prepared agreement conceding Hitler's

Boys of the Hitler Youth *(below)* adopt the steely gaze and rigid postures expected of them as future soldiers. Hitler was determined to create a young male generation imbued with physical fitness, martial courage and dedication to their leader as the hero and saviour of his people. Their female counterparts were expected to be paragons of femininity, an ideal implicit in the dress and deportment of members of the League of German Girls *(right)*. Legally excluded from holding any high party office, university professorships or judicial posts, women were encouraged to seek no role other than that of devoted mothers. "With each child that she brings into the nation," Hitler declared, "she is fighting her fight on behalf of the nation."

demands, or the issue would be settled by force. "Think it over, Herr Schuschnigg, think it over well. I can only wait until this afternoon. If I tell you that, you will do well to take my words literally. I don't believe in bluffing. All my past is proof of that." After thinking it over, the browbeaten Schuschnigg signed.

Back in Vienna, however, his courage revived and he announced that there would be a plebiscite for the people to decide whether or not Austria should remain independent. The enraged Hitler demanded that he cancel the plebiscite or face invasion. Schuschnigg capitulated, then resigned. His provisional successor, interior minister Arthur Seyss-Inquart, a Nazi stooge acting on orders from Berlin, promptly requested a German invasion to "restore order".

Before he acted, Hitler took pains to clear his decision with Mussolini, who offered no objections. Hitler was delighted. "I shall stick with him whatever may

happen," he said – one of the few promises he would keep.

German troops crossed the border on March 12, to a tumultuous reception. Hitler followed two days later, making a triumphant return to the city where he had once starved in obscurity. A month later, in a plebiscite, 99.75 per cent of Austrians approved the Anschluss. Socialists, Communists and Jews were publicly humiliated. Schuschnigg was sent to a concentration camp.

Once again, no country did anything to stop him. Just as with the Rhineland, Hitler had publicly declared his commitment to peace, gambled that other countries would not want violence, and had then taken what he wanted. The first of the targets he had listed to his generals had been acquired without a single shot being fired; now he was beginning to think about the next. On the flight back to Germany from Vienna, Hitler showed a crumpled newspaper cutting to his chief of staff, Wilhelm Keitel. It was a sketch map of the Reich's new frontiers, which now hemmed in Czechoslovakia on three sides. Placing his left hand on the map so that his forefinger and thumb were on Czechoslovakia's frontiers, he winked at Keitel, slowly pinching finger and thumb together.

The nations most concerned by Germany's expansion were the old war-time allies, France and Britain. Yet, apart from increasing their own military strength, neither took any positive steps to thwart Hitler. True, the French and the British were not in a position to impose their will on Germany by force. French generals had opted for a defensive military strategy, believing themselves to be safe behind the concrete blockhouses of the Maginot line that guarded their eastern frontier, while British leaders put their faith in a deliberate policy of "appeasement", by which was meant an understanding response to legitimate grievances and a way to reconcile former enemies. At the time it was seen as a noble ideal: magnanimous, sound security, good business.

Appeasement had a tireless champion in Neville Chamberlain, a former businessman and lord mayor of Birmingham who became British prime minister in May 1937. Courageous and self-confident, he was determined to go down in history as a great peacemaker, and for this, according to Winston Churchill, Chamberlain's successor and Hitler's implacable foe (but only an ordinary Member of Parliament in 1937), "he was prepared to strive continually in the teeth of facts". It never occurred to Chamberlain that Hitler did not want peace, that his whole personality, the personality of the Nazi regime, demanded the waging of war.

In the event of war with Czechoslovakia, Hitler's generals cautioned, conquest was not a foregone conclusion. Although only a young country, carved from the

LEGITIMIZING RACIAL HATRED

Anti-Semitism was Hitler's emotional bedrock. As a young man in Vienna, he had convinced himself that Jews were responsible for all of the political and economic woes that beset European society, and when he came to power he introduced drastic measures to eliminate them from public life. Jewish shops, lawyers and doctors were officially boycotted. Jewish children were banned from state schools, where Nazi ideas concerning race were introduced into the curriculum. Some of the most odious anti-Semitic children's literature was published by Julius Streicher, a sadistic pornographer whose tabloid newspaper *Der Stürmer* ("The Storm-Trooper") had functioned as a mouthpiece for Hitler's racist views since the 1920s.

In 1935, Hitler formalized his prejudices in the notorious Nuremberg Laws, which deprived Jews of their citizenship and prohibited intermarriage between Jew and "Aryan" – the Nazis' term for the hypothetical German ethnic type.

But how to tell Jew from Aryan? Pseudo-scientists were soon found to provide definitions of Aryan and Jewish physical characteristics. By such means, Hitler isolated the Jews from the rest of society, leaving them defenceless against the Nazi violence that would culminate in their systematic mass-murder.

In an attempt to confer respectability on a pseudo-science, a Nazi "race identification table" used for classroom display *(left)* purports to portray typical heads of the German "races". The classification is quite without basis in anthropology.

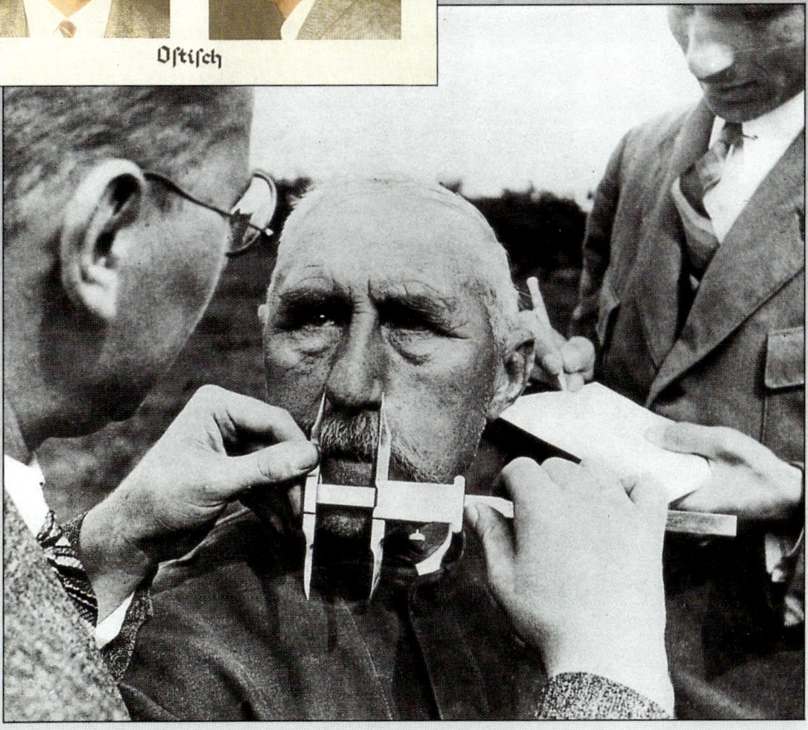

An illustration from one of Julius Streicher's anti-Semitic children's books shows blond Germanic pupils rejoicing as grossly caricatured Jewish children together with their teacher are expelled from school so that "order and discipline" can be restored.

Two "experts" measure the width of an old man's nose in an effort to compile a series of statistics supposed to determine his racial origin. In 1936, a League for Propagation of Racial Knowledge opened offices in larger German cities, inviting people to prove their "racial purity".

ruins of the Austro-Hungarian empire in 1919, it was a healthy democracy, with thriving industries – including an important armaments industry – a well-trained army, alliances with France and Russia, and strong western defences. Its weakness lay in its many minorities, including some three million German-speakers in the heavily industrialized Sudetenland bordering Germany. These were to provide Hitler with his pretext for invasion.

Only two weeks after the seizure of Austria, Hitler briefed the Sudetenland leader, Konrad Henlein, on how to proceed. "Always demand so much that we can never be satisfied," he said. Refusal could then be met by outrage and civil unrest – subversive action that would be supported by Germany. Henlein therefore demanded of Czechoslovakia's president, Eduard Benes, nothing less than independence for the Sudetenland. Benes responded with a number of counter-offers guaranteeing greater freedom for the Sudeten Germans, but as Henlein always found something to object to, the President turned for support to his principal ally, France. The French premier, Edouard Daladier, appealed to Neville Chamberlain to find a solution to the problem.

To Hitler's delight and astonishment, the British prime minister at once sent a message proposing that he should fly to Germany for talks to settle the dispute. On September 15, 1938, after a seven-hour flight – his first – Chamberlain was greeted by the Fuhrer at Berchtesgaden. Hitler reiterated his intention to see justice done for the Sudeten Germans, even if it meant backing Henlein with an invasion. Chamberlain became impatient. Why had Hitler allowed him to come, if he was determined to settle the matter by force? Hitler's mood softened. He suggested that the cession of the Sudetenland to Germany might offer a way out of the impasse. Chamberlain agreed in principle and then departed, leaving Hitler confident that Czechoslovakia would never agree to such a proposal. Preparations for invasion, set for October 1, continued.

But Benes, under pressure from the British and the French, did agree. Delighted, Chamberlain again flew to Germany on September 22 and told Hitler that his terms had been accepted. It was precisely the opposite of what Hitler wanted; he planned to take all of Czechoslovakia. "I am exceedingly sorry," he told the bemused prime minister, "but after the events of the last few days this solution is no longer of any use." Now he demanded immediate German occupation of the Sudetenland by September 28. Chamberlain protested, at which Hitler agreed to a delay of three days – until October 1.

Benes rejected this new set of demands. France at last stated that it would stand by its obligations and defend Czechoslovakia. Britain, too, prepared for war. "How horrible, fantastic, incredible it is," Chamberlain said in a broadcast to the nation, "that we should be digging trenches and laying gas masks here because of a quarrel in a faraway country between peoples of whom we know nothing."

On September 26, Hitler addressed a huge crowd in Berlin's Palace of Sport. In a speech full of extreme distortion and invective, he painted a lurid picture of Sudeten Germans being

Barefoot Ethiopian troops parade before marching off to fight the Italian armies that invaded their country in 1935. The poor state of the nation's forces convinced Mussolini that what he called the "greatest colonial war in all history" would be a "war without tears". But, although the Ethiopian defenders never had any real chance against the Duce's motorized columns, bombers and poison gas, it took the Italians eight months to take the capital Addis Ababa. During the campaign, the Italian side lost about 5,000 soldiers. They were mostly troops from Italy's African colonies – a fact that prompted Mussolini to comment that he wished more Italians had been killed so as to make the war seem more serious.

JAPAN TAKES THE WARPATH

Japan appeared to be firmly set on a course towards parliamentary democracy until, in the early 1930s, world depression brought it to economic ruin. Rejecting the liberal policies favoured by the then government, ultra-nationalist groups led by the armed forces embarked on a campaign to establish a military dictatorship whose ultimate aim was Japanese hegemony in the Far East.

Their first target was Chinese Manchuria and its huge natural resources, which the Japanese war minister – a serving officer who was therefore outside government control – believed to be a prerequisite for the successful waging of war. In 1931, army officers acting without the approval of the Japanese cabinet provoked an incident which they then used as an excuse to seize Manchurian towns.

Japanese politicians who were opposed to the Manchurian adventure were assassinated by young army officers dedicated to the code of *bushido*, the "way of the warrior". When, in 1932, the League of Nations condemned Japanese aggression, Japan simply quit the League. Supported by a wave of nationalist sentiment back home, the Japanese army took over the whole of Manchuria by 1933.

Four years later, the military fabricated an excuse to launch a full-scale attack on China, beginning an undeclared war that would last eight years. As pressure to resist Japanese expansion mounted in the United States, the Asian warlords looked for allies overseas. On September 27, 1940, Japan joined with Germany and Italy in a tripartite pact, by which each recognized the other's imperial ambitions.

General Hideki Tojo, the Japanese war minister, makes a ritual bow to the emperor, Hirohito, at a military review in October 1940. The real balance of power, however, was the other way around. Hirohito, although revered by the Japanese as a living god, had little part in shaping Japanese foreign policy, while Tojo, former chief of staff of Japanese forces in Manchuria, was a major force behind the growth of Japanese militarism. A year later, he would become prime minister and lead his country into war with the Western Allies.

forced to flee a ravaged countryside, portraying himself as a simple, pacific German and Benes as a lying, cheating warmonger. Benes, he yelled, pounding the podium, must agree now to hand over the Sudetenland. This "is the last territorial claim which I have to make in Europe . . . The decision now lies in his hands: peace or war." The deadline was 2.00 p.m. on September 28.

Hours before the deadline was due to expire, feverish representations from the British government persuaded Mussolini to intervene with a last-minute appeal to Hitler for a 24-hour delay in his war plans. Chamberlain, Mussolini explained, wanted a conference to discuss a negotiated settlement. Hitler agreed, provided that the meeting was held within the 24 hours. Invitations to attend were sent to Chamberlain and Daladier. Benes was not invited.

On September 29, the leaders of the four powers gathered in Munich to consider the terms of a draft treaty which was presented by Mussolini (but prepared by the German foreign ministry and Göring). In substance, the treaty merely repeated the demands already made by Hitler at his last meeting with Chamberlain: the Czechs were to complete their evacuation of the Sudetenland by October 10. Just after midnight on September 30, the British and French leaders agreed to the proposals. Czechoslovakia was to be partitioned.

Chamberlain returned to Britain convinced that he had averted war — the more so because he had persuaded Hitler to sign another sheet of paper, hastily typed, recording "the desire of our two peoples never to go to war with one another again". Arriving at London's Heston airport, Chamberlain uttered words that were soon to be given a tragic irony by events: "I believe it is peace for our time," he said, waving his piece of paper. "Peace with honour."

Once again, Hitler was assured of a major prize without firing a shot, but it was not the way he wanted it. "That fellow Chamberlain has spoilt my entry into Prague," he complained to his SS entourage back in Berlin. Nevertheless, Czechoslovakia was a corpse, ready for dismemberment. Benes resigned and went into exile in Britain. In March 1939, Hitler and his aides lambasted the new president, the ailing Emil Hacha (at one point the old man actually fainted when Göring threatened to destroy Prague with bombs), until he signed away the other western provinces of Bohemia and Moravia. Hours later, encountering no resistance, German troops rolled eastwards.

There were others, too, who were eager to tear at the dying country. Poland seized for itself a northern pocket known as Teschen; Hungary grabbed a strip of land along the border, and then the eastern province of Ruthenia. All that was left was a rump, Slovakia, which had nominal independence as a German protectorate. Czechoslovakia had simply ceased to exist.

Hard upon Munich, more German demands followed. First Hitler forced Lithuania to cede the German-speaking city of Memel. Next he turned his attention to Poland. The root of dissension here was the Baltic port of Danzig, a city of Germans isolated within Poland. Hitler demanded that a corridor be established between Danzig and the Reich. Confident that the Poles would not refuse, at first he did not contemplate using military action.

But at this moment — March 31, 1939 — Chamberlain, seeking ways to counter criticism of his betrayal of Czechoslovakia, offered to guarantee Poland's security. He still did not believe that Hitler would actually go to war, but he had become

THE SPANISH CRUCIBLE

In 1936, when Spain collapsed into civil war, it seemed to outsiders that the ideologies that were dividing Europe – fascism and communism – were formally opposed for the first time.

But the war, which began when army chiefs in Spanish Morocco rose against the Republican government in Madrid, was a far more complex affair: of employers against workers, landless peasants against property owners, Church against state, armed forces against civilian powers.

The government was a diverse coalition of left-wing groups. The rebels, alarmed that the country was about to surrender to communism, were supported by the Catholic church, the middle class and a small fascist party, the Falangists. They were eventually welded together by the austere General Francisco Franco – portrayed in the postwar mural above as a crusader who united army and Church.

With aid from Hitler and Mussolini, Franco rapidly gained control of the west and south of Spain. Hitler had a particular interest in the war: here he could test out his new air force. German planes ferried Franco's troops from Africa, and the 100 aircraft of the Condor Legion gave the Nationalists command of the air. Mussolini, eager not be outdone, sent almost 50,000 troops to fight for the Nationalists.

None of Europe's democratic governments responded to Republican pleas for help, but individuals did: some 40,000 of them enlisted in the International Brigades that were organized by Communist International. The Soviet Union also sent military aid; in October 1936, Russian aircraft and tanks temporarily saved Madrid for the Republicans.

Both sides fought with equal brutality and with scant regard for the lives of noncombatants. In one notorious atrocity that foreshadowed the terrors of World War II, Guernica, the Basque capital, was completely destroyed by German bombers, with heavy loss of civilian life.

The war dragged on for over two years, until Franco's better-disciplined, better-equipped forces cut through depleted Republican lines. By April 1939, it was over, leaving almost a million Spaniards dead, with Franco the dictator of a new military regime. Shattered, Spain stayed out of World War II, recovering slowly thereafter under Franco's stern control.

convinced that Britain needed an ally in eastern Europe. That ally could have been the Soviet Union, which had made overtures to Britain, but West and East were divided by a gulf of mistrust. The West had sought the destruction of Bolshevik Russia in 1918; and the Bolsheviks were in theory committed to undermining capitalist countries. Besides, Western politicians were convinced that Stalin was a savage, his armies in tatters, his political system teetering on the verge of collapse. In brief, Russia was both too dangerous and too weak to be an ally.

Exuberant Londoners cheer Prime Minister Neville Chamberlain on the night of September 30, 1938. Two days earlier, he had signed the Munich Agreement, conceding Hitler's demand that German troops be allowed to occupy the Sudetenland, Czechoslovakia's German-speaking border region. Although one of Chamberlain's cabinet colleagues resigned in protest at this betrayal of a friendly democracy, the Prime Minister's belief that by sacrificing Czech territory he had won "peace for our time" was widely shared, and not only in England. In Germany, where the military had been openly dubious about the prospects of conquering Czechoslovakia, a wave of relief swept the country. Hitler, however, saw Britain's policy of appeasement as a sign of weakness, which encouraged him to make further territorial demands.

Poland's foreign minister, Joseph Beck accepted Chamberlain's offer instantly and then firmly rejected Hitler's demands. The Fuhrer was astonished by the appeaser's new-found resilience. "They are little worms," he said, "I saw them in Munich." And again, in fury: "I'll cook them a stew they'll choke on!" The stew that Hitler planned was nothing less than war on Poland. The date was set for September 1.

That summer, Hitler received a much-needed reassurance. A perpetual worry for Germany was the possibility of war on two fronts simultaneously – in the west against France and Britain, and in the east against Russia. The problem had dominated German planning before World War I, and it remained a nightmare for German generals – or would have done, had not the Soviet Union itself signalled a desire to improve relations with Germany. It did so because Stalin had finally given up the idea of an alliance with Britain.

Although they remained long-term enemies, Hitler and Stalin both had a cynical interest in a short-term alliance. It would ensure that Hitler would not be faced with a conflict on two fronts at the same time should Britain and France actually fight on behalf of Poland; and it would also give Stalin the time to rebuild his army, which had been seriously weakened by ideological purges. Neither had any illusions about the other's long-term aims. "Everything that I undertake is directed against Russia," Hitler said. "If the West is too stupid and too blind to understand this, then I will be forced to reach an understanding with the Russians, smash the West, and then turn all my concentrated strength on the Soviet Union." "I know what Hitler's up to," Stalin confided to a colleague. "He thinks he's outsmarted me, but actually it is I who have outsmarted him."

On August 23, Nazi Germany and the Soviet Union signed what was ostensibly a nonaggression pact. But under a secret protocol, the two simply divided up Poland and other territories. Hitler would take western Poland, while Stalin would seize eastern Poland, part of Finland, the Baltic states of Lithuania, Latvia and Estonia, and part of Romania. It was perhaps the most astonishing event of an astonishing

Registering dull shock or helpless anger, a crowd of Czechs watch helplessly as German troops enter Prague on March 15, 1939. After their country's frontier defences had been signed away at Munich, the Czechoslovak government tried rigorously to comply with the terms of the agreement so as to save the rest of the country from annexation. But Hitler, whose intention had always been to seize the entire Czechoslovak state, used the excuse of a Slovak separatist uprising to occupy Prague less than six months after the Sudetenland. In contravention of the Munich Agreement, most of the country was declared a German protectorate, but Britain and France again did nothing, arguing that the voluntary severance of Slovakia from the country nullified their guarantee to protect the integrity of the Czechoslovak state.

decade. Both leaders had simply tossed all their well-rehearsed convictions aside, and the political world was suddenly turned upside down.

Only Chamberlain's guarantee to Poland could deter Hitler now, but convinced that Britain would do no more than "just put on an act of waging war" he set zero hour for 4.45 a.m. on September 1. "I've given the order," he told his foreign minister. "I've set the ball rolling."

This time, he lost his gamble. Chamberlain was still talking about a negotiated settlement when German bombs fell on Warsaw, but the House of Commons had had enough. Under pressure, Chamberlain sent an ultimatum to Hitler telling him to desist by 11.00 a.m. on September 3. When it expired, Britain announced that it was at war with Germany, and France unwillingly followed suit that afternoon.

Hitler's weapon against Poland was blitzkrieg (lightning war) – a new concept that had emerged in the 1920s and 1930s among military strategists who were anxious to avoid a repetition of the dogged stalemates that had characterized the First

Armed with lances and sabres, a Polish cavalry unit practises manoeuvres in April 1939, four months before the German invasion of their country that was to pit them against fast-moving tanks and screaming dive bombers. During the early days of the attack, some Polish cavalry charged the tanks in the belief that they were nothing but cars covered by painted plywood – a training device used by the Germany army before it had proper armoured vehicles. Hitler's invasion of Poland finally led Britain and France to declare war on Germany. But the two powers could do little to aid their far-off ally, and within a month Poland was vanquished, its lands divided between Nazi Germany and its new, short-term ally, the Soviet Union.

World War. In Germany, a number of more progressive generals, most notably Heinz Guderian, devised strategies that were based on fast-moving armoured units of tanks, trucks and self-propelled artillery. The ground forces would be supported by aircraft, including reconnaissance planes, fighters, and dive bombers which would act as airborne artillery. A few radical military thinkers in England, Italy and France (among them an abrasive young staff college lecturer named Charles de Gaulle, the future leader of France) also shared this vision, but they were outnumbered by traditionalists who continued to insist that battlegrounds were the domain of infantry and static defences. Hitler, however, had been quick to see the advantages of fast and decisive campaigns.

Put to the test against Poland, blitzkrieg proved to be an overwhelming success. First, bombers droned deep behind the enemy lines to destroy airfields, railway stations, bridges and fuel dumps. All along the front, Polish troops were assaulted by the terrifying Junkers-87 *Sturzkampfflieger* (dive bomber), better known as the Stuka, which plunged almost vertically, its siren wailing, to release bombs with devastating accuracy. Then came the tanks, bursting through weak points in the defences, fanning out to split the enemy forces, wheeling to destroy and capture. If the Polish troops stayed to fight, they were surrounded; if they attempted to retreat, they ran into the chaos caused by the bombers.

Even the weather seemed to be on the side of the Germans. Clear, sunny skies baked the ground hard for the tanks and kept the rivers – Poland's only natural lines of defence – low. Within days, western Poland was in German hands. Any hopes that the Poles could regroup in the east were dashed on September 17, when Stalin, fulfilling his agreement with Hitler, invaded across the eastern frontier. The armies of the two aggressors met at the River Bug, the new demarcation between the Third Reich and the Soviet Union.

In western Europe there was a brief flurry of activity. The French mobilized five million men. The British started a blockade of German ports and dispatched two divisions, the British Expeditionary Force, to help the French forces. Then all fell quiet again. Tradition dictated that no attack could be mounted without massive artillery bombardments, and the guns were not yet ready. The Polish campaign was over and the German army was ready to meet any threat before the Western allies were able to do anything effective.

Hitler was all for making a pre-emptive strike, with the aim of occupying the Low Countries and the Channel coastline down to Calais; but his generals, who had counted on several weeks' lull to build up strength, were so appalled that some of them considered deposing him. In the end they simply stalled for time, then produced an unoriginal plan involving a massive thrust through Belgium, similar to the German opening advance of 1914. Hitler did not like it; he himself favoured a push through the hilly, forested Ardennes region of southern Belgium, an area that his experts assured him was impenetrable by heavy armour. The onset of winter forced a postponement, but essentially the conservative plan was accepted – until, in January, it fell into Allied hands when a Luftwaffe plane crashed in Belgium. In something of a panic, the Germans went back to the drawing board.

In a work entitled *Rendezvous*, the British cartoonist David Low portrays Adolf Hitler and Joseph Stalin greeting one another over the prostrate body of a defeated Poland. On August 23, 1939, the two dictators, for long the bitterest of ideological enemies, had made a secret agreement to partition Poland as part of a hastily negotiated nonaggression pact. Stalin thereby bought time to build up his armed forces, while Hitler secured his eastern frontiers, enabling him to plan his 1940 invasion of Belgium and France. The Fuhrer's hatred of Soviet communism remained undimmed, however, and within two years of signing the pact with Stalin he was to launch a full-scale invasion of his supposed ally.

Soldiers of the British Expeditionary Force wade away from the beaches at Dunkirk, in northern France, to a waiting ship – one of the 900 small vessels that helped rescue over 300,000 Allied troops between May 27 and June 4, 1940. Trapped in a German pincer, these men would have had no alternative but surrender had Hitler not stopped the advance. He wanted to preserve his armour for a final offensive against the French army, whose defeat he felt sure would bring Britain to the negotiating table. In addition he was under pressure from Hermann Göring to leave the rest of the battle to the Luftwaffe. Two days later, Hitler reversed his decision, but the British had used the respite to strengthen their defences, enabling them to hold off the Germans long enough to complete one of the most dramatic evacuations in military history.

And so, for the first nine months of the war, neither side did anything of strategic importance. A German U-boat sank the battleship *Royal Oak* as it lay at anchor in the Orkneys. The British distributed gas masks, sent children out of London to live in foster homes where they would be safe from the threat of bombs, and banned the use of car headlights at night (thereby doubling the number of traffic accidents). But that was about all. If this was war, it was a very odd one. The Germans called it sitzkrieg, the sitting war. In Britain, it was known as the "phoney war".

Prewar apathy regained its former hold. The Belgians refused to allow any Allied troops on their soil; it would, they said, compromise their neutrality. The French commander-in-chief, General Maurice Gamelin, buried himself in the ancient fortress of Vincennes on the outskirts of Paris, making little contact with his officers. Mussolini, though Hitler's ally, had declared Italy nonbelligerent. When Churchill, who was appointed first lord of the admiralty on the outbreak of hostilities, said the war was not really about Poland – "We are fighting to save the whole world from the pestilence of Nazi tyranny" – few took him seriously. It was widely assumed that Hitler had made a fatal error in not attacking westwards immediately Poland fell. He "had missed the bus," said Chamberlain, in another famous phrase.

But it was Hitler, again, who seized the initiative. His more radical generals shared his belief that it would be possible to make an armoured thrust through the Ardennes, and that tanks could cross the River Meuse and penetrate the light French defences there. Hitler was delighted to have his earlier suggestion fed back as a fully fledged plan. The attack was set for May, 1940.

Before then, however, he conceived another action that would give Germany a strategic edge. He planned to invade neutral Norway in order to safeguard imports of Swedish iron ore, which were shipped either from the Baltic or from the ice-free Norwegian port of Narvik. Britain, too, planned an invasion of Scandinavia, but Hitler was one step ahead of the Allies. Even as British troops were embarking in the Firth of Forth on April 9, 1940, German invaders were quietly slipping ashore at various points along the Norwegian coastline. Early the next morning, German forces also entered neutral Denmark. Surprise was total. In Denmark there was virtually no resistance. The Norwegians resisted bravely – most dramatically by sinking the heavy cruiser *Blücher* in the Oslo fjord, with the loss of 1,000 lives. Allied naval actions sank two German cruisers and 10 destroyers, but on land the small British relief force was repelled. The Norwegian king, Haakon, escaped to Britain, and the Germans marched into Oslo unopposed.

In Britain, the fall of Norway had a dramatic effect. The public had become deeply dissatisfied with the bumbling complacency that had marked the phoney war. Now they were confronted with military failure. On May 7, an ageing Conservative Member of Parliament, Leo Amery, put the powerful feelings of many into words. Turning to Chamberlain in the House of Commons, he quoted Oliver Cromwell's words when he dissolved Parliament in 1653: "Depart, I say, and let us have done. In the name of God, go!" Already ill with a cancer that would soon kill him, Chamberlain resigned, to be replaced three days later by Winston Churchill at the head of a wartime coalition government. On the same day, the German armed forces swept westwards.

One month after the German invasion of France on May 13, 1940, a field gun lays down covering shellfire to protect forces about to cross the River Seine at Rouen, on their way to Paris. The capital fell in just five weeks, largely because the French military planners deployed their troops in expectation of an attack from the coastal plain of Belgium. But the German high command took them by surprise by attacking from southern Belgium, sending their armoured divisions through the hilly and forested Ardennes, and prising open weak links in the Maginot line, the supposedly impregnable chain of defences that protected France's eastern border.

The French commander-in-chief, General Gamelin, had been expecting an attack, and expecting it through Belgium. Nor were his preconceptions disappointed at first, for Hitler had devised a brilliant feint to disguise his true intentions: the German army would lure the French north with an invasion of Belgium and Holland, then Guderian's panzers – armoured divisions – would attack through the Ardennes, race for the sea, and slice the Allies in two.

Holland capitulated after only four days. Spirited resistance was broken by German threats to bomb Rotterdam; two hours before the deadline expired, the Germans dropped their bombs on the city anyway, killing almost 1,000 people. Queen Wilhelmina and her court fled to London. Belgium fell almost as quickly. Supposedly, the way into Belgium was barred by the great fortress of Eben Emael, north of the city of Liège, which could pour devastating fire for miles in any direction – except upwards. German parachutists, delivered silently by gliders, landed directly on the fortress, crammed explosives into its fire-slits, and then blasted and burnt out its occupants.

Allied divisions sped north to reinforce the Belgians, while Hitler rejoiced. "I could have wept for joy," he said. "They have fallen into my trap." Even as the fighting in Belgium continued, the main German force advanced through the weakly defended Ardennes. On May 13, it crossed the River Meuse into France, then swung north to slice into the flank of the Allied forces advancing into Belgium. Protected from above by Stukas, 71 German divisions whipped across France, cutting the Allied armies in half and scattering tens of thousands of refugees.

The Allies, their entire war plan shattered by the brilliance of the German advance, were left in complete confusion. The only conceivable response to this crisis – to sever the German arrowhead from its narrow shaft – was out of the question, for most units were exhausted and short of vital supplies. The French reserves were already cut off in Lorraine, far to the southeast, and the French commanders were always a beat behind events. The ineffectual Gamelin was replaced by General Maxime Weygand, an elderly World War I hero. Weygand was still issuing confident orders and encouraging messages when the German forces reached the Channel. It had taken them just a week.

Meanwhile, the Allies in Belgium and northern France were in rapid retreat. For the British there was only one thing to do: evacuate. Commanders back in London were still swayed by Weygand's misplaced optimism, but the BEF commander, General Lord Gort, a stolid realist, knew better. On May 27, he withdrew the British into the last coastal pocket around Dunkirk.

While Hitler inexplicably hesitated to attack the enclave, an extraordinary rescue operation went into action. It would take an armada to save the British troops, and since only 41 of the Royal Navy's destroyers were available, a call went out for all ships that could sail to lend assistance. The response was astonishing. Hundreds of civilian owners made ready their trawlers, paddle-wheelers, barges, ferries, launches, schooners, ketches and private yachts. Braving mines, shellfire and dive bombers, and guided by the columns of smoke from Dunkirk, 900 vessels carefully manoeuvred inshore towards the lines of men waiting on Dunkirk's jetties and beaches. During the next eight days, more than 200,000 British and over 100,000 French, Belgian and Dutch troops were rescued in an operation that became a byword for heroism in the face of defeat.

But France now stood ready for conquest; already, 370,000 Frenchmen were dead, wounded or taken prisoner. In the first half of June, both German army groups wheeled south, broke through the weakened French lines and scattered what remained of the French army. The roads leading to the south were choked with as many as 10 million refugees desperately fleeing the German advance, and thousands of cars, abandoned when they had run out of fuel. Officers' vehicles tried to force a way through the disordered procession, while German planes roared unopposed above, strafing the columns.

There were three possible courses open to the premier, Paul Reynaud: to surrender to the Germans, to accept yet more destruction in a futile defence of the nation, or to set up government-in-exile in North Africa. Those who were in favour of capitulation looked to the new vice-premier, Marshal Philippe Pétain, an 84-year-old hero of World War I, to negotiate a surrender. Others, notably the young undersecretary of state for national defence, Charles de Gaulle, refused to admit defeat. He was all for continuing the war from North Africa, or from anywhere else that French forces could be rallied.

Paris emptied. And after a final few days of bitter-sweet normality – the cafés crowded, the theatres full – some two million Parisians spilt southwards, in an "interminable treacle" of queues, going they knew not where. The French government also left and fled to Bordeaux, while the last remaining British troops made a hurried dash for the port of Cherbourg, where they steamed out of harbour just in front of General Erwin Rommel's Seventh Panzer Division. On June 14, three days before Marshal Pétain capitulated, the German forces entered the French capital, goose-stepping down the Champs Elysée.

"Our most dangerous enemy is Britain," Hitler had said after the defeat of Poland. Britain had now to be eliminated before he could turn to his main objective, Russia. He tried to secure a negotiated peace, but was coldly rebuffed. In August

At once conqueror and tourist, Hitler strolls away from the Eiffel Tower on June 23, 1940, the day after he had accepted the surrender of France. The document was signed in the Forest of Compiègne, at the exact spot where, in a restaurant car on a railway track, the Allies had imposed armistice terms on the German army in 1918. To complete the revenge he had promised his followers, Hitler even ordered the same railway car to be brought from a Paris museum for the occasion. He then spent a day sightseeing in Paris, which he called "one of the jewels of Europe", before leaving, never to return.

Vapour trails mark the pattern of an aerial dogfight over London during the Battle of Britain in August 1940. The Luftwaffe never succeeded in dominating the skies, partly because its fighter planes, operating at the limits of their range, could not provide adequate protection for its bombers, and partly because of the quality of the Royal Air Force's pilots. This tightknit little team – some 1,500 men in all, including many Polish, Czech and Commonwealth flyers – succeeded in thwarting Hitler's plans to invade Britain at the cost of more than 400 dead. Churchill acknowledged his countrymen's debt in a succinct, much-quoted phrase: "Never in the field of human conflict was so much owed by so many to so few."

he reluctantly decided that there was no alternative to an invasion, which was set for September 15. That meant first securing control of the skies – a task which the vainglorious Reichsmarshal Hermann Göring, commander of the Luftwaffe, claimed would be fulfilled in four days.

The Battle of Britain, as it later came to be called, started on August 12, with the first of many aerial attacks on coastal radar stations and air bases. The German planes were met by the Royal Air Force's single-engined Hurricanes and Spitfires, which were not as heavily armed as the Messerschmidt 109s that escorted the German bombers, but which were more manoeuvrable. Another advantage enjoyed by the RAF fighters was an excellent system of radar stations that could direct the aircraft to intercept enemy formations quickly and accurately, allowing the pilots to remain on the ground until the last possible minute, thus saving maximum fuel for combat. The German pilots, lacking adequate radar guidance themselves and operating at the limits of their aircraft's range, were at an immediate disadvantage. By the end of August, the Luftwaffe had lost over 600 fighters and bombers for the loss of less than 300 RAF fighters. Then, by concentrating his raids on airfields, Göring began to redress the balance.

But before it could tip firmly Germany's way, Hitler intervened. Incensed by a Bomber Command raid on Berlin, he diverted the Luftwaffe to attacks on London. On September 7, almost 400 German bombers, escorted by 600 fighters, attacked London's East End, killing 1,500 people. Hitler's purpose was to destroy the British people's determination to resist, but the "Blitz" had the opposite effect and, more important, it gave the RAF valuable time in which to rebuild their airfields and train new pilots. As a consequence, further German raids on civilian targets were broken up with heavy losses by British Fighter Command.

Realizing that Göring could not win control of the skies, Hitler cancelled the invasion of Britain – a project that had never excited his enthusiasm. On September 17 it was postponed "indefinitely", and two days later Hitler ordered the invasion fleet to be dispersed. The night-bombing raids would continue, as would U-boat attacks on British shipping, but for the remainder of 1940 Hitler concentrated his attention on plans for invasion of the Soviet Union.

Far to the south, off stage, Mussolini had watched Hitler's successes with growing envy. He wanted to share what he called the "booty" with "those who keep ferociously to themselves all the riches and all the gold of the earth". After the British defeat in Scandinavia, he announced that he could no longer delay his "appointment with history", but waited nonetheless until the French army had been broken before entering the war on Germany's side. Neither the Italian economy nor the army was in any shape to sustain a war, but Mussolini was convinced that Germany would emerge as the victor, giving Italy the opportunity to win its own "living space" in the Mediterranean. Indeed, he had already undertaken a quick little campaign against near-helpless Albania, seizing it in just five days in April 1939. Now he declared war on France, hoping to annex a few border areas in the south, but his troops were stopped dead in the Alps by snow and the few French troops who were still guarding the passes.

Mussolini blamed the failure in the south on the "softness" of his troops – a defect that would be remedied in a "parallel war" against Britain in the Mediterranean and African theatres. Indeed, he had sizable forces in Africa – 215,000 men in Libya and more than 250,000 in Italian East Africa – which he planned to throw against British-held Egypt. But these forces were woefully short of supplies, and when the Libyan troops did invade, they came to an ignominious halt in the desert when they ran out of fuel only 100 kilometres across the border. And after the East African troops had taken British Somaliland in August – Italy's only single-handed success on land throughout the whole course of the war – they too ran low on supplies and were rendered incapable of further attack.

In the light of Italy's military weakness, Mussolini's next actions were little short of mad. He planned to launch simultaneous invasions of Switzerland, Yugoslavia and Greece. Fortunately, he did not have sufficient troops for all three projects and, on advice from his commanders, he agreed to abandon his plans against Switzerland and Yugoslavia. That left Greece. Angered by an understanding which Hitler had secretly reached with Romania in September 1940, Mussolini blurted to Count Ciano, his son-in-law and foreign minister: "Hitler always faces me with a *fait accompli*. This time I am going to pay him back in his own coin. He will find out from the newspapers that I have occupied Greece. In this way the equilibrium will be re-established. I shall send in my resignation as an Italian if anyone objects to our fighting the Greeks."

Italian troops invaded Greece from Albania on October 28, 1940, and were expelled within a week. This further humiliation, combined as it was with a British raid on the port of Taranto that destroyed a large part of the Italian navy, plus a British counterattack on Libya in December, persuaded Hitler that Mussolini must have German help. Over the next few weeks, German troops arrived to support Italy in Greece, Libya, and also in Sicily (to strengthen Italian attacks on British ships in the Mediterranean). Not only was Libya held and Greece taken, but Yugoslavia, too, was overwhelmed.

These conquests, which were of such importance to Mussolini, were a strategically irrelevant distraction for Hitler, who by this time had approved the plans for Operation *Barbarossa*, the invasion of the Soviet Union. In readiness for the attack on Russia, he withdrew Luftwaffe units from Sicily to the eastern front, with catastrophic results for Italy. Operating out of Malta, the British air force and navy destroyed many Italian convoys to North Africa. Once again, Hitler had to come to the rescue, giving Field Marshal Albert Kesselring the task of capturing Malta and winning all North Africa for the Axis.

In the end, there was no German invasion of Malta, and the British in Egypt held firm, retaining a foothold in Africa that would become the springboard for a subsequent Allied invasion of Europe through Italy. Mussolini's involvement in the war had been disastrous for Germany, as Hitler himself admitted. "My unshakable friendship for Italy and the Duce may well be held to be an error on my part," he wrote. "It is in fact quite obvious that our Italian alliance has been of more service to our enemies than to ourselves."

In particular, Hitler claimed – with the wisdom of hindsight – the unplanned German intervention in the Balkans had "led to a catastrophic delay in the launching of our attack on Russia. Ah, if only the Italians had remained aloof from this war!"

Almost certainly, he was exaggerating. In June 1941, there were only seven German divisions in the Balkans, compared to some 150 along the border with the Soviet Union. At that moment, before the release of the greatest invasion in history, Hitler was supremely confident of victory.

THE RED TSAR

When Vladimir Ilyich Lenin, first leader of the Soviet Union, died after a 20-month illness on January 21, 1924, all the funeral arrangements were made by the one man he did not want to succeed him – former seminarian and Bolshevik revolutionary Joseph Stalin, photographed here at his leader's left side in 1922.

Lenin was so opposed to Stalin, whom he regarded as too crude for high office, that he had recommended in a letter to the Communist Party Central Committee that the shoemaker's son from Georgia should be stripped of his post as its secretary-general. But Stalin, a brilliant political tactician, had recruited so many of his own supporters on to the committee that it voted to ignore even the deathbed wishes of the Soviet state's founder.

This crucial hurdle overcome, Stalin spent the next four years consolidating his personal power. He eliminated rivals by first allying himself with them against political opponents and then abruptly shifting his allegiance, isolating his former supporters and exposing them to charges of political divisiveness which he himself would bring. In this way he disposed of his most formidable rival, Leon Trotsky.

In 1928, Stalin abandoned Lenin's New Economic Policy, which permitted small-scale private enterprise, replacing it with forced "collectivization", of small peasant plots. Collectivization was accompanied by a programme of industrialization – forced through at breakneck speed. In a single decade, the Soviet Union aimed to reach levels of industrial productivity that it had taken the Western democracies more than a century to achieve.

But the upheavals that the economic revolution set in train caused horrendous suffering and widespread discontent. Fearing conspiracies everywhere, Stalin in the 1930s launched a mass terror campaign to crush all opposition. In a climate of fear whipped up by government propaganda, two thirds of the Communist Party Central Committee, half the army officers over the rank of major, and most managers holding key industrial posts were eliminated as "enemies of the people".

The Great Purge ended only when it became clear that the Soviet Union's internal convulsions had sharpened the predatory intentions of Stalin's fellow dictator, Adolf Hitler. Lacking European allies, Stalin abandoned his anti-Nazi stance and signed a nonaggression pact with Hitler, hoping peace would give him time to build up the Soviet Union's industrial and military muscle for the inevitable confrontation with Germany.

ПОБЕДА СОЦИАЛИЗМА
В НАШЕЙ СТРАНЕ ОБЕСПЕЧЕНА
ФУНДАМЕНТ СОЦИАЛИСТИЧЕСКОЙ
ЭКОНОМИКИ ЗАВЕРШЕН
„РЕАЛЬНОСТЬ НАШЕГО ПРОИЗВОДСТВЕННОГО
ПЛАНА-ЭТО МИЛЛИОНЫ ТРУДЯЩИХСЯ
ТВОРЯЩИЕ НОВУЮ ЖИЗНЬ"
И. СТАЛИН

In terms of manpower and raw materials, post-revolutionary Russia was a giant, but when compared to the Western powers it was woefully deficient in skilled labour, machinery and in efficient management. Conscious of the Soviet Union's weakness, Stalin ordered an entire overhaul of the economy, launching a series of Five-Year Plans which were designed to turn the Soviet Union into a major industrial power. Failure to meet the set targets was considered a crime against the state, and punished accordingly.

As a first step, Stalin ordered the collectivization of agriculture. Small farms were combined into units sufficiently large to make mechanization cost-effective; those peasants who resisted were dispossessed of their holdings, and deported to labour camps or executed. Others slaughtered their livestock and fled the countryside for the towns, where they were hired at miserable wages to work in factories partly financed by the export of agricultural output extracted from the state farms at rock-bottom prices. Food production by the demoralized and alienated farmers actually fell, and poor distribution of the harvest meant that millions went hungry. Farm output did not rise to pre-collectivization levels until 1938, but by 1937 Soviet industrial output was second only to that of the United States.

A portrait of a steadfast Stalin dominates this poster celebrating the construction of a steel plant in the Ural Mountains, 1,400 kilometres east of Moscow. Exhorted by slogans such as "The victory of socialism is achieved in our country", Soviet workers did fulfil some of the economic goals set by the first two Five-Year Plans, which concentrated on what Stalin called "the means of production". Between 1929 and 1938, coal output rose by 230 per cent, electric power by 540 per cent, and motor vehicle manufacture by an amazing 15,000 per cent.

While peasants gather the harvest on a Ukrainian collective farm, a truckload of government officials produce a propaganda sheet extolling Stalin's agricultural policies. In reality, the effects of collectivization were disastrous in the Ukraine, where an estimated two million starved when the harvest failed in 1932 and the central government refused to send relief supplies of grain destined for export.

Stalin's model worker, Alexei Stakhanov, smiles for a publicity photograph. In a carefully orchestrated campaign to impose higher production targets, the state organized an entire movement around this Ukrainian coal miner who, it was claimed, had hewn 15 times the norm during a single six-hour night shift. In fact, the feat was a sham. Stakhanov had two helpers, and the chase after increased output which he encouraged seriously damaged quality and workers' safety.

In December of 1934, the popular and talented Leningrad Communist party chief Sergei Kirov was murdered by unknown assailants. Almost certainly the assassination had been ordered by Stalin, who used the crime as a pretext to launch his Great Purge of political rivals – real, potential, and, by the end of the five-year witch-hunt, imaginary.

Stalin's first targets were his closest party colleagues. They were arrested on trumped-up charges, forced to confess imaginary crimes at widely publicized show trials, and then either sent to prison camps or executed. Lower-ranking party officials soon shared their fate, often for alleged support of Trotsky, the now-disgraced organizer of the 1917 Russian Revolution. With all political opposition crushed, Stalin turned on the Red Army, liquidating its commander and no less than 14 of his 16 generals.

As the purge accelerated, it fed on itself, with citizens denouncing each other and then being denounced in turn. Even when the accusations were patently absurd, the police and public prosecutors did not dare dismiss them in case they, too, laid themselves open to charges of treason. That did not save them; in the end Stalin, realizing that the country was bleeding to death from the wounds he had inflicted, ordered a purge of the purgers themselves.

The doomed Marshal Mikhail Tukhachevsky, seventh from left, lines up with fellow senior Red Army officers at the 1934 Communist party congress. Three years later, Tukhachevsky was removed from his post as commander in chief, charged with spying for Germany, and executed with most of his generals. So began a purge that claimed the lives of more senior officers than died in World War II.

A top-hatted symbol of foreign capitalism drives a team of ravening dogs on a 1930 propaganda float. Behind marches a caricature of Leon Trotsky, Lenin's likely successor until Stalin manoeuvred him out of the running, then out of the party, and finally, in 1929, out of the country. Trotsky continued his opposition from abroad until 1940, when he was murdered in Mexico by one of Stalin's agents.

Communist officials pose at the 40th anniversary of the Moscow Arts Theatre, in 1938 *(top)*. Standing fourth from right is the head of the secret police, Nikolai Yezhov. That same year, he was removed from office and sent to a criminal lunatic asylum. When the same picture was republished in 1949 *(bottom)*, his image had gone. Also missing was the theatre's director – a victim of clumsy photographic retouching rather than the purge.

Joseph Stalin, champion of world communism, shakes hands with Nazi Germany's foreign minister, Joachim von Ribbentrop, at a reception to celebrate the signing of the Nazi-Soviet nonaggression pact on August 23, 1939. Although the partnership was a marriage of convenience between irreconcilable ideological enemies, the pact served the short-term interests of both parties. For Hitler, aware that his planned conquest of Poland might lead to conflict with France and Britain, it removed the risk of war on two fronts. For Stalin, it provided a precious breathing space in which he could rebuild the Soviet Union's military and industrial strength. The agreement also gave him a licence to bolster his western defences by annexing the Baltic states of Estonia, Latvia and Lithuania, as well as parts of Poland, Finland and Romania. But though his interests were entirely cynical, Stalin came to place a misguided and obsessive faith in the pact.

A white-clad Finnish soldier stands over the frozen corpses of Russian invaders of his country, one of them still in the crouching position in which he died. The "Winter War" began in November 1940, when the Soviet Union set out to strengthen its northern defences at the expense of Finnish territory. But the Red Army, incompetently led and poorly equipped for winter warfare, suffered some 200,000 casualties in four months before sheer weight of numbers and fire power made further Finnish resistance impossible.

AN OPPORTUNIST ALLIANCE

Throughout the 1920s, Stalin concentrated on domestic policy rather than on foreign affairs. Whereas the discredited Trotsky wanted to spread communism around the globe, Stalin's expressed intention was to create "pure" socialism inside the Soviet Union before making any attempt to export it.

As a result of this introspective attitude, by 1933 the Soviet Union had become diplomatically isolated, and was exposed to threats from two hostile neighbours: Nazi Germany in the West, and expansionist Japan in the East.

Stalin therefore instructed Communist agents to form hitherto discouraged alliances with leftist groups outside the Soviet Union; their efforts assisted Communist-backed governments to gain power in both Spain and France. Meanwhile, Stalin's foreign minister, Maxim Litvonov, was winning international support for a policy of unified resistance to German aggression.

The policy came to nought, however, when Britain and France signed the 1938 Munich Agreement with Germany, which effectively sanctioned Hitler's seizure of Czechoslovakia. When Hitler, anxious to complete his conquests in western Europe before embarking on his planned invasion of Russia, offered Stalin a 10-year treaty of nonaggression, the dictator hastily accepted. He also took steps to secure his eastern frontier by concluding a similar pact with Japan.

THE WORLD AT WAR

2

It was midsummer night, 1941, the shortest of the year. Along the Soviet Union's western borders between the Baltic and the Black Sea, there was barely enough darkness to conceal the German troops massed in their forward positions. But the Soviet commanders turned a blind eye to the menace that confronted them; Stalin himself had ordered them to avoid any posture that Hitler could interpret as a "provocation". None was needed. At 3.15 a.m. on June 22, while squadrons of Luftwaffe dive bombers were already approaching sleepy Soviet airfields, the armed array – some 150 divisions, more than 3 million men with 3,580 armoured fighting vehicles – advanced across the border virtually unopposed. The 22-month-old conflict that had transformed the face of Europe was about to assume new dimensions of space and ferocity. Operation *Barbarossa*, Adolf Hitler's dream made military reality, was under way.

Until that June morning when the *Wehrmacht* came crashing through the muddled Soviet defences, the war in Europe had seemed to all intents and purposes over, leaving Germany in a position of unassailable dominance. The Third Reich had swallowed half of Poland and controlled Austria, Czechoslovakia, France, Belgium and the Netherlands, as well as Denmark, Norway, Greece and Yugoslavia. Fascist Italy was a solid ally, and Hungary, Finland and Romania had thrown in their lot with Hitler. Sweden was compliantly neutral, her iron ore feeding the furnaces of the Ruhr's steelworks. Even Stalin, still placing his faith in the non-aggression pact he had signed with the Fuhrer in 1939, was shipping vital supplies of oil and grain to Germany. The United States remained politically hostile to the Nazi regime, but isolationist sentiment – President Franklin D. Roosevelt had won the 1940 elections on a "no war" platform – seemed certain to keep the world's greatest industrial power well clear of the conflict in Europe.

Only Britain, battered and near bankrupt, still stood against Hitler. The air battles of 1940 had shown him the near-impossibility of launching a successful invasion of his island opponent. It was equally clear that American aid in the form of the lend-lease arms transfer scheme, which had started in April 1941, would keep Britain in the struggle after her own resources were exhausted. But even under the implacable leadership of Winston Churchill, the British were incapable of causing any serious harm to Germany's military power. It was only a matter of time, it seemed, before Churchill or a less obdurate successor realized the hopelessness of the situation and sued for a peace that Hitler would be more than happy to grant.

There were, to be sure, a few problems – caused less by Hitler's enemies than by his friends. His efforts to save the Italians from their self-inflicted disasters in North Africa and Greece had involved Germany in expensive sideshows: the German airborne assault on the island of Crete alone had cost some 4,000 German dead.

Wives and mothers seek out their dead after a German massacre of Russian partisans during fighting in the Crimea in 1942. Millions would share these women's grief before the world's first total war was over. Of the estimated 100 million men and women mobilized to fight, some 20 million died in battle. Civilian deaths were even higher. About seven million noncombatants perished in the Soviet Union alone, which bore the brunt of conflict in the war's European theatre.

By the autumn of 1942, Germany and its allies controlled almost all of Europe — from the River Volga, where German troops were fighting in the streets of Stalingrad, to the French Atlantic coast, from which U-boats harried Allied shipping. In North Africa, German and Italian troops had approached within striking distance of the Suez Canal. But the Greater German Reich *(shaded red on map)*, which Hitler had vowed would endure a thousand years, had less than a thousand days to run. November 1942 brought a devastating Russian counteroffensive at Stalingrad and an Anglo-American invasion of North Africa. The first marked the beginning of the German army's long westward retreat back to Berlin; the second would lead to Allied control of the Mediterranean and the eventual seaborne invasion of Europe.

More seriously still, the fighting in Greece involved troops earmarked for the attack on Russia, originally scheduled for May. And although the unusually wet spring of 1941 would almost certainly have postponed *Barbarossa* in any event, the fighting around the Mediterranean was an unwelcome distraction for the German army on the eve of the greatest military operation in history.

Hitler, though, was determined to proceed with what he had always regarded as his true mission in life: an eastwards war of conquest and extermination that in time would leave a Germanic population of 250 million people ruling the entire area between the Atlantic and the Urals. Whatever some of his generals might say about the dangers of fighting a war on two fronts, he himself had no doubts that Germany had the might to translate his murderous dream into reality. Two months, he reckoned, would finish the business. "We have only to kick in the door," he declared, "and the whole rotten structure will come crashing down."

In fact, Hitler had seriously underestimated the real strength of the Soviet Union. When Hitler was confronted with reasonably accurate intelligence estimates of the

Soviets' tank-building capacity, for example, he simply dismissed most of them, and he considered those that he did believe as all the more reason for an immediate attack, before the Russians had had the opportunity to reach their full military strength. It was the first in a long series of errors that would end with the ruin of Germany — not to mention most of the rest of Europe — and the red flag of the Soviets flying in triumph over Berlin.

In that summer of 1941, though, a Nazi victory seemed a foregone conclusion. For Operation *Barbarossa* began brilliantly. Three powerful army groups were involved: group North, which was launched through Latvia and Lithuania towards Leningrad; Centre, battering past the fortress of Brest-Litovsk along the Minsk-Smolensk high road to Moscow; and South, charged with the occupation of the Ukraine. Everywhere, deep armoured penetrations not only tore through Soviet border defences but smashed and surrounded entire armies behind the front. The Red Army's high command, which had been gutted by the purges of the late 1930s, could not match the skill and experience of Germany's generals and their staffs.

At its greatest extent, in January 1943, Japan's Greater East Asia Co-Prosperity Sphere *(within yellow line on map)* covered most of China and Southeast Asia. Despite its name, it brought little prosperity: like Nazi Germany, imperial Japan treated its conquests as loot to enrich the homeland. And the new Japanese empire proved as fragile as its German equivalent. On land, the endless defeats the Japanese inflicted upon China were patiently absorbed, bringing victory no nearer. The seaward side of the empire was dependent on a naval dominance that Japan could not maintain in the face of American industrial strength. Island-hopping counterattacks were followed by aerial bombardment of Japanese cities and, in August 1945, a final, terrible scourging in nuclear fire.

Stalin himself, the "Man of Steel", spent the first 11 days of the war in shocked, near-catatonic isolation from his suffering troops and people. Hundreds of thousands of Soviet prisoners shambled westwards in the despair of defeat. On July 3, Colonel-General Franz Halder, chief of the German general staff, wrote confidently in his diary: "It is probably no overstatement to say that the Russian campaign has been won in the space of two weeks."

There were some ill omens, however. The invaders had already encountered Russian KV and T-34 tanks, which were more powerfully armed, better armoured and more mobile than their German equivalents. Even Hitler was perturbed by reports of dogged Soviet resistance: he told Mussolini that "the Russians fight with a truly stupid fanaticism. Pillbox crews blow themselves up rather than surrender." The sacrifice of hundreds of thousands of troops gave the Soviets time to dismantle the important industrial facilities that stood in the Germans' path and ship them, lock, stock and barrel, to new sites beyond the Ural Mountains, where they would resume production by the spring of 1942.

Not all Soviet units, however, were fighting to the last man. The fact was that Stalin's long rule of terror had made him a figure of hate to many of his subjects. In the Baltic provinces of Latvia, Estonia and Lithuania, which had been independent

In July 1941, during the initial German onslaught on the Soviet Union, German panzer grenadiers rush from the cover of their armoured troop carrier to clear Russian defenders from a burning village near Smolensk. Motorized to keep pace with the tanks that spearheaded the assault, the grenadiers were generally on hand to deal with troublesome enemy positions, while less mobile foot soldiers brought up the rear. The Germans' shrewd combination of troops of different disciplines – infantry, armour and artillery, backed up by Luftwaffe dive bombers – was the main reason for the astonishing speed of their advance through the shocked Soviet Union in the first stages of the operation, code-named *Barbarossa*.

states until the Soviet Union virtually annexed them in 1939, and in the western Ukraine, where there was a long tradition of nationalism, the advancing Germans were frequently received as liberators. But Hitler rejected suggestions that anti-Soviet prisoners be re-enlisted as German allies: he had no intention of owing any favours to people whose country was no more than a "big cake", as he put it, to be sliced up for Germany's advantage.

In any event, pro-German sentiments generally evaporated quickly. On the heels of the *Wehrmacht*'s combat troops came the *Einsatzgruppen* of SS chief Heinrich Himmler – "special forces" entrusted with the murder of Jews, Communist officials and other potential troublemakers, which latter category could and did include just about everyone. Indeed, by a colossal irony, the indiscriminate German onslaught achieved something that a generation of Five-Year Plans, secret policemen, midnight executions and Siberian labour camps had scarcely accomplished: it was legitimizing Soviet rule in the hearts and minds of the Soviet Union's people.

From the first days of Operation *Barbarossa*, the war was seen as a murderous affront not to the Bolshevik regime but to the holy soil of Mother Russia. It was a mood quickly sensed by Stalin. On July 3 he broke his long silence with a broadcast to the nation. In a speech that deeply affected his listeners – many of whom had never heard their leader's voice before – he talked not of Marx and Lenin but of a "national patriotic war . . . for the freedom of our motherland". Churches, long closed for ideological reasons, were reopened, and cities rang with the sombre pealing of formerly silenced bells.

Hitler paid no heed to the enemy's new spirit of resistance. Convinced that his eastern campaign was already as good as won, he even ordered a cut in tank production to increase the amount of scarce steel allocated to the U-boat building programme. After the capture of Smolensk in late July, he decided to divert the main attack on Moscow southwards, to bring the whole of the Ukraine's rich agricultural land under German control. Many of his generals protested, arguing that Moscow was the key to the Soviet Union's overcentralized railway communications, the seat of political power and the one clear objective that their troops, as well as the watching world, could understand. Hitler, increasingly obsessed with the economic exploitation of his new territory, overruled them.

The first result of the switch was a colossal battle at Kiev in September, when more than 600,000 prisoners and a vast amount of military booty fell into German hands. Another consequence was that the attack on Moscow could not be resumed until October 2 – a day on which the first ominous snowflakes of the coming winter fell. For most of October, however, rain was the greatest obstacle to progress, bogging down the invaders on Russia's unpaved roads. The frost, when it came, actually sped the German armour on its way. But as October turned to November, the steadily dropping temperatures brought misery to the lightly clad German troops and chaos to their supply system. Hitler had been so confident of achieving victory in 1941 that he had not provided for a winter campaign.

The very speed and scale of the German offensive contributed to its undoing. By late November, Hitler's armies had conquered an area more than three times the size of France. Leningrad was locked in a siege that would ultimately cost more than a million civilian lives, and advanced German patrols could see the spires of the Kremlin from Moscow's suburbs. But the *Wehrmacht*'s supply system could not keep pace with the advance. Even round the great Russian cities there were few

roads, and most of these were no more than dirt tracks. The railway system was badly damaged, and the *Wehrmacht*'s horse-drawn wagons – the Germans never had enough motor transport to mechanize their infantry units, let alone their supply services – could furnish only a fraction of the fuel and spares that were needed. Even without the mounting numbers of battle casualties inflicted by stubborn Soviet defenders, wear and tear that could not be swiftly made good kept German tank and aircraft strength dangerously low.

Yet the 1941 battles for Moscow were close-run indeed. In mid-October the city was in the grip of panic, and many senior party officials fled. Stalin himself, his nerve recovered, stayed behind. By November 7, the 24th anniversary of the Bolshevik Revolution, when Soviet troops marched straight from the traditional celebration parade to the nearby front line, fear had been replaced by grim determination. As winter closed in and temperatures fell to minus 30 degrees Celsius, the Germans clawed their way slowly closer against a Soviet defence that inflicted 250,000 casualties for a 160-kilometre advance. Frostbite claimed thousands more victims. At the end of the month, Chief of Staff Halder warned, "We have reached the end of our human and material resources".

Bomb-bursts garland the U.S. Pacific Fleet's capital ships during the surprise Japanese attack on Pearl Harbor in Hawaii. The stately line *(left)*, moored tranquilly in the base's "battleship row", made an easy target for Japan's carrier-launched strike pilots, who sank or crippled eight battleships as well as 13 smaller vessels at the cost of only 29 aircraft. But the raid was not an unmitigated disaster for the United States; the Pacific Fleet's own carriers, far out at sea on exercise when the Japanese blow fell, escaped unharmed. And far from shaking American morale, the attack, which was delivered without any declaration of war, united the country in a quest for vengeance. It would be many months before the U.S. could hit back, however, and in the meantime the nation's anger vented itself on America's Japanese community. More than 100,000 men, women and children *(above)*, most of them loyal U.S. citizens and many of them from families resident for generations, were bundled into makeshift resettlement camps.

Then, on December 6, the Soviets launched a massive offensive of their own. There had been Soviet counterattacks before: usually ill-timed and badly coordinated, they had simply added to the Red Army's horrifying losses. This time, though, Stalin had 20 fresh divisions of experienced troops. They were tough Siberian units transferred from the Soviet Union's eastern frontier, where they had been standing guard against a possible Japanese attack from Manchuria. Japan had signed the Tripartite Pact with Germany and Italy in September 1940, and though the Japanese foreign minister had concluded a neutrality agreement with Stalin a few months later, it was known that many of his colleagues favoured a strategic offensive against the Soviet Union. No such attack would now come, Soviet intelligence chiefs had assured Stalin: the Japanese had laid other plans.

Stalin's judgment would soon be proved right. In the early hours of December 7, far from the icy death struggle on the outskirts of Moscow, two soldiers training on newly installed radar at the U.S. Navy's Pacific Fleet base in Pearl Harbor, Hawaii, reported some puzzling blips upon their screen. "Hell," said a bored officer, "it's probably just a pigeon with a metal band around its legs." Fifty minutes later, hundreds of Japanese strike aircraft caught the huge base off guard. In less than two hours they sank or damaged eight battleships and three cruisers, destroyed 188 planes and killed almost 2,500 men. A shocked America found herself at war.

British prime minister Churchill, informed of the attack by BBC radio, telephoned Roosevelt. "What's this about Japan?" he demanded. "It's quite true," said the U.S. president. "We're all in the same boat." "This actually simplifies things," said Churchill, and calmly went to bed. Three days later – on December 11 by GMT – Adolf Hitler "simplified things" still further by declaring war on the United States himself. The conflict was now global: not just a continent but an entire planet was locked in combat.

The Second World War stands out in a war-stained century not just for the unprecedented scale of the fighting – at least 50 million people died as a result of it – but for the political upheavals that it set in train. By 1945 German power in Europe – a key political force for 70 years – had been smashed. And Europe itself, including victorious Britain, had lost its former supremacy in a world that was now uneasily divided between the United States and the Soviet Union, forged by the fires of war into superpowers. Japan's attempt to build a "Greater East Asia Co-Prosperity Sphere" collapsed in ruins; but Asians could not forget the defeats that the Japanese had inflicted upon their white colonial overlords. Nationalism and independence were the dominant themes in what, postwar, would become known as the Third World.

The war brought other huge changes too. It saw a massive growth in industrial capacity, matched by enormous advances in technology – the atom bomb was the most fearful example, but radar, rocketry, computers, mass-produced antibiotics and organo-chlorine insecticides such as DDT were also among the conflict's enduring legacies. For the first time in history, the fate of nations was largely determined by the obscure research of unseen scientists. It was a war fought on the "home front" as well as on the field of battle. Whole populations were mobilized to work and fight, the routines of their daily lives conditioned by the struggle, their very thinking shaped by the mass propaganda used by all the belligerents. It was a war without limits in space or morality, courage or cruelty. There were few true "non-combatants", for death rained from the sky upon men, women and children, workers and housewives and soldiers alike. It was war carried to the extreme: absolute, pitiless and world-changing.

Vividly pictured in a 1942 Italian poster, a colossal Japanese samurai slashes through a helpless Anglo-American fleet. The artist's work reflected Axis enthusiasm for Japan's drive of conquest, but there was little real cooperation between Germany and Italy and their far-off ally. Physical distance was one disadvantage, but politically, too, there was little attempt to act in unison. Thus Japan never declared war on the Soviet Union, and until 1945 American ships flying the flag of the Soviet Union sailed unmolested across the Pacific, carrying vital lend-lease supplies to the Russian port of Vladivostok.

Throughout December 1941, the *Wehrmacht* found itself fighting desperately against Soviet armies that were better motivated than its own. By that time, the Soviets had clear strategic directions and commanders capable of achieving their objectives. In Georgy Zhukov, Stalin had found a general with a will as unshakable – and as ruthless – as his own. A sample order to one of his officers during the Moscow fighting was typical of his style: "If Antonov's division has not reached its position by dawn, I shall shoot you like a traitor." Such "unwarranted abruptness", as a fellow general later called it, was not by itself enough to make a great commander, but when Zhukov ordered a formation to a position, it was usually the right position. And he also had plenty of able subordinates, for six months of disaster had brutally winnowed incompetent party hacks from the Soviet command structure. In effect, the "subhuman" Slavs had turned into winter supermen, and German morale would never completely recover from the shock.

On several occasions, the whole central front was near to collapse. But when Hitler's commanders pleaded for a general retreat, he was obdurate: "They must dig into the ground where they are," he ordered, "and hold every square metre of land." Almost certainly the dictator was right. In the snowbound confusion, any attempt to effect an organized withdrawal to better positions would have been impossible to coordinate, and total rout might well have followed. Nevertheless, the stand-fast orders cost the Germans men and equipment that could not easily be replaced, and in any event the Soviets succeeded in pushing the German front back more than 150 kilometres before the deepening winter made conditions impossible even for the well-clad Siberians.

Hard-pressed as he was on the Eastern Front, Hitler's declaration of war on the United States, which was by far the world's richest and most industrialized state, was an incredible act of folly. Certainly, Roosevelt's support for the British war effort had been galling, and Japan was Germany's ally; but Hitler could not take the war to America – he could only wait for the Americans to bring it to him. Germany throughout its history as a united nation had feared a war on two fronts. Hitler, by act of his own megalomaniac will, had gone further: he now had almost the whole world in arms against him.

His Japanese allies made no reciprocal gesture of support, maintaining carefully correct relations with the Soviet Union. But elsewhere, Japan's war plan was even more of a gamble than Nazi Germany's. The war party in Japan's government – a clear majority, since pacifists were frequently assassinated by ultra-patriots – saw conflict with America as inevitable sooner or later, and urged immediate action. Japan, they reasoned, had reached a near-peak in military might. Her fleet in 1941 was superior to the U.S. Pacific Fleet, but Japan could not hope to match the shipbuilding effort the Americans had already begun, and Japan's relative strength could only decline. By striking hard at once, Japan could seize almost all of Southeast Asia, including the strategically vital oilfields of the Dutch East Indies, as well as a perimeter fence of islands halfway across the Pacific that would deny the Americans the forward bases they would need for any sort of counterattack.

Hands raised in surrender, British troops captured at Singapore in February 1942 await their fate. The speed with which Japan's bicycle-borne soldiers overran the Malay Peninsula had unnerved British and Australian commanders, and the city, supposedly the impregnable bastion of Britain's Far Eastern empire, fell with little resistance. The jubilant Japanese could scarcely believe their good fortune, for their men had reached Singapore's defences exhausted by their rapid advance. They were far lower in food, fuel and ammunition than the defenders, whose generals cited their own shortages to justify the capitulation to an enraged prime minister Winston Churchill.

For six months at least, the Japanese planners were certain, their offensive would be unstoppable. Britain, embroiled with Nazi Germany, could offer no serious resistance. As for the United States, it would eventually come to terms with the new situation – or so Japan's warlords thought. However deluded their hopes would prove to be, they were based on more than mere wishful thinking. The U.S. economy was barely out of the doldrums of the 1930s Depression, and in 1941 few Americans could have predicted the astonishing production levels the war industries would achieve in the course of hostilities. Unemployment and dissatisfaction were rife; President Roosevelt was unpopular with a large section of the public. Even so, few of his opponents disagreed with the peace-at-any-price policy with which he had narrowly won the 1940 election. But most significant of all in the minds of the Japanese war leaders, the August 1941 renewal of conscription legislation, in a time of unprecedented world crisis, had been approved in

During the battle for Stalingrad in 1942, Soviet infantrymen, quilted against the cold of autumn, find firing positions in the gutted shell of a building. Weeks of fighting reduced the city to little more than rubble, its fallen homes and factories a warren of dugouts for attacker and defender alike. Control of the city was essential for Germany's grand strategy *(above)*, which involved an enormous pincer movement intended to link troops fighting in Russia with their comrades in North Africa; the prizes would have included the oil wells of the Middle East. But the Germans could not quite overcome Stalingrad's defenders, and when the snows of winter came in November it was the Germans who were the victims of a pincer movement — a huge Russian counterattack that first encircled and then annihilated an entire German army.

the U.S. House of Representatives by only one vote. The American people, Japan's military believed, would never have the stomach to slog it out at close quarters against Japanese troops battle-hardened in Manchuria, imbued with the samurai warrior tradition, and fanatically loyal to their emperor.

These were dangerous assumptions on which to hazard the fate of a nation, for no Japanese leader had the least idea of how Japan could win if the Americans, with their huge advantages in industry, natural resources and manpower, decided to fight to the finish. In fact, Japan's militarily brilliant surprise attack on Pearl Harbor achieved a political near-impossibility. It united the American people in a way no act of Roosevelt's could have done, and it provided them with a sense of moral outrage that made any aim short of total victory unthinkable. As war-winning weapons, such unity and purpose were well worth the cost of a few battleships. Ironically, the attack's master-planner, Admiral Isoroku Yamamoto, suspected as much himself. English-speaking and widely travelled in Europe and America, Yamamoto dismissed his fellow officers' congratulations after the Pearl Harbor raid: "I fear that we have only succeeded in awakening a sleeping tiger."

But for the time being, it was the Japanese tiger that was on the rampage. As predicted, the Pacific offensive began with six months of unbroken success. In a dazzling sequence of operations, Japanese troops seized the great entrepôt of Hong Kong, the American dependency of the Philippines, British Malaya – source of most of the world's natural rubber – and the fortress of Singapore. The oil-rich Dutch colonies of Indonesia fell by April 1942, while the Emperor's warriors were driving the last demoralized British, Indian and Chinese defenders from Burma and threatening the Indian frontier itself. To the south, Japanese troops were firmly established in New Guinea; to the east, the strategically important islands of the Solomons and the Gilberts had been swallowed up early in the offensive, along with the luckless American outposts at Guam and Wake.

In most places, the Japanese advance was met by the ignominious surrender of Southeast Asia's white overlords. Usually, the victorious troops were given at least a guarded welcome by local populations, glad to see their colonial masters humiliated by fellow Asians. Asian nationalism stirred even beyond the conquered territories: the British, their prestige never lower, found India almost ungovernable when the Indian Congress party called for a "mass struggle" against them.

But the Japanese were no more liberators than the Germans had been in the Ukraine. Their purpose was exploitation, and they went about it with a brutal thoroughness that made British or Dutch rule seem a pleasant memory. (The region's large Chinese community was treated with special cruelty.) Thus, though Japan's victories gave the local nationalists a healthy dose of pride in Asian accomplishment, within a few months many of the Greater East Asia Co-Prosperity Sphere's new subjects were involved in clandestine resistance operations and guerrilla warfare – skills that would prove useful for the post-colonial future.

The first check to the Japanese advance came even as Burma was falling. In early May, 1942, a Japanese invasion force, covered by three aircraft carriers, was heading for Port Moresby in New Guinea when it encountered an American carrier task force in the Coral Sea. The confused and blundering battle that followed was the first naval engagement in history fought by fleets that were never in sight of each other. Instead, swarms of carrier-borne aircraft searched – and struck. "Scratch one flat-top!" radioed a jubilant American pilot: the carrier *Shoho* was the first major

LIFE ON THE HOME FRONT

As part of their efforts to defeat Adolf Hitler, the Allied democracies together with their Soviet partner mobilized their populations to an extent that was unmatched by totalitarian Germany until the latter stages of the conflict.

While Germany enjoyed peacetime standards of consumption until 1941, the Allies put their economies on a war footing at the start of hostilities, increasing industrial output at the expense of consumer items, and imposing rationing. In Britain, a frugal weekly allowance of meat, fat and sugar actually rendered healthier the diet of many of its citizens. For Soviet office workers – who received shorter rations than manual labourers – the weekly food allotment was only one third that of the British level, and nonessential items were not available to civilians at all. Dentists, for example, had to pull teeth without using an anaesthetic, and cigarettes were in such short supply that owners could charge passers-by two roubles a puff. Even Americans had to make sacrifices: some 20 items, ranging from petrol to tomato ketchup, were rationed.

Women welders break for a chat at the Bethlehem Steel shipyard in Pennsylvania. Working long shifts, women in all areas of the armaments industry were a powerful weapon in Roosevelt's "arsenal of democracy", contributing to a sixfold increase in the tonnage of American shipping, and helping to increase aircraft production fivefold between 1939 and 1944.

During the siege of Leningrad, which claimed a million civilian lives, a teacher takes a class outside their shell-torn

Another important difference between Nazi Germany and the Western Allies lay in the extent to which the latter harnessed their female populations to the war effort. Fully 51 per cent of the Soviet labour force were women, while in the U.S. some six million additional female workers helped to double industrial production during the course of the war.

In Germany, by contrast, only one third of the potential female workers joined the labour force. Drawing on a tradition that women should confine their activities to "children, church and kitchen", the Nazi propaganda chief Joseph Goebbels declared that the function of women was "being beautiful and bringing children into the world".

A banner advertises a Christmas sale in a bomb-damaged Cologne street in 1944. Until late in the war, Germany imported luxury items from occupied countries; the availability of French perfume, Dutch dairy products and Norwegian furs helped to soften the hardships of an urban population living under the constant peril of bombs.

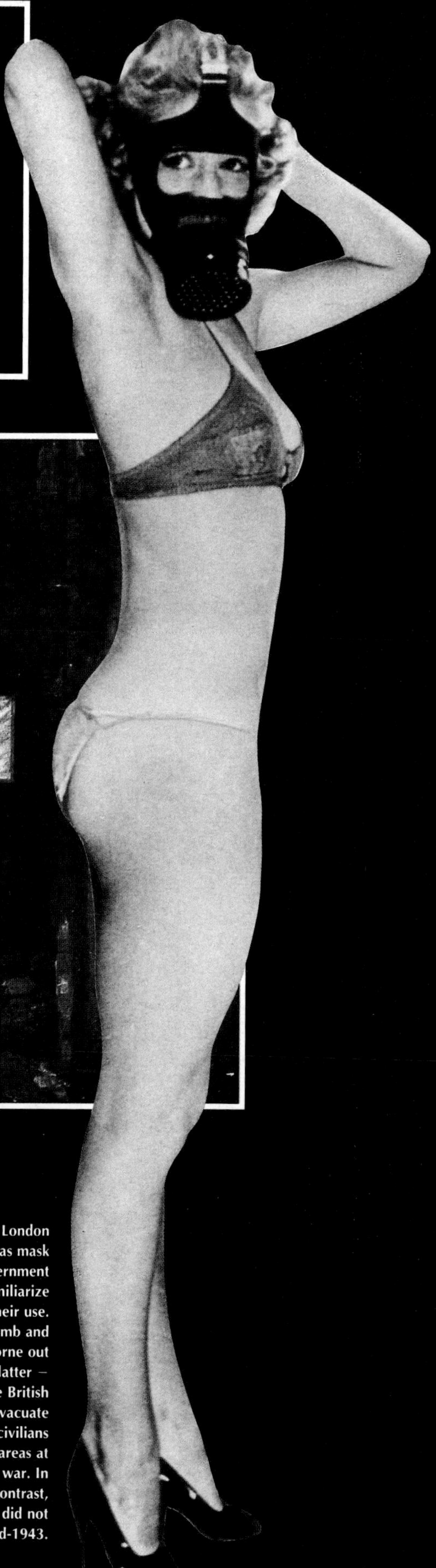

A scantily clad London chorus girl dons a gas mask as part of a government campaign to familiarize people with their use. Fears of enemy bomb and gas attack – not borne out in the case of the latter – persuaded the British government to evacuate nearly two million civilians from likely target areas at the outbreak of war. In Germany, by contrast, mass evacuation did not begin until mid-1943.

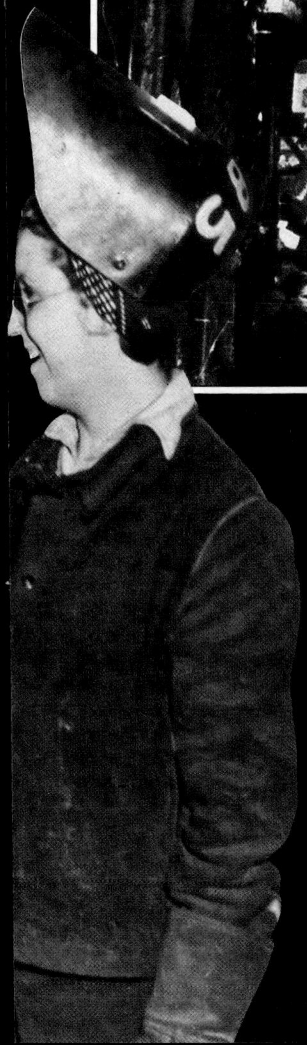

With the tortured bodies of eight hanged comrades dangling behind him as an example of Nazi cruelty, a Soviet partisan commander urges his men to greater efforts. Partisans were active from the early days of the German invasion, and by 1942 Moscow had developed a vast organization to train, supply and direct them. In large areas of the occupied Soviet Union, German control was confined to towns and the main roads that linked them, and partisan attacks were a constant drain on the German supply system. But the fighting inflicted grievous suffering on the peasant communities amid whom the irregular forces operated. The partisans themselves were ruthless with collaborators, willing or unwilling, while the Germans responded to their actions with reprisals that were savage even by Nazi standards.

Japanese naval loss of the war. One of the other Japanese carriers was seriously hit and had to return to base for repairs. But the Japanese scored, too. Their aircraft destroyed the carrier *Lexington* and so badly damaged her sister-ship, the *Yorktown,* that her captain reckoned she would need three months in a dockyard before she could fight again. In terms of losses, the battle was more of a draw than a Japanese defeat; but it gave notice that the season of easy victories was over.

Confirmation came a month later, when Admiral Yamamoto launched a complex assault on the key island outpost of Midway. His plan involved a coordinated attack by eight carriers, 11 battleships, 20 cruisers and scores of lesser craft. He would first seize the island, then use his massive striking power to destroy the U.S. Pacific Fleet when it steamed to the rescue. As far as he knew, after the Coral Sea fighting the Americans had only two intact carriers left, and Japanese intelligence placed them far from Midway.

In fact, the Americans had three carriers, for the damaged *Yorktown* had been patched up in 72 frenzied hours at Pearl Harbor. And all three were moving to intercept the Japanese main carrier force. They already knew its course and general whereabouts — information supplied by American cryptanalysts, who had broken the main Japanese naval code in April. The Americans found the Japanese first and, at heavy cost in aircraft, left four carriers sinking in flames. Japanese counterstrikes finally put paid to the *Yorktown,* but the outcome was a decisive American victory. Not only was Midway safe from invasion: Japan would make no more conquests of significance in the Pacific. Henceforth, the Japanese fleet would fight on the defensive, in an increasingly desperate attempt to hold on to its early gains.

These two battles did much to disabuse the Japanese of their illusion of U.S. weakness. American pilots had pressed home their attacks through murderously effective anti-aircraft defences — they lost 150 planes — with near-suicidal courage. A Japanese admiral who watched the airmen die was moved to say, in troubled admiration, "These men are samurai". Back in the U.S. a huge training programme was producing more such men, but the 150 or so strike pilots lost by the Japanese could not be so easily replaced. As for the machines they flew, American factories were turning them out at least five times as fast as the Japanese rate, and production was increasing. The achievement of the damaged *Yorktown*'s resurrection was another indication of the technological disparity between the two sides: Japan's injured carriers lingered far longer in port before they were battle-ready again.

The Pacific war, in fact, would be a war of high technology, where relatively small groups of trained men with expensive, complicated machines were worth infinitely more than ordinary soldiers. In other words, it was precisely the kind of war that Japan was least able to wage effectively. Japan's formidable infantrymen, scattered throughout the Pacific conquests, would eventually be a liability – immobile mouths to be fed at the end of long supply lines in a huge new short-lived empire that would prove far harder to defend than it had been to conquer.

While American forces recovered confidence and strength in the Pacific, the Allies were planning strategies for the war in Europe. As early as December 1940, the U.S. had identified Germany as potentially the most dangerous enemy; and despite the sting of the Pearl Harbor raid, Roosevelt reaffirmed that the destruction of Germany should receive the highest priority. The Soviet Union, of course, was still at peace with Japan. In many ways, the "United Nations" – Roosevelt's name for the grand coalition against Germany – was an uncomfortable alliance: the two democracies had found a strange bedfellow in Stalin's totalitarian Soviet Union.

The British and the Americans began combined planning sessions in December 1941. For the remainder of the war, Anglo-American coordination of policy and resources was remarkably close, though not without friction. Relations with the Soviets were more difficult. Essentially, Stalin wanted a "Second Front" – an Anglo-American invasion of Europe – and he wanted it instantly, to take pressure off the Red Army. Although the Americans broadly supported him, the British, who were frankly appalled at the likely cost of a premature assault on Hitler's home ground, demurred. With the reluctant consent of the Americans, more modest invasion plans, aimed at North Africa and the Mediterranean, were put into effect, and a decisive landing in France was postponed until 1943 or 1944. But there was no doubt of the prime objective of the "Big Three", and at a conference at Casablanca in January 1943, Roosevelt spelt it out: unconditional surrender from Germany and the other Axis powers.

In early 1942, however, any sort of German surrender remained a distant dream. The year began as grimly in Europe as in Asia. Elated by the Red Army's December triumph before Moscow, Stalin ordered a further series of winter offensives, against the advice of his best commanders. As Zhukov wrote later, with politic tact, "Stalin was very attentive to advice, but, regrettably, sometimes took decisions not in accord with the situation". The Soviets were short of equipment and munitions, and suffered heavy losses with very little to show for them. At Vyazma on the Moscow front, most of one attacking army was surrounded and destroyed; an attempt to cut through to Leningrad left the Second Shock Army isolated, though still fighting; in the south, an amphibious assault aimed at relieving the besieged fortress-city of Sevastopol in the Crimea ended in bloody disaster. Yet in March and April, Stalin attacked again, both in the north and in the south – with even worse results. A

COMBATING THE U-BOAT MENACE

The Atlantic sea lanes were the Allies' most vital supply artery; if German submarines could close them to Allied merchant shipping, then America's industrial power would be of no help in Europe.

In the first few years of the war, the Germans nearly achieved their aim, but by 1943 the vulnerable merchantmen were sailing in convoys protected by purpose-built submarine hunter-killers and close escorts. The boats were carefully deployed to provide minimum exposure to attack; because they presented a bigger target from bow to stern than head-on, they sailed only five deep over a wide front (sometimes with a rescue ship in the rear to pick up survivors). Long-range aircraft and aircraft carriers were soon added to the convoys' defences, and more and more U-boats littered the sea beds, fulfilling the "iron coffin" nickname bestowed upon them by their own crews.

A merchant officer, a few feet from an emergency life raft, surveys the slow-moving columns of a 1942 Atlantic convoy. Since most U-boat attacks were pressed home in the hours of darkness, counting surviving ships at dawn became an obsession with many convoy sailors during the three or four weeks of their voyage.

Carefully planned escort deployment gave convoys the maximum protection possible – at least on paper. Various types of vessel, including converted trawlers, were used for escort duty. All of them were equipped with asdic – sonar apparatus that could detect submerged submarines in an area indicated by the shaded cones. In addition, most escorts had radar with a range of some 4,000 metres – greater than the effective torpedo range of U-boats. But during the Atlantic battles, warships were regularly detached to hunt down possible submarine contacts or to search for survivors, giving a brave and enterprising U-boat skipper the opportunity to find a gap in the escort screen.

massive effort to save the Second Shock Army failed at the cost of 100,000 men. On the southern front, a drive to recapture the industrial city of Kharkov drove deep into German-held territory, only to be annihilated by a German pincer attack. This time the losses amounted to 200,000 men, as well as most of the Red Army's tanks. An April assault in the Crimea also failed. Since January, Stalin's offensives had cost, on all fronts, almost half a million prisoners and nearly as many dead and wounded. Not even the Soviets, with their huge reserves of manpower, could continue to sustain casualties at such a rate.

Now it was the Germans' turn to go on to the attack. Hitler had taken personal charge of the grand offensive that was planned for 1942: Operation *Blue*. For the time being, Moscow and its enormously reinforced defences was to be left alone. Instead, the blow would fall in the south.

The plan was ambitious in the extreme. German troops would first smash through the heavily industrialized basin of the River Don. Then, while the attack's northernmost element seized the city of Stalingrad as a bastion, the main force would swing southwards into the oilfields of the Caucasus, all the way to the Turkish border. Even that was only part of the gigantic pincer movement Hitler had planned. If all went well, German and Italian troops would drive the British out of Egypt and capture the oilfields of the Middle East. In such circumstances, Turkey would surely

As shell-bursts fountain on the horizon, Soviet infantry advance behind T-34 tanks during the 1943 battle for the Kursk salient, in central Russia. The fighting, waged over open steppe country, began with a German attack that was fiercely resisted by the massed Red Army defenders. It ended with victory salutes fired in Moscow and a general Soviet advance along much of the Eastern Front.

enter the war as a German ally, as she had been in 1914. When the operation was over, a gigantic east wall would seal off the remnants of the Soviet Union, which in any case would have nothing left to wage war with. The British and Americans, deprived of Soviet support, would soon come to terms; and Nazi Germany, like a well-fed beast of prey, would quietly digest her conquests.

The big question was whether the nation had the resources to achieve such grandiose objectives. Compared to the task before it, the German army in the East was woefully undermanned and underequipped. Its 1941 strength had already proved insufficient, and it began 1942 with 625,000 soldiers less. The manpower problem was partly eased by trimming unit sizes to create more divisions, by paring home-based reserves to the bone, and by enlisting major aid from allies. Between them, the Hungarians, Romanians, Slovakians, Finns and Italians provided 51 divisions. But the new, smaller divisions were weaker than the 1941 versions; moreover, the allied troops were rarely as reliable as German units and seldom had anything like a full quota of tanks and artillery.

The Germans themselves were dangerously short of equipment. Their factories had been able to replace only 10 per cent of the vehicles lost so far, and the supply of tanks and aircraft was not much better. Even in horses and mules, the mainstay of German army transport, there was a shortfall of 160,000 beasts.

The sluggishness of German industrial production was largely a self-inflicted wound, for the machines and skills existed to do much better. But in a curious way, Hitler had failed to understand the nature of the total war that he himself had unleashed. While Britain, the Soviet Union and the United States had all put their economies on to an emergency war footing, German factories operated much as they had in peacetime, often with only one shift per day. Consumer goods, impossible to obtain in Britain and Russia and growing scarce even in the United States, were widely available in the Reich. Women, by now a large part of the Allies' workforce, stayed at home in Germany with their children — in accordance with Nazi ideology, but not with the needs of the hour.

The truth was that Hitler, who expected his troops to lay down their lives for him without a murmur, was reluctant to ask for even modest sacrifices on the home front. The Nazis' prewar popularity had depended more on the prosperity they had brought than on torchlit parades and racial ranting, and Hitler knew it. Until much too late, he chose not to impose upon his people the kind of tightly directed economy that Britain, America and the Soviet Union had come to take for granted.

Nazi ideology was itself the cause of many difficulties, and not only because it relegated German women to the home. Throughout the war, Germany was plagued with a chronic manpower problem: the army was always trying to snatch workers from the factories, where they were needed just as much as in the front line. To fill the gaps, millions of workers from the occupied territories were conscripted into the Reich, but their productivity was dismally low, and the bolder spirits regularly resorted to sabotage. These workers would have contributed more to the Nazi war effort if they had been left at home — or could have, if the Nazis had not systematically looted factories throughout the occupied lands of their machinery, much of which spent the rest of the war, abandoned and forgotten, in railway sidings.

The vast numbers of Soviet prisoners captured by German troops were another squandered resource. A high proportion of them were simply allowed to die,

Armed with 13 machine guns and protected by a liberal provision of armour plate, the American B-17 Flying Fortress seemed to live up to its name. U.S. planners were convinced that its interlocking fields of fire would make the bomber almost invulnerable to enemy fighter attack. But Luftwaffe pilots soon found the bomber's weak point. Ball and upper turrets were barely able to respond to a head-on attack, and the other forward-firing guns were rubber-mounted weapons which were manned by the bombardier and the engineer, whose gunnery training was skimpy.

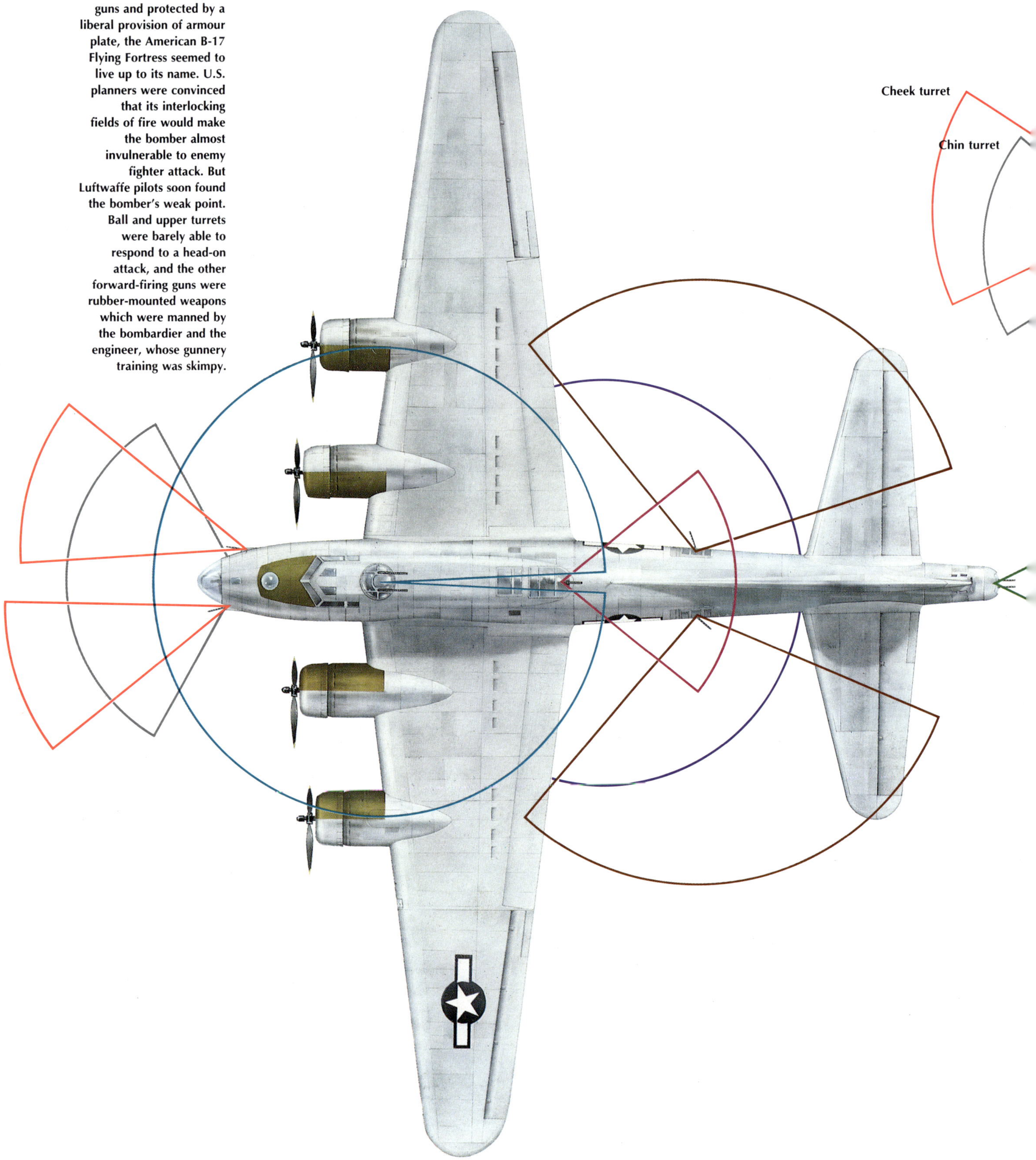

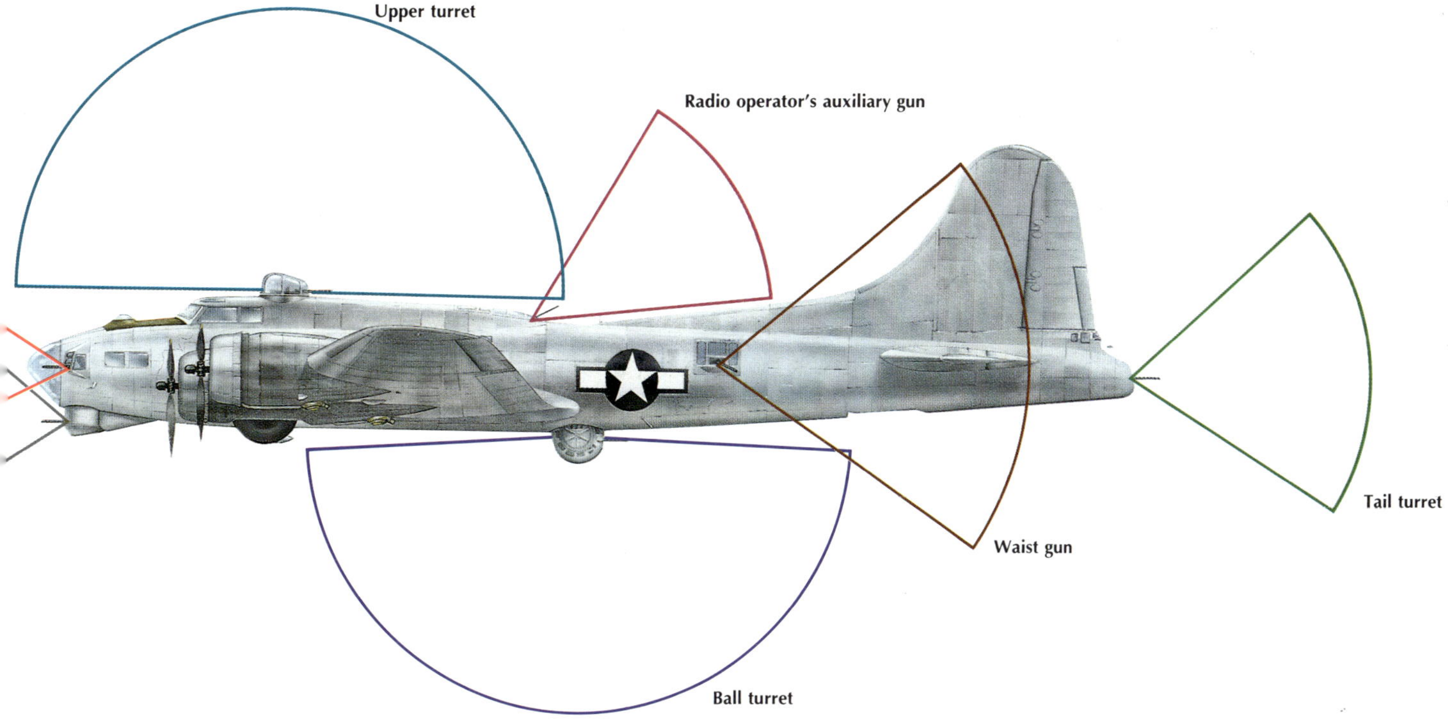

FLYING FIRE POWER

In the air war against Germany, the British pursued a strategy of area bombing by night, while the Americans favoured precision daylight bombing. They were sure that their heavily armed B-17 Flying Fortresses and B-24 Liberators would be able to defend themselves against enemy fighters, and they believed that their Norden bombsights would enable them to hit their targets with pinpoint accuracy. But though the B-17s were excellent bombers, they were no match for fast enemy interceptors, and it was not until long-range escort fighters became available near the end of 1943 that daylight bombing became possible without intolerable losses. Even then, the difficulty of sighting on targets in bad weather meant that, on average, less than one third of the bombs dropped fell within 300 metres of the specific target.

A B-17 ball turret gunner demonstrates his cramped station. On a mission, he would spend up to 10 hours there, encumbered by about 20 kilograms of protective clothing and breathing equipment. The B-17 carried four gunners, plus the pilot, co-pilot, navigator, bombardier, flight engineer and radio operator.

American troops wade chest-deep into heavy German fire at Omaha Beach, one of the five landing areas on the coast of Normandy chosen for the great Allied invasion on D-day – June 6, 1944. In the greatest amphibious operation in history, 176,000 men were set ashore in a 24-hour period, supported by 600 warships and more than 10,000 aircraft. The devastating fire power they provided numbed most of the defenders, and D-day casualties were lower than Allied commanders had feared – except at Omaha, where a fiercely held seafront embankment *(background)* kept the issue in doubt until evening.

through starvation and neglect, for respect for human life certainly did not hinder Germany. By the middle of 1942 there were already huge slave labour camps – Auschwitz, for example – whose purpose was unashamedly to work their inmates to death; those who were too old, too young or otherwise unfit to work were killed immediately upon arrival. But the German economy gained little from the suffering of its victims. The crowning Nazi madness came in late 1942 and 1943, when the so-called "final solution" – the mass murder of Europe's Jews, together with gypsies and other "undesirables" – got into full swing. Scarce transport resources were tied up for months at a time in order to carry millions of able-bodied and often highly skilled people not to German workshops, where they were desperately needed, but to German gas ovens. Their only economic contribution to the Reich was to be bundles of shoes and soiled clothing, human hair for mattresses, and the gold fillings from their teeth.

Nazi organizational methods were another war-loser. Hitler had always believed in the principle of "divide and rule". High party officials were given overlapping areas of responsibility; mutual suspicion and bureaucratic empire-building were both encouraged. Himmler's SS, for example, was virtually a state within a state, running its own factories and scientific research programmes which guaranteed duplication – and waste – of effort. Major decisions were taken for reasons of internal politics, sometimes merely on Hitler's whim. There was none of the careful committee work that characterized British, American and, indeed, Russian planning. It was a nice irony that Hitler the dictator exercised no real central control over his economy – far less than Churchill or Roosevelt. Matters did improve somewhat after mid-1942, when Albert Speer, a young architect and gifted amateur economist, was appointed chief of German production. But with an effective time-lag of 18 months between production decisions and their effects upon the battlefield, his reforms came too late to turn the tide.

For on the Eastern Front, Operation *Blue* ended in disaster. The offensive got off to a good start in late June. Within days, the key city of Rostov, on the River Don, was in German hands, and Army Group B was driving steadily onwards towards Stalingrad on the River Volga, while Army Group A swung southwards into the Caucasus. In late August and early September, General Friedrich Paulus' Sixth Army broke through to the Volga both north and south of Stalingrad, and the battle for the city itself – it was built almost entirely on the west bank of the river – began. It was a fearful struggle, in which every ruined building was a strongpoint to be captured and recaptured at a terrible cost in the lives of the best troops of both sides. Inch by inch, the Sixth Army gained ground.

But General Zhukov had devised a plan to break the German stranglehold on Stalingrad and in so doing to trap the entire German Sixth Army. If the Soviets kept their nerve, he explained to Stalin, then the dictator's name-city could be held with minimum reinforcements, while powerful reserve forces were assembled well to the north and south of the battlefront. Then, when everything was ready, a great Russian pincer movement would pull a double ring of steel around the Germans. Stalin agreed; the plan proceeded.

Wearing an armband to mark him as a legitimate combatant, a resistance fighter of the French Forces of the Interior takes cover behind a truck during the Allied advance on Paris in August 1944. FFI men appeared in thousands to offer aid to Allied units, and their efforts gave their nominal leader, General Charles de Gaulle, a valuable political stake in Allied councils. But the liberation of Paris itself was entrusted to the more orthodox soldiers of Free France's only armoured division, built round a core of émigrés who had fought in Allied ranks since 1940.

Throughout September, the fighting in the city continued. Hitler had become obsessed with the place, as much for its name as for its strategic importance. In October, he ordered troops moved from Army Group B's vulnerable flanks to take part in a final push that would surely leave the Germans in possession of Stalingrad's rubble. The flank guards were replaced by Romanian and Italian divisions, low in tanks, guns and, in many cases, morale. By early November, only a few Soviet bridgeheads remained on the west bank, but the Germans were too exhausted to shift them.

Then, on November 19, the great blow fell – precisely on the second-grade formations on the Germans' northern and southern flanks. Within four days, the two arms of the Soviet pincer, scattering or annihilating everything before them, joined together. Twenty-two Axis divisions were trapped – 250,000 men, with all their armour and artillery. A rapid attempt at a breakout might have succeeded, but Hitler was adamant that Stalingrad should be held. And besides, Hermann Göring had promised that his Luftwaffe could keep the Sixth Army supplied until the spring.

In December, troops from a force commanded by Field Marshal von Manstein came close to cutting an escape corridor through the encirclement. But a new Soviet attack in the middle Don area put the relief force, too, in jeopardy, and though von Manstein succeeded in pulling his own troops back more or less intact, Paulus' Sixth Army was doomed. All through January 1943, the soldiers endured agonies of cold, hunger and disease. When the Sixth Army finally surrendered in February, there were only 90,000 men left alive. And the Soviets were attacking elsewhere, too. Before the winter was over, they had regained Kursk and Kharkov, and partly broken the siege of Leningrad. All told, the fighting had cost Hitler almost a quarter of his troops in Russia. Stalin, promoting himself marshal of the Soviet Union, declared, "The mass expulsion of the enemy from the Soviet Union has begun".

There was precious little good news for Germany in 1942. Shortage of materiel hampered German efforts everywhere – not just on the vital Eastern Front. In the North African desert, General Erwin Rommel's Afrika Korps were always short of tanks, though German tactical skill and British blundering brought Rommel close to triumph in May. But the Afrika Korps was painfully difficult to supply. The overstretched Luftwaffe – scarcely 15,000 aircraft were produced in 1942, compared with 23,672 in Britain, 25,436 in the Soviet Union and 47,836 in America – could no longer maintain its previous air superiority over the Mediterranean; by late 1942 the British were sinking up to 70 per cent of the Axis freighters that attempted the crossing, while their own build-up in Egypt continued almost unmolested.

The result was that Rommel's 1942 desert offensives could never pack enough punch to rout the British. After his failure to break through at El Alamein in Egypt during July 1942, he had little choice but to wait until Britain's Eighth Army, with a new commander – General Bernard Montgomery – and a carefully assembled advantage of 600 tanks, was ready to attack. The second battle of El Alamein, lasting for 12 days in late October and November, drove Rommel into headlong retreat.

A few days later, in Operation *Torch*, a huge Anglo-American armada landed an army in Algeria and Morocco. Rather than staging an immediate evacuation, Hitler reinforced: the thought of the whole North African coast in Allied hands made him fear for the security of what he was already beginning to call "Fortress Europe".

The Germans at first made some headway against the raw American invaders: the rapid expansion of the U.S. army from 185,000 in 1938 to a three-million man

General Charles de Gaulle, since 1940 the self-appointed leader of Free France, is greeted by ecstatic crowds in the French town of Laval in August 1944. De Gaulle was not always so popular with his fellow countrymen; after the fall of France, many of them regarded his broadcasts from exile in London as provocations from an officer acting without authority. But de Gaulle was a consummate politician, with a sense not only of his own destiny but also that of his country. From a small group of supporters – and with the sometimes reluctant aid of his allies, Churchill and later Roosevelt – he built up a military and political organization that made him the most respected figure in post-war France and went a long way to restoring the pride his nation had lost in the 1940 debacle.

Prime Minister Winston Churchill, President Franklin D. Roosevelt and Secretary-General Joseph Stalin pose happily for the cameras at their February 1945 summit meeting in the Crimean resort town of Yalta. Although the "Big Three" almost always presented a public image of harmony, there were disagreements in private – and not only between the two democrats on one side and the Soviet dictator on the other. Churchill mistrusted Stalin, while Roosevelt was sure that "Uncle Joe" would respond generously to generous treatment; Stalin played the Americans against the British. The main outcome of the meeting was Churchill's and Roosevelt's acceptance of the future Soviet domination of eastern Europe. In return, Stalin pledged to keep out of the Mediterranean, withholding support from the communist parties of Italy and Greece despite their loyalty to Moscow.

force only four years later had inevitably meant sketchy training and an acute shortage of experienced officers. But the Germans – including Rommel – were awestruck at the quantity and quality of American equipment; as for training and experience, these would be provided in the hard school of battle by the Germans themselves. Although the campaign dragged on until May 1943, the outcome was inevitable: the Axis lost 300,000 soldiers, including 215,000 prisoners.

In addition to the defeats in Russia and North Africa, the Germans had to fight on a new front – the skies above the Reich. The Royal Air Force's Bomber Command had begun its strategic offensive as early as July 1940, but for almost two years its achievements had been negligible. Daylight raids had proved suicidal, and Britain lacked both suitable aircraft and the navigational equipment necessary to find targets at night. Churchill had authorized the attacks more to bolster British morale than in the hope of inflicting decisive damage.

But Churchill allowed himself to be persuaded by air power theorists that strategic bombing, properly directed, could bring Germany to her knees without the heavy land fighting and consequent casualties that he and most senior British officers remembered with horror from the First World War. Britain chose to invest immense resources in the construction of heavy, four-engined bombers, which by the end of 1942 formed the backbone of the attacking force. British scientists developed new target-finding techniques, and in Air Marshal Arthur Harris, Churchill found an aggressive and single-minded exponent of stategic bombing. The new weapons would be used not for precision raids – Harris reckoned that a waste of effort, and results so far largely bore him out – but for area attacks against cities. The German population would be "de-housed".

A concentrated attack on the old Baltic port of Lübeck showed the kind of damage that could now be done. The place was of no particular importance, but it was easy to find and its wooden buildings burnt well. In March 1942, Bomber Command flattened half the city. Two months later, by using every crew and aircraft he could muster, including training units, Harris sent over 1,000 bombers, by far the largest raid so far, to Cologne. The next morning, the flames of the burning city were brighter than the rising sun. The "Terror Fliers", as the Germans called the bomber crews, were bringing the horrors of war to the German homeland.

Such concentrated attacks were difficult to organize and, even with the new electronic navigation gear, required clear weather for success. There were no more thousand-bomber raids in 1942. But nights in an air-raid shelter became a depressingly regular experience for a large part of Germany's population. And before the end of the year, American day-bombers, heavily armed and armoured against fighters and flak, were joining the campaign. After "practice" missions against relatively undefended targets in the occupied territories, they launched their first raid

Much aged by defeat, and scarcely recognizable as Italy's once-triumphant Duce, Mussolini gives a last interview in April 1945 *(above)*. A few days later, he was captured by Italian communist partisans. Fearing the political consequences of a drawn-out trial, their leaders summarily shot the ex-dictator, along with his mistress, Clara Petacci. Their bodies *(right)*, together with that of a Fascist official, were later strung up in a Milan square. Standing before the firing squad, Mussolini apparently recovered some of his old style. "Shoot me here," he reportedly said, tapping his chest. "Do not spoil my profile." And he could still inspire loyalty, for though Petacci could have escaped arrest, she chose to accompany her lover to the end.

on Germany itself in January 1943. The air defence of the Reich would make yet another claim on Germany's limited resources.

Strategic bombing was high-technology war *par excellence*. The gadgets of the attacker were met by counter-gadgets as each side's scientists tried to outguess and thwart their opponents. Target-finding beams and radar would be jammed, jamming would be counterjammed, and the cycle would begin again at a higher and usually much more expensive level. Germany, the best-educated nation in Europe, should have acquitted itself well in such a contest, but given the general muddle that marked Nazi scientific planning, it was not surprising that the Anglo-American system, in which information and ideas were freely exchanged between combat units and research stations, usually managed to stay ahead.

With the improving weather of spring and summer 1943, the Anglo-American bombing campaign steadily increased in intensity. In what the publicity-minded Harris called "the Battle of the Ruhr", hundreds of British bombers belaboured Germany's industrial heartland night after night, while the Americans launched what they hoped were pinpoint raids on targets on the fringe of the Reich. The climax came in July, when a succession of massive raids came close to destroying the great port of Hamburg. The endless showers of incendiaries created a firestorm in the centre of the city: temperatures reached more than 1,000 degrees Celsius and at least 40,000 civilians died.

As the Red Army closes in on Berlin during April 1945, Adolf Hitler inspects his last storm-troopers: boys of the Hitler Youth, whom the Fuhrer expected to die for him in the coming street-fighting. The annihilation of Germany's next generation meant little to Hitler, who felt that the nation had somehow betrayed him and should go down with him in utter ruin. He even issued orders for the destruction of such industry and communications as remained. If carried out, they would have meant inevitable starvation for the survivors of the Reich, but for once Hitler's deputies – even SS chief Heinrich Himmler – ignored their master. And army officers in the last, doomed battles did what they could to send the militarily useless Hitler Youth home, although many of these child-fanatics were killed.

The bomber campaign took a heavy toll of Allied aircrews, too. American long-distance penetrations later in the year brought insupportable losses at the hands of the Luftwaffe, and when Harris tried a "Battle of Berlin" in the winter of 1943 to 1944, German nightfighters slaughtered his crews. There was some controversy as to the effectiveness of the bombing campaign. German production was almost always less badly disrupted than the Allies imagined, for it was much easier to hit the centres of towns, where people lived, than the outskirts, where industries were generally located. Besides, the incendiaries which were favoured by the Allies for city-wrecking purposes did little harm to machinery, and the Germans proved adept at patching up damaged war factories.

The destruction of non-essential plant often freed bombed-out workers for the labour-hungry arms industry, and the skilful way in which the Nazi party made itself responsible for relief work in the scarred cities kept the population remarkably loyal. In any case, indiscriminate bombing of civilian targets was a poor advertisement for the Allied cause and provided the Germans with a rich source of propaganda. The costs, too, were staggering: in 1942 a B-17 Flying Fortress bomber cost more than $250,000. Moreover, the airmen usually represented the cream of Allied manpower; as a result of the bombing offensive's demands, Britain and the United States would later find themselves seriously short of junior infantry officers. But if the bombing campaign was hurting the resource-rich Allies, it was hurting the Germans more. The necessity for home air defence put an intolerable strain upon the Luftwaffe, and for the rest of the war German soldiers on every front could expect little or no air support.

There was one Western campaign that still seemed to hold some hopes for Hitler, if not of outright victory then at least of stalemate: the long-drawn-out Battle of the Atlantic. Since 1939, German U-boats had been trying to block the sea lanes on which first British survival and later the American build-up depended. But here, too, Allied superiority in production and technology eventually swung the balance. Germany had begun the war with too few U-boats to force a decision, even against Britain's slender force of unpractised antisubmarine escorts, equipped with primitive sonar – equipment for detecting underwater objects by means of reflected sonic waves. By the time U-boat numbers had reached a dangerous level, there were more escorts, equipped with increasingly sophisticated technology, including radar, improved sonar and depth charges, and a radio-location system that could pinpoint a submarine's position from its brief, coded signals to headquarters.

There were still some bad moments for the Allies. In November 1942, for instance, they lost over 700,000 tonnes of shipping, and in the first three months of 1943 the U-boats did enough damage to cause real fears that the planned invasion of Europe would have to be delayed. But most U-boat successes were against unescorted merchantmen. As more escorts became available, fewer ships travelled alone, and attacks on convoys imposed a steady attrition on U-boat strength. By 1943, Americans were turning out freighters far faster than the U-boats could sink them: one of these so-called "liberty ships", a standardized design prefabricated for speed of manufacture, was actually built in 80 hours and 30 minutes.

Finally, after April 1943, the Allies possessed a fleet of long-range aircraft capable of patrolling the entire North Atlantic. It was the last straw. By then it often cost more than one submarine for every merchantman destroyed. The U-boat campaign was reduced to nuisance level, at high cost to Admiral Dönitz's German navy: of every eight men who served in his submarines, seven failed to return.

There was one other important sea lane: the North Cape route to Russia. In the face of strong air, sea and surface attack, the Western Allies had been sending aid to the embattled Soviet Union since 1941. Initially it was not much more than token assistance, which was of more value politically than militarily. Even when the volume of aid increased, arms shipments were never of the highest importance: Russia's own tanks, for example, were far better than anything the Anglo-Americans produced throughout the war. But vast quantities of foodstuffs eased the

Skeletal corpses of Jewish prisoners litter the ground at Bergen-Belsen concentration camp in western Germany. The British, who liberated the camp in April 1945, found 10,000 dead and 40,000 inmates still barely alive; their SS guards were still shooting them even as the British arrived – to keep order, they claimed. Reports of German murder camps had circulated for years, but had generally been dismissed as propaganda-inspired atrocity stories. The fall of the Third Reich brought incontrovertible evidence of massacre and cruelty on an unimaginable scale. Although a few of its perpetrators were shot out of hand by liberating troops, and others were prosecuted by war crimes tribunals in later years, most merged quietly back into civilian life.

problems of war-stricken Soviet agriculture, and from late 1942 onwards a steady supply of jeeps and trucks gave the Red Army a degree of mobility which it would put to devastating effect in the campaigns of 1943 and 1944.

As if the technical superiority of the Allies were not enough, they also had huge advantages in military intelligence. Stalin could rely on reports sent from loyal communists throughout the world, in London and Washington as well as in Berlin, to keep him informed; such sources had warned him repeatedly of *Barbarossa*, and it was not their fault that the dictator had failed to act on their reports.

The British had another kind of access to Axis secrets. In 1940, a group of their cryptanalysts succeeded in cracking the supposedly unbreakable German cipher system, which was based on a complex encoding machine called "Enigma". So

confident were the Germans in Enigma's security that they used it for almost all their radio transmissions. With the assistance of one of the world's first computers, British and American intelligence officers could often read vital enemy signals within hours of their interception.

Another aspect of the secret war was the underground movements scattered throughout occupied Europe. In the Soviet Union and the Balkans, partisan forces were of major military importance; in Yugoslavia, for example, the leader nicknamed "Tito" had 150,000 men and women under arms. Elsewhere, resistance activity was less overt. Despite harsh German punishments, there was a constant trickle of sabotage, and Allied fliers shot down in occupied Europe had a fair chance of finding an "underground railway" to get them safely home through neutral Spain or Switzerland. Just as usefully, the forced labourers on whom Germany's factories had come to depend were a valuable source of information for Allied planners. In time, and as an Allied victory became more certain, men and women of the resistance would increase both in numbers and daring.

The events of 1943 left no doubt as to who was winning in Europe. In the Soviet Union, the Red Army had learnt its lessons well. After Stalingrad it had pushed the Germans back along most of the Eastern Front. And almost all of its offensives were well calculated; seldom again would Soviet troops push forwards recklessly only to be encircled and destroyed by canny German commanders. From now on, they themselves would do the encircling – with just one exception. A vigorous

German attack in March 1943 recaptured the city of Kharkov, taken by the Soviets only days before. The Kharkov battle, modest by the standards of the gargantuan Eastern Front, would be the German army's last victory.

There were still four million Axis soldiers in the Soviet Union – only slightly less than the number of troops fielded by the Red Army. In terms of tanks, artillery and aircraft, though, they could no longer match their opponents. But Hitler was determined to stage one more offensive, if only to avoid passing the initiative completely to the Soviets: Operation *Citadel* would pinch out the great Soviet-held salient around Kursk, destroying the best of the Red Army's men and equipment. Even Hitler recognized the risks. "Whenever I think of this attack," he told one of his generals, "my stomach turns over."

Originally, Operation *Citadel* had been scheduled for May, when it might have stood some chance of success; but Hitler decided to postpone the offensive to give his panzer divisions a chance to re-equip themselves with new and more deadly machines – the Panther and Tiger tanks. In the meantime, a Soviet spy ring based in Switzerland had passed details of *Citadel* to Moscow. The Soviets, who had been considering an offensive of their own in the same area, massively reinforced the salient. When the German attack was finally launched on July 5, it stormed into the strongest position on the front.

The Battle of Kursk, fought over steppe and farmland, was the greatest armoured clash of all time. Almost two million men, with 6,000 tanks, took part. The Soviet air force, rebuilt almost from scratch after its 1941 humiliation, flew some 28,000

Against a background of urban desolation, Russian tanks and guns grind their way across Berlin's River Spree. Even before the Russian onslaught, Anglo-American air attacks had left much of the city in ruins. The Red Army's battle with Berlin's last-ditch defenders accounted for most of the rest, and cost the Soviets some 300,000 casualties. The Western Allies lost about 800,000 during the entire campaign that took them from Normandy into the heart of Germany.

sorties, and even the battered Luftwaffe managed to put together 140 squadrons. Within a few days, the German attack began to falter. Despite their powerful new tanks, which, untried upon the battlefield, gave plenty of technical problems, they could make no real headway against the deeply layered Soviet defences.

But the contest was not pushed to a final resolution. On July 10, Anglo-American armies invaded Sicily. Three days later Hitler summoned his commanders to tell them that he would have to transfer his Kursk forces to protect his European southern flank. In fact the Germans released only one division for the fighting in Sicily, and *Citadel* dragged on until the end of July. When the Germans did finally withdraw, disengaging themselves as best they could, it was in response less to the Sicilian landings than to Soviet offensives aimed at cities north and south of Kursk.

The Sicily invasion was nonetheless a decisive event, for it opened a new theatre of war. On July 21, Mussolini was deposed by members of his own grand council who wanted to pull Italy out of the war. Not one of the Fascist party's four million members raised a finger to save him, and some of his captors proposed that he should be handed over to the Anglo-Americans as proof of Italy's intention to abandon its German ally. But the surrender negotiations were mishandled, and within days of the Allied landing on the mainland in September, at Salerno, just south of Naples, the Germans had rescued Mussolini, disarmed most of the war-weary Italian army and seized the country's strategic strongpoints.

Churchill had once called Italy and the Balkans "the soft underbelly of Europe". Politically, the British prime minister had a point. Militarily, though, the mountainous Italian peninsula with its series of rivers and ridgelines was perfect defensive country, and the Germans made the most of it, fighting with skill and tenacity.

The key to Italy was its long coastline. Thanks to Allied sea power, troops could land almost anywhere along it. But a shortage of landing craft – the Pacific war was using far more than expected, and others were being hoarded for the invasion of France – delayed a further Allied landing until January 1944, at Anzio just south of Rome. The landing achieved complete surprise, but once safely ashore the Allied commanders moved too slowly, giving the Germans time to mount an assault that bottled up the invaders on their beachhead – "the largest self-supporting prison camp in the world", as German propaganda boasted. Not until May 1944 was there a successful breakout, and by the time the Anzio force joined up with other Allied units advancing from the south, most of the Germans had escaped northwards with their equipment. Rome fell on June 4, but the Italian campaign would drag on for almost another year before German resistance at last collapsed.

Meanwhile, in Russia the German defence was less successful. After Kursk, the Red Army thrust westwards on a wide front. German casualties and transfers had reduced their forces to around three-and-a-half million men, against whom the Soviets could field six million, with another million in reserve. The Red Army still could not match the Germans in small-scale tactics, and its advances cost heavily in blood, but Soviet lives were seldom spent pointlessly. Red Army attacks persistently sought and found the weak points in the shaky German line, for the Soviet commanders who had learnt to outfight the Germans at Stalingrad were fast learning how to outthink them, too. The list of liberated towns grew steadily longer.

The Soviet advance gave a new urgency to the most horrific Nazi policy of all: the annihilation of the Jews. Hitler, his dreams of conquest fast collapsing, was determined to succeed in this objective, at least. His regime had been murdering

Only three kilometres long, the key islet of Betio in the Tarawa atoll (*left*) saw some of the fiercest fighting in the Pacific campaign. The well-entrenched Japanese defenders inflicted 3,000 casualties on an inexperienced American invasion force before they themselves were killed. The Americans learnt quickly from their mistakes, building replicas of Betio's blockhouses in Hawaii to test new and more effective demolition techniques. Their ambitious, two-pronged attack on Japan's conquests, under General Douglas MacArthur in the south and Admiral Chester Nimitz in the north, went ahead as planned (*below*) with minimal losses, at least to the American troops. Japanese soldiers died by the thousand in their pulverized bunkers, often without even seeing their enemies.

Displaying only a fraction of the 90 to 100 aircraft she could accommodate below decks, the 27,000-tonne carrier U.S.S. *Essex* steams across the Pacific in May 1943. Fast carriers of the *Essex* class, capable of making 33 knots, formed the core of the hard-hitting strike forces with which the U.S. Navy dominated the Pacific after mid-1943. Sailing at the centre of a battle group bristling with anti-aircraft guns, the carriers inflicted devastating damage on Japanese fleets, shore installations and merchant shipping.

Jews since 1939, but generally by the messy, uneconomic means of a bullet in the head. In 1942 and 1943, the Nazis began to use mass-extermination methods, including poison gas. By early 1945 Hitler had killed almost six million Jews; three out of every four in his crumbling empire.

Not even Hitler believed that slaughtering Jews would help him win the war. For that he placed his hopes on either a great falling-out between the Western Allies and the Soviet Union, or on the secret weapons his scientists were developing. There was little chance of the former. Relations between them would become distinctly uneasy as the Red Army pushed past the old Russian frontier and it became clear that the countries of eastern Europe were destined for a future inside a new, totalitarian Soviet sphere; but the desire for the complete destruction of Nazi Germany proved a powerful cement, and the alliance held until the end.

Secret weapons were almost as much of a pipe dream. Of scores of German projects – including a long-range bomber capable of attacking New York and a gun powered by liquid explosives – only two came to fruition. The first, the so-called V-1, was a small pilotless plane that could carry 1,000 kilograms of explosive from France or Belgium to London. It was an ingenious device, cheap to make and requiring no scarce materials. When it was first used in 1944, it greatly alarmed the British, who had to resort to highly expensive countermeasures. The second weapon, though, was the one that most appealed to Hitler. The V-2, a liquid-fuel rocket with a range of about 350 kilometres – a longer-range version was on the drawing board – was the forerunner of the intercontinental ballistic missile. Since it rose out of the atmosphere on firing, and descended at more than 5,000 kilometres per hour, there was no defence against it. But its cost was huge – 50 times that of a V-1, which carried roughly the same payload – and it absorbed resources that were in short supply, including many of Germany's best technicians.

A deck officer on the U.S.S. *Enterprise* clambers on to the wing of a burning Hellcat fighter to drag its injured pilot to safety from his cockpit. Carrier-borne planes frequently crashed while attempting to land on rolling and pitching flight decks which were little more than 250 metres long.

To make the V-2 a war-winning weapon, something more powerful than conventional explosives would have been needed. Since 1939, a number of British and American scientists had feared that Hitler might be developing just that. Even before the war, the theoretical possibility of an atomic bomb had been explored, and Germany had been a world leader in atomic research. To Western physicists, including a high proportion of German-Jewish exiles, it was imperative that the Allies develop such a fearful weapon first. By 1941, the British had done the theoretical groundwork; then, when America entered the war and British research was made available to U.S. scientists, President Roosevelt authorized the start-up of the Manhattan Project, the greatest scientific and engineering enterprise of the century so far.

The Americans spent lavishly and well, their research teams driven by the fear that Hitler's scientists would beat them to their goal. In fact, the Manhattan Project was a one-horse race, for Germany's nuclear programme never received any kind of priority, and research was dilatory. But not even the prodigal expenditures and industrial skills of the Americans would have the bomb ready before 1945. Germany would have to be defeated the hard way.

Since 1941 Stalin had been demanding from his allies a second front: a full-scale invasion of Europe. Nineteen forty-two came and went without it. A raid on the French port of Dieppe, ostensibly to test German reactions, ended in disaster. As 1943 passed without an invasion, Stalin grew noisily suspicious of Anglo-American intentions, but the Allies' obligation would soon be fulfilled. North Africa, Sicily

In the minutes before taking off on his suicide mission, a kamikaze pilot (*right*) calmly waits while a smiling comrade ties his headband – formerly worn by samurai warriors as symbols of courage in the face of death. The example above carries the Japanese legend "divine wind".

A burning kamikaze falls like a meteor into the sea between two American aircraft carriers in July 1945. The knowledge that they were under attack from suicide pilots greatly improved the reaction times and accuracy of American gunners.

Kamikaze

In the heat of combat, pilots of all the warring nations had occasionally been known to use suicidal ramming tactics against their enemies. Only the Japanese, though, went so far as to organize squadrons of airmen formally sworn to die – the kamikazes. Named after the "divine wind" that had saved 13th-century Japan from a Mongol invasion, the corps was formed in an hour of equal peril, on the eve of the 1944 American attack on the Philippines. There was certainly cold logic behind the plan: with pilots flying deliberate, one-way missions, even the obsolete aircraft that Japan had available might inflict devastating blows.

But there was nothing cold about the response. In a mood of exaltation, young men flocked to volunteer, for courage and patriotic devotion were among the few resources the Japanese did not lack. Those selected were usually the most inexperienced; battle-seasoned pilots were too valuable to be lost. They spent their last days calmly, awaiting the summons to their final flight. Many wrote moving letters home: "I have been given a splendid opportunity to die," explained one kamikaze to his parents. "Let my death be as sudden and clean as the shattering of crystal."

When the time came, they drank a last glass of sake with their comrades, then sought their end in fiery collision with the biggest American ship they could find – for though their leaders exhorted them to return and wait for another opportunity if there was no suitably valuable target, few ever did.

In fact, their impact on the war was negligible. Between the kamikazes' foundation in October 1944 and Japan's surrender, 1,228 gave their lives to sink 34 American ships, only three of them larger than destroyers, and damage 288 others.

and Italy – not to mention the Pacific – had taught the Western Allies, sometimes painfully, the art of seaborne landing. American industry had built enough of the specialized craft that were required. By the spring of 1944, the British Isles creaked under the weight of the troops, tanks and aircraft massed for the great assault.

Operation *Overlord* was launched on June 6, 1944, when American, British and Canadian troops landed on five beaches in Normandy. Massive air superiority made it difficult for the Germans to counterattack in force; besides, a skilful Allied deception convinced the Germans that a second invasion was likely in the Calais area, and Hitler refused to transfer all the reserves available to him. A stubborn German defence kept the Allies within a confined area for almost two months, but the fighting cost them irreplaceable equipment. When German resistance finally collapsed in August, there was nothing between the Allies and the River Seine.

A crushing defeat of the long-expected Allied invasion had been Hitler's last hope of wresting something other than total ruin from the war. Now that hope was gone. And while German forces in Normandy bled to death, the Soviets launched a series of attacks that led to the complete destruction of the German army Group Centre. By August, the Red Army was on the banks of the Vistula in Poland.

Between the hammer of the Soviets and the anvil of the Western Allies, Germany could expect no mercy. Recognizing this, a group of senior German officers tried to assassinate Hitler on July 20. They failed – a matter of little importance to the Allies, who were determined to enforce an unconditional surrender on the Reich and had no intention of negotiating terms with a military junta. Hitler, convinced he had been saved by divine providence, was equally determined to fight to the death.

In a bold gamble aimed at ending the war in 1944, the Anglo-Americans risked a huge airborne operation to capture the Rhine bridges in the Netherlands. But the attack was smashed, and in December Hitler even managed a daring offensive of his own. Against the advice of his commanders, he sent some of his carefully hoarded panzers through the snow-covered and thickly forested Ardennes in an effort to slice between the British and the Americans, and recapture Antwerp. Although the attack caused panic initially, it had no real chance of triumph: even on the first day there were Allied commanders who welcomed the chance to draw German armour forwards in order to crush it. Hitler only succeeded in wasting German reserves that might otherwise have prolonged the war for a few months.

Germany's cities were spared the ultimate agony of nuclear attack, but they were exempted from very little else. The year 1944 saw an intensification of the Allied air offensive, which reached its destructive height on February 13 and 14, 1945, when great raids on the baroque city of Dresden reduced it to a scorched necropolis. The Luftwaffe could offer only feeble resistance. Many of its planes had been shot from the sky by the long-range fighter escorts the Americans had used throughout 1944; more still were immobilized by lack of fuel.

With the end of war in sight, the Allies set about dividing the spoils. Roosevelt, Churchill and Stalin met early in 1945 at Yalta in the Crimea; although their "Declaration on liberated Europe" was filled with high-sounding rhetoric about free elections and the rights of people to choose their governments, the future Soviet domination of Poland and other eastern European countries was tacitly recognized. There could be no arguing with the huge Soviet forces already in occupation.

The Red Army entered Germany in January of 1945 and started driving towards Berlin. The Soviet troops inflicted a savage revenge on the German population as

Mushrooming high above the Japanese city of Hiroshima, a colossal cloud marks the death of 80,000 of its people — victims of the world's first nuclear attack, on August 6, 1945. The bomb, one of only two in the U.S. arsenal, was dropped in the hope that its terrible power would force the Japanese to surrender without the need for a bloody invasion of their home islands. When no immediate answer was forthcoming, the Americans dropped their remaining "device" on Nagasaki, and the Russians launched a promised invasion of Manchuria. Within a week the Japanese government had agreed on surrender terms, and a formal capitulation was signed on September 2.

they went and soon millions of German refugees were fleeing westwards. The Anglo-Americans crossed the River Rhine two months later, in March. In early April the final Soviet assault on Berlin began, and on April 25 the Red Army and the Americans met on the River Elbe. In what was left of the Third Reich, squads of Nazi fanatics shot and hanged "defeatists" by the score, while Hitler raved in his Berlin bunker, ordering nonexistent units into impossible counterattacks. "Afterwards," he said on one of those last days, "you rue the fact you have been so kind." On April 30, as the Russians were fighting their way through Berlin's streets, the Fuhrer committed suicide.

For another week, remnants of the German army kept fighting, buying time to allow as many refugees as possible to reach zones under Anglo-American control.

The final, unconditional surrender came on May 8. From Moscow to Normandy most of the continent lay in ruins, and the dead would never be accurately counted. But the war in Europe was over.

The last message received by Berlin's telegraph office as the Soviets closed in was brief: "Good luck to you all." It came from Tokyo. Whatever happened in Europe, Japan was still fighting with the courage of despair against ever-lengthening odds.

After Midway in June 1942, the initiative had passed firmly to the Americans. In their first offensive action of the war, they landed on Guadalcanal in the Solomons, where the Japanese had been building an airfield to threaten communications between the United States and Australia. The savage struggle for the island lasted nearly six months and cost the Japanese two thirds of their 36,000-strong force. The Japanese navy did better in the sea battles around the island, inflicting more damage than it suffered, but, unlike the Americans, it could not make good its losses. At the same time, a largely Australian force halted the Japanese in New Guinea and began to claw back lost territory.

The pattern for the next three years was set, as the Americans, with their increasing air and naval superiority, island-hopped their way towards Japan. While U.S.

The razed centre of Hiroshima shows what lay beneath the nuclear mushroom's terrible beauty. Although the bombing undoubtedly shortened the war, even the American military planners were shocked by the devastation their weapon had caused. There were other, unseen, effects too. As at Nagasaki, Hiroshima's survivors were stricken by a numb, helpless lethargy that remained with them for weeks. In the months and years that followed, many apparently uninjured by the blast would die of radiation-induced ailments.

submarines waged a highly successful campaign against Japanese supply lines, a two-fold offensive moved into gear. South-West Pacific Area Command, based in Australia under General Douglas MacArthur, took the route through New Guinea and the Philippines; Central Pacific Command, led by Admiral Nimitz from his headquarters in Hawaii, took the direct westerly route through the Marshalls, Marianas and Iwo Jima and Okinawa. Whenever possible, Japanese garrisons were bypassed and left to "wither on the vine", as Nimitz put it; but the campaign still required more than 100 island invasions, 68 of them involving heavy fighting.

A U.S. sailor snatches a kiss from a passing girl in New York's Times Square on August 15, 1945 – V-J Day, the end of World War II. The war's conclusion provoked euphoria in the victor nations, at least for a brief moment, and even for the defeated there was as much relief as anger and humiliation.

Guadalcanal, Tarawa, Eniwetok, Saipan, Ulithi: tiny places with names no-one had heard of became graveyards for Japan's army in the Pacific. American casualties, though painful enough for an unmilitary democracy, were comparatively light; American fire power and technology saw to that. The capture of the little atoll of Tarawa in the Gilberts chain, for example, cost almost 1,100 U.S. dead; a few months later the Americans took the whole Marshalls group for less than 600. The Japanese, in both cases, fought almost to the last man. At Tarawa, there were only 17 prisoners taken from almost 5,000 defenders.

As the ring closed around Japan, she was forced to desperate expedients. The invasion of the Philippines in late 1944 brought the Japanese navy to all-out action. Since an American success would cut them off from their East Indies oil supply, the Japanese risked everything on the disastrous Battle of Leyte Gulf – after which they had neither oil nor fleet. Short of experienced pilots, they introduced a new kind of air warfare: the suicide attack, named after the legendary *kamikaze*, or "divine wind", which had saved Japan from a Mongol invasion in the 13th century. In the Philippines, more than 400 kamikazes set out on one-way missions that sank 16 ships and damaged 80 more, but a scarcity of planes – there were plenty of volunteer pilots – ensured that the suicide air corps could never turn back the tide of invasion.

Direct air attacks on Japan began in June 1944, from China. With the capture of the Mariana Islands and Iwo Jima, bases for the gigantic new American B-29 bombers were even closer. Systematic firebombing reduced most Japanese cities to ashes: one raid on Tokyo, in March 1945, killed more than 80,000 citizens.

The Japanese fared no better on mainland Asia. A rash 1944 attack on Imphal on the Burma-India frontier, at a time when Japan had barely enough resources to sustain a coherent defence, ended in a crushing defeat at the hands of the British and their Indian army. In 1945, British and Indian troops advanced to destroy the hard core of Japanese resistance in central Burma.

But the Japanese continued fighting – with no hope of victory but with no fear of death. The Americans were now faced with the appalling prospect of an invasion of Japan itself. The Soviet Union had agreed to declare war within three months of Germany's defeat, and a Soviet attack on Japanese-held Manchuria was considered essential to the final and total defeat of Japan. Even so, realistic estimates for U.S. casualties were as high as 250,000; and no-one tried to count how many Japanese would die in a suicidal defence of their homeland. But there was another way to force Japan to admit defeat.

The Manhattan Project had at last borne its dark fruit. On July 16, 1945, as plans were being made for the invasion of Japan, a nuclear "device" was successfully detonated in the desert of New Mexico. Harry Truman, who had become president on Roosevelt's death in April, was convinced that the monstrous weapon his scientists had created would end the war at far less cost in human lives than a conventional invasion. On August 6, a solitary B-29 dropped an atomic bomb, as powerful as 20,000 tonnes of TNT, over the hitherto undamaged city of Hiroshima. Almost 80,000 civilians died in seconds; many more were hideously injured. On August 9, the day after the Soviet Union made its declaration of war on Japan, a second bomb fell on Nagasaki.

It was enough, more than enough. A few more days passed before the Japanese government, racked in the hour of its dissolution by assassinations and suicides, could come to its decision, but on August 15 Japan announced its surrender, which was formally accepted on September 2. The world was at peace, six years and one day from the moment that Adolf Hitler had ordered his legions across the Polish border. By 1945, that first attack was ancient history. As victors and vanquished alike were coming to understand, the world they shared in smouldering, sullen peace was no longer the same world that had gone to war.

A refugee sobs amid the shattered bricks of the home she had left behind. It was a scene repeated in countless villages, towns and cities throughout the world in 1945. In Germany and Russia alone, at least 7.5 million dwellings were destroyed, and even the photographer could not later recall where he had taken this shot. But though grief would always remain, reconstruction, of nations and values as well as of houses, could now begin in earnest.

RETURN TO THE PROMISED LAND

Israel was conceived in oppression and born in war. It was Hitler's "final solution", the wholesale massacre of Jews, which convinced European Jewry that any hope of a secure and peaceful future must lie within the borders of their own, independent state. As victims of Nazism, their cause attracted widespread sympathy, but tragically, the high ideals on which Israel was founded were soon to be eroded by bitter sectarian violence.

Jewish nationalism found its political expression in late 19th-century tsarist Russia, where violent anti-Semitism inspired in many Jews a longing, after 1,800 years of Diaspora – "dispersal" – to return to their original homeland of Israel and its ancient capital, Zion, part of Jerusalem. A Zionist movement, which had been founded by a Viennese journalist named Theodor Herzl in 1897, encouraged Jews to emigrate to Palestine, which was then part of the moribund Ottoman empire. There existed already a long-established 25,000-strong Jewish community in Palestine consisting mainly of pious men and women who had come to the land of the Bible to study their religion. By 1914 they had been joined by around 60,000 immigrants who were fired by nationalist rather than religious ideals. Thus by the outbreak of World War I, there were 85,000 Jews living in Palestine, compared with about 650,000 non-Jews – mainly Arabic-speaking Muslims.

During World War I, the Zionists won from Britain a promise of extraordinary significance. Hoping to attract the support of American and Russian Jewry for the Allies, the Foreign Secretary, Arthur Balfour, declared British approval for "the establishment in Palestine of a national home for the Jewish people". As Britain also supported the local Arabs in their desire to throw off Turkish rule, there was no mention of statehood. And there was a qualification: "that nothing shall be done which may prejudice the civil and religious rights of existing non-Jewish communities in Palestine." At the time of the Foreign Secretary's statement, very few saw the two ideals as contradictory.

The Balfour Declaration of 1917 was given international sanction in 1922, when the recently founded League of Nations granted Britain a mandate, or temporary trust, over Palestine, which was to be encouraged towards independence. The Balfour pledge was incorporated into the terms of the mandate, and the Zionist movement was recognized as the appropriate "Jewish agency" for assisting the British in building the national home.

Immediately, there was a violent outcry from the Palestinian Arabs. This was their land; they too had political aspirations within an Arab world of newly independent nations emerging from the ashes of the now defunct Ottoman empire; and Jerusalem was as holy a city to Muslims as it was to Jews and Christians. That year, clashes between Jews and Arabs left some 50 dead on each side.

Despite further trouble in the ensuing years, Jewish immigration into Palestine increased with Adolf Hitler's accession to power in 1933. From 1929 to 1932, emigration from Germany had averaged about 5,000 a year; but as the menace of Nazism became apparent, the figures shot up, from 30,000 in 1933 to more than 60,000 in 1935, by which time the Jews formed 25 per cent of Palestine's population. In 1936, when the British authorities refused to halt immigration, Arab insurgents called a strike and began to attack Jews, British officials and fellow Arabs who refused to join the rebellion.

To counter such attacks, the Zionist organization set about building a national defence force, the Haganah, inspired by the semi-official Jewish "Special Night Squads", which had been established with British help to protect scattered settlements. Some Jews prepared for more savage measures by founding a terrorist group, the National Military Organization, or Irgun. Among its ranks was an ultranationalist called Abraham Stern, who would later set up his own terrorist force.

By now it was clear that Balfour's ideals were irreconcilable and that no solution would work for both sides. The outbreak of World War II further complicated the picture. The British authorities, dependent on Arab oil to sustain the war effort, adopted a policy of limiting Jewish immigration; when the quotas were filled, additional immigrants were turned away. It was a harsh policy, and when the first authenticated reports of the final solution reached the outside world in 1942, it could be seen as downright murderous. Certainly extremists viewed it in that light, and acted accordingly. On November 4, 1944, Lord Moyne, British minister of state in the Middle East, was shot dead by two members of the Stern Gang.

The next month, Britain's opposition Labour party made a rash commitment to allow unlimited Jewish immigration to Palestine. In the meantime, however, the oreign secretary, Anthony Eden, had assured the Arab world that the British government would "give their full support" to an Arab union. The hope was that a coalition of Arab states would regard a Jewish national home in their midst as a small thing; in fact, the seven-nation Arab League that was established in March 1945 was united on very little except anti-Zionism. When the Labour party leader Clement Attlee became prime minister a few months later, he found the Arab League determined to oppose Jewish immigration at all costs.

By now, however, the British were increasingly losing control of the situation. Every action intended to suppress disorder merely escalated the violence. In June 1946 the Haganah blew up all bridges across the River Jordan. Jewish leaders were arrested. On July 22 the Irgun retaliated for the arrests by blowing up a wing of the King David Hotel, the British army's Jerusalem headquarters, killing 91 Britons, Jews and Arabs.

Finally Prime Minister Attlee decided — as he did at approximately the same time

Two small ships crammed with 1,300 illegal Jewish immigrants lie tantalizingly close to the coast of Palestine, on August 12, 1946. Refused permission to land by Palestine's British authorities, who had promised the country's Arab majority that they would restrict Jewish immigration from Europe, the refugees were eventually put on board a British freighter and sent to internment on the island of Cyprus. In a vain attempt to prevent their deportation, Jewish sympathizers attached mines to the hull of the ship and blew a hole in its side.

with regard to India — to pull out. Ernest Bevin, the foreign secretary, made an announcement in February of 1947 that Britain would hand over its mandate of Palestine to the United Nations, the successor to the League of Nations. A UN Special Committee arrived in Palestine to study the issue of partition in June. Their inquiries were conducted under the threat of yet more violence: three Irgun terrorists were under penalty of death by hanging, and two British soldiers were being held hostage in an attempt to force the terrorists' release. In addition, many shiploads of illegal Jewish refugees were making for Palestine.

One boat, the *President Warfield,* soon to be renamed the *Exodus,* was carrying some 4,500 German Jews, survivors of the Belsen concentration camp, who had embarked at Marseilles. The vessel was intercepted off Haifa by British warships. As the destroyers closed in, the immigrants on board maintained a continuous radio commentary to the outside world. Finally, with her siren wailing like "a wounded cow bellowing through the night", the *Exodus* surrendered. Sent back to Marseilles again, the refugees were refused sanctuary in France and were eventually landed in Hamburg — a grim irony that was not lost on the public.

On the day that the *Exodus* returned to Marseilles, the three condemned Irgun terrorists were hanged; the two British soldiers being held hostage were killed by the Irgun on the next day, and their bodies were booby-trapped with mines. "We repaid our enemies in kind," said the Irgun leader, and future prime minister, Menachem Begin. "He forced us to answer gallows with gallows." The news of the killings aroused anti-Semitic feeling in Britain, where there were anti-Jewish riots in several cities.

On November 29, 1947, the United Nations proposed its own solution to the problem: an end to the British mandate and partition of Palestine into an Arab and a Jewish state; the city of Jerusalem would come under international administration. The Zionists accepted the UN plan with alacrity. The Arabs rejected it and began to prepare for war.

Both the United States and the Soviet Union — which regarded a Jewish state in Palestine as an anti-imperialist wedge in the Middle East — voted in favour of the UN resolution. Britain voted against, but it was no longer willing or able to control events. In December of 1947, as riots raged unchecked, the British announced that they would withdraw from Palestine by May 15, 1948.

Fierce fighting broke out even while the British mandate still ran, and by the end of March 1948 Jews and Arabs had sustained over a thousand casualties. On the morning of May 14, one day before the mandate was due to end, the Union Jack was lowered at Government House in Jerusalem, as Jews and Arabs were seizing positions in and around the city. At 4.00 p.m., 200 Jewish leaders gathered in the Tel Aviv Museum of Modern Art to hear David Ben-Gurion, who was to be the country's first prime minister, read out a short declaration proclaiming the establishment of the state of Israel.

Within hours, Israel was recognized by the United States and the Soviet Union. Early the next morning the neighbouring Arab League countries — Lebanon, Syria, Iraq, Jordan and Egypt — invaded.

In sheer numbers the opposing forces were evenly matched — around 35,000 Israeli troops against about 40,000 Arab soldiers. In terms of military equipment, however, the Israelis were at a disadvantage, and Arab fire power soon began to tell. In the first month of the war, the Syrians advanced into Upper Galilee, the Iraqis drove westwards to reach a point that was only 15 kilometres from the Mediterranean, and the Jordanian Arab Legion besieged Jerusalem, capturing the Old City with its Jewish quarter. The Egyptian army threatened the rest of Jerusalem from the south.

At this point, a UN mediator, Count Folke Bernadotte of Sweden, arranged a month-long truce. The Israelis used the time profitably, flying in arms which they had bought from France and Czechoslovakia, and then, in a vital 10-day period in mid-July, putting into action several well-planned offensives. On July 18 a second truce came into effect.

Count Bernadotte was keen to arrange for the return of the many Arab refugees who had fled from Palestine. On September 17, members of the Stern Gang, which actively tried to terrorize Arabs into fleeing the country, murdered him. Shocked at such an act, which could only result in the alienation of world opinion, Ben-Gurion ordered the dissolution of both the Stern Gang and the Irgun.

By this time, the Israeli forces were better-armed and were going over to the offensive. The Arab military effort broke down in disunity over political and military goals. Feeling that they had don-enough, the Syrians and the Iraqis both withdrew across their borders. The Jordanians had taken Old Jerusalem, which was all they had set out to do, and were now willing to arrange a ceasefire with Israel, which then retook the south from the Egyptians. On December 29, the UN Security Council ordered a ceasefire, and Israel's war of independence eventually came to an end early in 1949 in a series of armistice agreements.

When the smoke had finally settled, Israel found itself in possession of 21 per cent more land than it had been assigned under the 1947 partition plan. More than half a million Arab refugees had sought sanctuary in the enclaves of the Egyptian Gaza Strip and the Jordanian West Bank, including Old Jerusalem, and in Lebanon. A million Jews now had a home of their own, and had demonstrated their willingness and ability to defend it. The politics of the Middle East had a new and volatile element; its stored resentments and unconcealed passions were to break out in three more wars over the course of the next four decades.

On May 14, 1948, one day before the British mandate in Palestine was due to expire, Jewish leaders gather in a Tel Aviv museum to hear the state of Israel proclaimed by David Ben-Gurion, soon to be elected its first prime minister. Above him is a portrait of Theodor Herzl, the founder of modern Zionism, who in the late 19th century championed the cause of a Jewish national home in the land of the Bible. Although Israel was immediately recognized by the United States and the Soviet Union, Ben-Gurion's announcement was the signal for a concerted attack on Israel by its Arab neighbours.

INDEPENDENCE FOR INDIA

3

On April 13, 1919, in the city of Amritsar in the Indian province of the Punjab, a crowd of more than 10,000 men, women and children filed down a narrow street that led into an expanse of open ground enclosed by high walls that was known as the Jallianwala Bagh. Many of them had come to attend a political meeting, but there were also many who were visiting the city for the annual horse fair and had followed the crowd out of curiosity. Few of those who came from outside the city were aware that the meeting was illegal.

During the previous three days, Amritsar had been the scene of some violent demonstrations against British residents and property. The town hall, the telegraph office, an Anglican church, a mission school and a railway goods yard had been set alight. Five British officials had been killed by angry mobs, and a woman missionary had been attacked. Brigadier General Reginald Dyer, commander of the nearest army units, had been called in to restore order. On April 12 he had forbidden public meetings, and on the following morning he had gone through the city with a drummer announcing that all mobs would be fired on.

But Dyer's threat was not sufficient to deter the citizens of Amritsar. Their quarrel with the British was based upon the reluctance of the British government – which had ruled India directly for more than 60 years – to grant the degree of independence demanded by Indian nationalist leaders, whose patience was running short. A British promise that India would become self-governing on the conclusion of the First World War had not been fulfilled; instead, the British Parliament had in March 1919 passed laws designed to suppress nationalist agitators. Known as the Rowlatt Acts after the judge appointed to advise the British government on security, this legislation provided for the internment of those suspected of subversive activity and for the trial of certain political offenders by judges sitting without juries. The riots in Amritsar had developed after the leaders of a peaceful protest against these repressive measures had been arrested.

When Brigadier General Dyer heard that his orders were being defied, he immediately set out for the Jallianwala Bagh with two armoured cars and 50 riflemen. The vehicles were left outside the compound as they were too wide to negotiate the narrow passageway through which the crowds had filed. The soldiers took up kneeling positions on the rising ground just inside the entrance, and released the safety catches on their rifles.

Without giving any warning, Dyer gave the order to open fire. In the moments before horror dawned, many of the Indians believed that the soldiers were firing blanks; but when bodies began to fall, uproar broke out. The crowd panicked, some seeking desperately to escape by climbing the walls, others crawling for shelter behind the bodies of their fellows, others trampling the wounded as they

The Indian nationalist leaders Jawaharlal Nehru and Mahatma Gandhi share a moment of relaxation during a political meeting in Bombay in 1946. Gandhi, a devout Hindu, believed India's vast rural population could be provided with food, clothing and health care without recourse to Western technology; to symbolize his views, he habitually wore the villager's traditional clothing, a homespun *dhoti*, or loincloth. Nehru, who was to become free India's first prime minister in 1947, was an agnostic socialist committed to modernization. Both men, however, were united in their conviction that India must be liberated from British rule. Together they led a massive campaign of nonviolent resistance to achieve that goal.

fled to the farthest reaches of the compound. A few jumped into a well, and were drowned by others falling on top of them. In just 10 minutes the soldiers fired 1,650 rounds of ammunition, very few of which were wasted. According to the official reports, 379 people were killed and 1,208 wounded.

While the screams of the wounded still filled the air, Dyer ordered his troops to rise, shoulder arms and leave the compound. "I fired and continued to fire until the crowd dispersed," he told a subsequent inquiry, "and I consider this is the least amount of firing which would produce the necessary moral and widespread effect it was my duty to produce if I was to justify my action." During the two months of martial law that followed the massacre, Dyer continued to carry out what he perceived to be his duty with the same thoroughness. Water and electricity supplies to the Indian quarters of Amritsar were disconnected, and six men who contravened the curfew were publicly flogged. Any Indian passing along the street

The campaign for Indian independence culminated in the creation of not one but two nations: Hindu India *(shaded yellow)* and Muslim Pakistan *(shaded green)*. As the map shows, the latter originally consisted of two separate enclaves some 1,500 kilometres apart. Muslim leaders, who feared that their coreligionists would have few political rights in a country that was dominated by a Hindu majority, had begun to demand their own homeland during the 1930s, but agreement was not reached until shortly before the British left India. Subsequently, civil war was to lead to the secession of East Pakistan, which in 1971 became the independent nation of Bangladesh.

where the woman missionary had been attacked was forced to crawl along the ground for 140 metres, spurred on by the heavy boots of British soldiers.

After the inquiry, Dyer was forced to retire. His actions were condemned by the Secretary of State for India. In a speech to the House of Commons, the Secretary of State for War, Winston Churchill, borrowed a phrase from the historian and poet Lord Macaulay to describe the massacre as "the most frightful of all spectacles, the strength of civilization without its mercy". "We have to make it clear," he continued, "some way or other, that this is not the British way of doing business."

But Dyer's actions at Jallianwala Bagh were approved by the House of Lords, by many individual Members of Parliament and by large sections of the British press. In India, money was collected for him by members of the exclusive clubs that were the centre of the social life of European residents. This widespread failure of the British to denounce General Dyer rubbed salt into the Indian wounds, and gave symbolic significance to the massacre itself as an example of the capricious use of force by a tyrannical overlord.

Since 1858, when India had been declared a Crown possession, the key decisions affecting the lives of a population of more than 350 million had been made by no more than a thousand senior British bureaucrats. Trust and a degree of goodwill had played as much a part in the working of this system as military force. After the atrocity at Amritsar, that trust no longer existed; many of the Indian leaders who had been prepared to cooperate with the British while seeking increased political rights for their own people now became ardent nationalists, and India was set irrevocably on the road to independence.

Britain had a closer relationship with India than with any other part of her empire. Although the British Raj – so called from a Hindi term for government – was not formally established until 1858, British interests in India extended back as far the early 17th century, when the first merchants had arrived and trading settlements had been founded. By the beginning of the 20th century, many British military and administrative officers who served in India came from families whose links with the country dated back for generations. In addition, many Indians had first-hand experience of life in England, having travelled there to study at universities. To the British and to many Indians also – in particular the several hundred Indian princes who were allowed to continue governing their states under British patronage – the destinies of the two countries appeared to be tightly interwoven.

But although the feelings of pride and of affection for the people of India that were expressed by the British were often deep and sincere, their actual experience of the country was very limited. Most were handicapped by prejudicial beliefs in their own racial superiority. Few learnt to speak any of India's almost 200 native languages, or sought to understand her culture. To the majority of the British, the beliefs and customs of the people who lived outside the walls of their comfortable compounds remained a baffling mystery. One British officer likened himself to "a man wandering about with a dim lantern in the dark".

In every province, adherents of different religious faiths lived side by side, often indistinguishable to European eyes but in fact following very different traditions. The largest community were the Hindus, who comprised well over half of the population; the most conspicuous aspects of their 4,000-year-old religion were its pantheon of gods and the caste system, which divided its adherents irreversibly

Seated in a gold-embossed howdah on an elaborately adorned elephant, the Viceroy of India, Lord Curzon, and his consort proceed at a stately pace through the streets of the capital city of Delhi. Following the tradition of the Indian *durbar*, at which a prince assembled all the members of his court, the British held ceremonial processions to mark occasions such as the coronation of a new monarch or a royal visit to India. These displays – which also served to impress the watching crowds with the majesty of the British Raj – were considered politically valuable in a country whose 350 million people were ruled by just a few thousand British administrators and army officers.

into different hereditary classes. A prominent minority of the population – more than 50 million in all – were Muslims, descendants of the conquerors from central Asia who had ruled in India for 700 years before the British arrived and of the people who had converted to Islam during this period. In addition, there were large numbers of Sikhs, members of a reformed Hindu sect who were especially prevalent in the Punjab; and also Parsees, Jains, Christians and Jews.

These various communities followed different religious leaders and observances. But they had in common the experience of being subjects of the British empire and, as such, second-class citizens in their own country. While the British hunted, danced, played polo or cricket, lived in spacious bungalows and travelled in luxurious first-class compartments, Indians stood by to serve their every need. To the Hindus, who took pride in the achievements of their ancient civilization and whose caste system made them acutely sensitive to matters of social status, this situation was especially irksome.

Many of the early leaders of the Indian independence movement emerged from the ranks of the middle-class professionals – lawyers, journalists, businessmen and teachers – who had been educated in the schools and colleges that were established during the early years of the Raj to train Indians for jobs in the middle and lower ranks of the civil service. The acquisition of the English language for these practical purposes also enabled them to read books about Western political philosophy and history, brought them into contact with new concepts of nationalism, liberalism and democracy, and gave them the intellectual tools with which to analyse the injustices of colonial rule.

One particular cause of resentment was Britain's economic exploitation. Raw Indian cotton, cheaply purchased, was used in British mills to manufacture textiles that were then sold back to India at a profit. Money from the Indian economy was sent back to London to run the India Office and to pay interest on British loans. Unemployment in India rose steadily, both among the ancient class of skilled artisans and also – as the universities turned out more graduates than the civil service could accommodate – among the new class of educated Indians.

In 1885 the British condoned the creation of the National Congress, an assembly consisting of 73 Indian representatives which, while it wielded no power, at least provided a forum for debate on nationalist issues. Year by year, the Congress leaders grew more radical in their demands. To begin with, most of them accepted British dominance and sought to obtain reforms simply by submitting petitions to the British viceroy; soon after the turn of the century, however, certain members of the Congress – at that time still a predominantly middle-class movement – set out to campaign for the support of the masses, and extremist factions began to resort to terrorist activity. But as support for the Congress increased, divisions between the Hindu and Muslim communities – each wary of being dominated by the other – threatened to cripple the nationalist cause. The National Congress was dominated by the Hindus. In 1906 the Muslims founded the All-India Muslim League to promote their own political interests.

During the First World War, 1,302,000 Indian soldiers fought alongside British troops, and the vast majority of the Indian people supported the British cause. But political activity – and also isolated acts of terrorism – had still continued. In 1916 Congress leaders surprised everyone by concluding the Lucknow Pact with the Muslims, by which the latter agreed to support the demands of the National Congress for self-government in return for a promise to accept the principle of separate Muslim constituencies – with Muslim representation greater than their numerical proportion of the population could justify – in any new constitution. In answer to widespread agitation, the British announced that, as soon as the war was over, India would become a dominion within the empire; this status would give India its own government under a British governor general.

Expectations were consequently high at the war's end, but the Government of India Act, which was passed by the British Parliament in 1919, fell far short of what was hoped for. The creation of new legislative assemblies, in which a proportion of the members would be elected by a limited franchise, was considered insufficient reward for a nation that had suffered over 100,000 casualties. When the United States had entered the First World War in 1917, many Indians had taken to heart President Wilson's definition of the Allies' goals as "freedom and justice and self-government amongst all the nations of the world". The British still regarded self-government as a privilege to be bestowed upon a subject people; but Indians were demanding it as an inalienable right.

The passing of the Rowlatt Acts during March 1919 – which removed two of the precious legal rights that were among the few undeniable benefits of British rule – added insult to injury. Mass protest meetings were called in many Indian cities. The massacre at Amritsar and other sternly repressive actions taken by the British only served to swell the ranks of the nationalists and strengthen their resolve. And in the following year, a leader emerged who possessed such charisma and such an intuitive gift for dramatic gestures that he would extend support for the National Congress among the illiterate millions of India's population.

Smartly turned out in European-style clothes, Gandhi poses with his staff outside the office of his Johannesburg legal practice in 1913. Following his arrival in South Africa in 1893 as a newly trained lawyer, Gandhi built up a prosperous business that specialized in safeguarding the political rights of his countrymen. During the course of this work, he advocated civil disobedience as a means of combating repressive government laws. Despite suffering imprisonment and often the loss of their livelihoods, thousands of Indians followed Gandhi, and the success of such tactics encouraged him to employ them on a wider scale after his return to India in 1915.

Mohandas Karamchand Gandhi was born on October 2, 1869, at Porbandar in western India, where his Hindu father was hereditary chief minister of a small state. Brought up as a pacifist and a vegetarian, he was married as a boy to a child bride. At the age of 18 he was sent to London to study law, and in 1891 he returned to India as a qualified barrister. But success eluded him in his own country. Two years later he set out to practise law in South Africa instead, and during the 22 years that he remained there he developed the personal philosophy that was to lie at the heart of his actions for the rest of his life.

Drawing upon a variety of sources – including Hinduism, Christianity and the works of the Russian novelist Leo Tolstoy, with whom he exchanged letters – Gandhi came to believe that the prime objective of life was the pursuit of truth, and that the two most vital allies in this task were nonviolence and self-discipline; later in his life, the specially trained followers who shared his ambitions and methods were to be known as "truth fighters". Suffering assaults and imprisonment in the course of his work for the political rights of Indians who had settled in South Africa, Gandhi remained always courteous and restrained towards his opponents. His faith in the moral power of passive resistance never wavered, and his persistence was rewarded by the repeal of several repressive laws. When he returned to India in 1915, the poet Rabindranath Tagore gave him the name Mahatma – "Great Soul" – in recognition of his work and teaching.

A thin, genial and self-effacing man in spectacles, the 46-year-old Gandhi did not much look like a man of action, but his demeanour disguised an iron will and boundless energy. For all his idealism, Gandhi was a very astute politician, and he possessed a talent for directing the energies of the various nationalist factions – Hindus and Muslims, moderates and radicals, urban intellectuals and rural peasants – towards a common goal.

On his return to his home country Gandhi spent several years studying the political situation, taking part in industrial disputes and setting up a community on the outskirts of Ahmadabad where he gathered together and trained his truth fighters with the help of subsidies provided by Hindu merchant princes. (As one of his followers somewhat cynically remarked: "It cost a great deal of money to keep Gandhi in poverty.") He made his own judgments of people and causes, and acted accordingly. A relentless enemy of the British empire, he numbered many English men and women among his friends. A champion of Hinduism, he was yet a stern critic of the caste system which had allowed the lowest-ranking and poorest of Hindus to become known as "untouchables" because the higher ranks were forbidden even to touch them.

To symbolize his empathy with the humblest people of India, Gandhi gave up wearing European clothes in 1921 and wore instead a *dhoti*, a peasant's homespun cotton loincloth. He also endeared himself to the rural masses – and convinced them that, among all the politicians who claimed to speak for their cause, he alone could be wholly trusted – by his observance of rigid codes of conduct. In 1906 he

Believing that only through renouncing all worldly needs and desires could he proceed towards spiritual truth, Gandhi limited his personal possessions to the bare minimum. Shown above are a selection of his belongings: two small food bowls with which he had been issued in prison and which he retained as souvenirs, a wooden fork and spoon, his diary, watch and spectacles, a copy of the Hindu sacred text *Bhagavad Gita*, a spittoon, a pencil case, one pair of leather sandals and one pair of wooden shower clogs. The only object of purely sentimental value was the ivory statuette of the three monkeys who "speak no evil, see no evil, hear no evil". These items accompanied Gandhi on all his travels, along with a simple spinning wheel which every day he made time to use.

Violence and excess were equally abhorrent to Gandhi. He lived on a vegetarian diet, and never ate more than he required; his sandals were made from the hides of cows that had died naturally. Millions revered Gandhi as a saint, his ascetic life style according with those of a long tradition of Indian spiritual leaders.

GANDHI'S ASCETIC LIFE STYLE

took a vow of chastity, and – although he considered that families should have no more than three or four children – the only form of birth control he countenanced was sexual abstinence. He refused to make use of any medication other than natural herbal remedies; so strict was his adherence to this principle that in 1944, when his wife was dying of acute bronchitis, he refused to allow her to be injected with the penicillin that might have saved her life.

Gandhi was at first prepared to cooperate with the British, but after the massacre at Amritsar, he declared: "Cooperation in any shape or form with this satanic government is sinful." Now committed to open opposition to the Raj, he sought two immediate objectives. The first was to present a united front by cementing an alliance between Hindus and Muslims; the second was to persuade the Congress to adopt a policy of widespread passive resistance.

The first of these goals was achieved in early 1920 when, after Gandhi himself had joined a Muslim protest organization, Hindus and Muslims demonstrated together throughout India. To attain the second, Gandhi outlined his doctrine of "progressive nonviolent noncooperation" to a special session of the National Congress in Calcutta in September 1920. The simple but revolutionary aim was to make India ungovernable. He called on Indians to boycott everything that was British – not just British goods but also the Raj's courts, the legislative assemblies and the schools and colleges.

Among those who opposed this programme was Muhammad Ali Jinnah, a lawyer and a former leader of the Muslim League. A reserved and dignified man, who always dressed immaculately in English suits, Jinnah was suspicious of the populism of Gandhi's approach and described his supporters as "inexperienced youths and the ignorant and illiterate". But the great majority of the Congress ratified Gandhi's proposal and proceeded to define its objective as self-government "by all peaceful and legitimate means".

The response to the noncooperation programme was enthusiastic. Imported cloth was burnt in public. Teachers abandoned their profession, students their studies. Many eminent lawyers relinquished lucrative practices. From Gandhi's point of view, the only cause for misgiving was the lack of self-discipline evident in many of the demonstrations. In November 1921, riots broke out in Bombay which lasted for five days and caused the deaths of 53 people. Then a month later, while Gandhi was preparing a programme of civil disobedience which was to include the nonpayment of taxes, 22 policemen were attacked and killed after firing on a political procession. As soon as he heard the news, Gandhi called off the entire campaign. Reluctantly, his followers obeyed.

By then, many of the demonstrators were in prison. After the Bombay rioting, the government had declared all Congress and Muslim protest organizations illegal. But instead of acting as a deterrent, this decree raised the morale of the Congress supporters and gave them a sense of suffering for a cause. The jails were crowded with as many as 30,000 political prisoners; and after the campaign had been called off and the violence had calmed down, Gandhi himself became one of them, arrested and sentenced to six years' imprisonment for sedition.

By 1924, when Gandhi was released early from prison after an appendicectomy, the accord that had previously existed between Hindus and Muslims had broken down and it seemed to many that his policies had achieved almost nothing. But attitudes had changed; the resignation of old was gone. Among the industrial workers of Bombay and Ahmadabad in particular, labour unrest and trade union organizations spread rapidly. Terrorists robbed post offices and railway stations.

The British were forced to make concessions. The Rowlatt Acts were repealed. A royal commission proposed that 50 per cent of India's civil servants should be Indian, and eight army units were set aside to be commanded entirely by Indian officers. In November 1927, the government appointed a further commission to look into the workings of the administration and recommend the next steps to be taken towards self-government.

The announcement of the names of the commissioners set off a fresh blaze of nationalist protest. They were all British, with not a single Indian among them. The National Congress voted to boycott the commission at every stage; and when Sir John Simon and his seven commissioners arrived in India early in the following year, they were met everywhere by demonstrators bearing banners inscribed with the words "Simon Go Back!".

At the same time, in a more positive vein, nationalists decided to draft their own constitution for India. Representatives of the Congress, the Muslim League, the Central Sikh League and every other political group met at the end of February 1928 and appointed a committee to take on the task under the chairmanship of Motilal Nehru, a lawyer from the highest Hindu caste, the Brahmans, who had given up a successful practice as part of the boycott. In August Nehru submitted

Mounted police armed with batons and revolvers send Indian demonstrators fleeing for safety in Calcutta in January 1931. A year previously, the Indian National Congress had pledged itself to the goal of complete independence; throughout the 1930s, breakdowns in negotiations between the British government and the nationalist leaders led to renewed campaigns of civil disobedience, and clashes between protest-marchers and the authorities became increasingly violent.

In 1940, a detachment of Indian soldiers march in step with their Scottish comrades-in-arms, the kilted Cameron Highlanders, past the pyramids of Egypt. Later that year, Indian contingents led a successful Allied attack against the Italian army at Sidi Barrani, on the country's northwest coast. Despite continuing opposition to British rule in India, the majority of Indians supported Britain's stand against Nazism during the Second World War, and supplied both men and equipment to support the Allied armies.

the committee's conclusions: he proposed a democratic federation of states with a two-chamber parliament for which the vote would be given to all adult men and women. In order to make the plan more acceptable to the British, he also indicated that India would step back from the goal of total independence and accept dominion status with a governor general as representative of the Crown.

Although this proposal was accepted by the majority of the Congress, it was vehemently opposed by certain young radical members and also by Muhammad Ali Jinnah. The latter was concerned that the proposed new constitution did not safeguard the rights of Muslims, while the former insisted that India should demand nothing less than complete independence from Britain.

The most forceful of the radical leaders within Congress were two graduates of Cambridge University in England: a zealous judge's son from Bengal, Subhas Chandra Bose, and Motilal Nehru's son Jawaharlal. While he was in England, the urbane young Jawaharlal Nehru had been entertained by some of Britain's noblest families; returning to India, he had been repeatedly snubbed by white, middle-class colonials. After meeting Gandhi in 1916 and being impressed by the latter's emphasis on action rather than speeches as a means of combating injustice, he had been arrested and imprisoned for demonstrating; and in his prison cell he had studied Karl Marx and added socialism to his philosophy. His radical education had been completed one night when he travelled on the same train as General Dyer, who was returning from the inquiry into the massacre at Amritsar. From the next sleeping compartment, Jawaharlal Nehru heard Dyer tell other officers that he had wanted to reduce Amritsar to "a heap of ashes", and had only held back because he "took pity on it". Nehru was deeply shocked, as he was by the approval of Dyer's action expressed by the House of Lords and most of the British élite in India. "I realized then," Nehru later wrote, "how brutal and immoral imperialism was and how it had eaten into the souls of the British upper classes."

When the Congress met at Calcutta in December 1928, the moderates and radicals were still implacably opposed. But it was at this moment that Gandhi returned to the centre of the stage by persuading a majority of the Congress members to accept dominion status, provided the British agreed to the new constitution within a year. If they did not, he promised a fresh campaign of civil disobedience.

The Viceroy, Lord Irwin, went to London to report the ultimatum. But the Labour government, which had only a tiny majority over its opponents in Parliament, was in no position to rush through legislation. A year passed. At the stroke of midnight on December 31, 1929, the newly elected president of the Congress, Jawaharlal Nehru, led a procession to the banks of the River Ravi and raised the national flag to shouts of "Long live the revolution!" Shortly afterwards, a declaration written by Gandhi was read throughout India, in which the objective of the Congress was proclaimed as *Purna Swaraj*, "complete independence".

Gandhi began the new campaign of civil disobedience with a gesture that won him the renewed enthusiasm of the masses and the attention of the entire world. He announced that he was going to march to the sea and make a cake of salt from the deposits on the shoreline. In so doing he would be breaking the law, which gave the government a monopoly on the manufacture and sale of salt.

On March 12, 1930, Gandhi left his home near Ahmadabad and set out with a bamboo pole in his hand to walk nearly 400 kilometres to the village of Dandi on the west coast. He was accompanied by 78 of his truth fighters and his progress was followed by representatives of the world's press. Every day for 24 days the peasants from the surrounding countryside lined the roads to greet him as he passed, cooling and softening the path beneath his feet by spraying it with water and strewing it with leaves. On April 6 he reached Dandi and spent the entire night in prayer. Next day, he went down to the beach and picked up some of the salt that had dried on the sand after the tide went out. Holding it above his head, he announced that he had manufactured salt.

This was the signal for nationwide demonstrations to begin. The campaign spread rapidly from the cities to the countryside; even middle-class Hindu women abandoned their traditional seclusion and took part in political meetings. But while

The haggard features of Muhammad Ali Jinnah, seated in front of the national flag of Pakistan, betray the ravages of the cancer from which he was to die in September 1948, just one year after becoming Pakistan's first governor general. Trained as a lawyer in England, Jinnah was not strict in his observance of Islamic traditions: he ate pork, attended prayers in a mosque only rarely, and addressed meetings in English rather than Urdu, the primary Muslim language of India. But the creation of an independent Muslim nation was largely due to his fierce ambition and his refusal to compromise with either the British or other nationalist leaders.

many millions adhered to the principle of peaceful protest, the hundreds who believed in violence also increased their activities, bombing buildings, raiding armouries and assassinating senior British officials. By the time the demonstrations were over, 60,000 people — including Gandhi himself and other leaders of the Congress — had been imprisoned.

While the frustrated authorities in India struggled to suppress the relentless civil disobedience, the Simon Commission published its report in England. Invitations to attend a conference in London in November 1930 were accepted by all interested parties and organizations except the Congress. When the conference ended, the representatives had agreed in principle to a constitution which made India a federation of states and a British dominion like Australia or Canada. But this agreement was worthless without the consent of Gandhi and the Congress, and the British government knew it: Lord Irwin released Gandhi from prison and invited him to the viceregal palace in Delhi to discuss a compromise.

After long and wary negotiations, Gandhi and Irwin made a pact. In return for a promise by Irwin to release all political prisoners, Gandhi persuaded the Congress to call off the civil disobedience campaign and send a representative to a second round-table conference to be held in London. Several Congress leaders were appalled; Jawaharlal Nehru wavered in his loyalty and Subhas Chandra Bose came out in opposition. But Gandhi had been persuaded by the Viceroy's sincerity. "I submitted," he said, "not to Lord Irwin, but to the honesty in him." The Viceroy was not quite so complimentary in his description of Gandhi: "a most baffling enemy, generous, irrational and elusive, and as hard to pin down on a point of logic as a butterfly on the plains of his native Gujarat."

Inevitably, Gandhi was the Congress representative at the second round-table conference. But he was not among friends. The government was unsympathetic to his demand for complete independence; and his efforts were hindered by both Muslim leaders — who wanted assurances that in any future constitution Muslims would be treated as a separate community with separate representation — and by representatives of the low-caste Hindus, who were demanding the same rights for themselves. The situation was described aptly by one of the Muslim leaders, who told the British: "It is the old maxim of divide and rule. But there is a division of labour here. We divide and you rule." Before the conference ended, Gandhi left in disgust and returned to India.

The civil disobedience campaign began again, and Gandhi was soon back in jail. This time, however, the Indian people had lost their enthusiasm. As Jawaharlal Nehru wrote later: "The initial push of inspiration was far less than in 1930. It was as if we entered unwillingly into battle." Many moderate Congress leaders began to drift back into cooperation with the British. Eventually, in May 1933, Gandhi gave orders from his prison cell to suspend the campaign.

Meanwhile, the British government had been enacting legislation to bring about some of the agreements reached at the second conference in London. In August 1932, the Prime Minister announced that low-caste Hindus would be granted their own electorates. Gandhi, who was implacably opposed to any system that kept the "untouchables" separate from the rest of the Hindu community, declared that he would fight the proposal with a "perpetual fast unto death". Shortly before noon on September 20 he took a last meal of honey and lemon juice, and then prepared himself to refuse all food and drink except water. He was 62 years old

Vultures pick over the remains of corpses littering a Calcutta alley in August 1946. Jinnah had organized a day of peaceful demonstrations in support of Muslim demands for a separate homeland; however, agitators spread rumours of a Hindu plot to murder Muslims, and violence erupted. Since only Hindu shops were open on the day of the demonstrations, it was easy for the mobs to identify their quarry. The Hindus retaliated, and 6,000 people were killed in the ensuing blood bath, more than in all previous communal riots in India under British rule.

and his frail, skinny body had no reserves of fat. Fearing that his death was imminent, the leaders of both the high-caste Hindus and the "untouchables" gathered round the bed in his prison cell, and within six days they had agreed a compromise. Low-caste Hindus would vote with other Hindus in joint constituencies, but for a period of years to come, until their lot had improved, a large number of places would be reserved for them in the legislatures. Gandhi had

effectively prevented the emergence of a third major political force of over 50 million people that might compete with the Congress and the Muslim League.

In 1935 the Government of India Act, which provided for a new constitution, was at last approved by the British government after long delays caused by right-wing Conservative opposition. The longest statute ever passed by the British Parliament, the Act proposed a federation of provinces that would elect their own governments, with a central administration of Indian politicians to be overseen by a British governor general. The compromise pleased nobody. Nehru denounced it as a "charter of slavery". Nevertheless, to the surprise of the British, all the Indian political parties took part in the election held at the beginning of 1937 as a first step towards implementing the constitution. When the votes were counted, the Congress was in a position to form governments in seven of the 11 provinces.

Flushed with their victory, the Congress representatives failed to recognize the dangers of not being magnanimous. In forming their cabinets, they refused to appoint any Muslim ministers unless they first dissociated themselves from the Muslim League and joined the Congress. Jinnah, to whom increasing numbers of Muslims looked to save them from Hindu dominance, now widened still further the divisions that lay between the Congress and the Muslim League by arguing for the creation of a separate Muslim homeland. "The majority community have clearly shown their hand," he said. "Hindustan is for the Hindu."

In 1930 the Muslim poet Sir Muhammad Iqbal had suggested to a meeting of the League that a state of their own in northwest India "must be the final destiny of Muslims". He did not suggest that this state should be independent of India, but soon afterwards a group of young Muslim students took up his idea and proposed an entirely separate country. Their name for it was derived from the first letters of most of the provinces and communities that the new country would comprise – P for Punjab, A for the Afghans in the North-West Frontier region, K for Kashmir, S for Sind – and the last part of Baluchistan. The acronym so formed was Pakistan, a word which meant "land of the pure". In 1940, although opinions still differed as to the precise status of the intended homeland, the creation of Pakistan became the official policy of the Muslim League.

On the outbreak of the Second World War in September 1939, the British governor general, Lord Linlithgow, tactlessly announced that India was at war with Germany without having consulted anybody. The Congress party responded by directing its ministries in the provinces to resign. But the Muslim ministries in Bengal, the Punjab and Sind refused to do so, and as a result the Muslim League began to rise steadily in prestige and influence. By the end of the war it had become too powerful to be denied its demands.

Meanwhile, the Congress leaders were not fundamentally opposed to the British war effort: "In a conflict between democracy and freedom on the one side and fascism and aggression on the other, our sympathies must be inevitably on the side of democracy," declared Nehru. Nevertheless, both he and his colleagues were determined to exact concessions, and asked that they should be allowed to form a national government in return for their cooperation.

A tide of rejoicing Indians surges round the carriage of Lord and Lady Mountbatten on Independence Day in Delhi. Mountbatten, the last viceroy of India and a great-grandson of Queen Victoria – in whose reign the British Raj had commenced – had won the respect of Indian leaders for the decisive manner in which he organized the transfer of power, but he was unprepared for such popular acclamation. When his passage to the official platform was blocked, Mountbatten had to stand up in his coach and salute the new flag of India across the heads of the densely packed crowds.

Predictably, the Governor General refused to hand over such authority to a body which would not be recognized by the Muslims. The attitude of the British government changed significantly, however, when Japanese armed forces advanced into Southeast Asia during early 1942. On March 8, the Japanese reached Rangoon in Burma, from where they threatened to invade India, and three days later the British prime minister, Winston Churchill, dispatched Sir Stafford Cripps to India with a proposal for compromise.

Cripps promised that, in return for their support, the British would allow the Indians to draw up their own constitution and would introduce dominion status as soon as the war was over. But the Muslims would not accept a proposal that did not concede the creation of a separate Pakistan, and the Congress held out for immediate self-government. To Gandhi, a promise from a country that looked as though it was about to lose a war was no better than "a postdated cheque on a crashing bank". When no better offer was made, his attitude hardened still further: "I used to say that my moral support was entirely with Britain. I am very sorry to confess that today my mind refused to give that moral support. British behaviour towards India has filled me with great pain."

Building on the momentum of an anti-British uprising in the east of the country, Gandhi persuaded the National Congress to authorize a new nonviolent campaign against the British under the slogan "Quit India!" Meanwhile, the Muslims campaigned under a slogan of their own: "Divide and Quit!" But the British were at war, and were in no mood to be conciliatory. Gandhi and most of the Congress leaders were arrested. Popular demonstrations were quelled by baton

In the panic caused by the partition of India, a train overladen with Muslim refugees prepares to leave Delhi for Pakistan. In all, around 14 million people crossed the borders between the two nations, but many who began the journey never completed it. Trains destined for Pakistan were frequently attacked en route by Hindus and Sikhs, and arrived with all their passengers slaughtered; similar atrocities were carried out by Muslims on trains travelling in the opposite direction. Many thousands of Hindus in Pakistan and Muslims in India who feared to risk the journey, or who delayed for too long the decision to leave, were also butchered.

charges and bullets. By the end of 1943 the British had gained firm control over the people of India, and the voice of the Congress was silent.

Outside the borders of their country, however, the continuing opposition of Indians to British rule was more dramatic. Unlike Gandhi and Nehru, Subhas Chandra Bose – whose favourite slogan was "Give me blood and I promise you freedom!" – had no qualms about collaborating with Britain's enemies. Early in 1941 Bose escaped from house arrest in Calcutta and made his way via Afghanistan and Moscow to Germany, where he married a German woman and became infatuated with Nazism. He broadcast on behalf of the Axis powers and persuaded about 2,000 Indian prisoners, who had been captured in North Africa, to join a German Indian Legion. In 1943, an organization called the Indian Independence

League invited him to visit the Japanese occupied territories in the Far East, where Indian soldiers who had been taken prisoner at Singapore were being used to form the basis of a much larger Indian National Army. Travelling in German and Japanese submarines, Bose went first to Tokyo and then visited Singapore, where he was elected president of the league and announced the establishment of a provisional government of free India.

Early in 1944 the soldiers of the Indian National Army advanced some 250 kilometres into their own country as allies of the Japanese. They were eventually driven back with the loss of 4,000 men; and when the British and loyal Indian forces counterattacked and took Rangoon, 20,000 of them surrendered. Although Subhas Chandra Bose escaped, the plane that was carrying him to Tokyo crashed near Taiwan, and he died a few days later in a Japanese hospital.

Despite continuing nationalist opposition to the British, India's contribution to the Allied cause was substantial. By the end of the war, the Indian army comprised more than two million men, of whom 700,000 were engaged in the final defeat of the Japanese in Burma. Total Indian casualties in the fighting numbered around 180,000. In addition, new steelworks were built, textile and cement industries were expanded, and shipbuilding was revived in aid of the war effort.

The war drained Britain of both the will and the economic power to hold on to India, and a general election in 1945 brought to power a Labour government that was eager to see the country self-governing as soon as possible. But there were still many obstacles to autonomy, chief of which were the irreconcilable demands of the Congress leaders, who insisted on a united India, and the Muslim League, which demanded a separate state. A conference was convened by Lord Wavell – a quiet intellectual soldier who had been appointed to the reinstated role of viceroy in 1943 – to discuss the formation of a transitional government; this broke down when Jinnah insisted that the League should be the sole representative of all Muslims, in spite of the fact that the Congress had the support of many Muslims in the Punjab and Bengal. In early 1946 a compromise scheme appeared at first to have satisfied both parties, but then Nehru gave a press conference in which he appeared to say that once the proposed new constitution was in operation, members of the Congress would be no longer bound to accept its original terms. From that moment the tension mounted rapidly, and the British, who had already begun to demobilize their army, were in no position to keep the peace for long.

In his demand for a Muslim country composed of the states where Muslims were in a majority, Jinnah was supported by Muslims from all over India, a third of whom actually lived in states where Hindus were in a majority. At the League's annual meeting at Lahore in 1940, where it had adopted the resolution calling for the creation of an independent homeland, it had recognized the problem by demanding "adequate, effective and mandatory safeguards" for the protection of Muslim minorities. But this was a demand that nobody could guarantee to fulfil.

On July 28, 1946, Jinnah proclaimed his opposition to both the Congress and the British government and called on all Muslims to demonstrate their solidarity by observing August 16 as Direct Action Day. When the day actually arrived many thousands demonstrated peacefully, but there were others whose passions could not be so safely contained.

At dawn small groups of Muslim thugs entered the city of Calcutta armed with sticks, iron bars, knives, bottles and shovels. As the city awoke they began their attacks, looting shops, burning buildings and hacking to death every Hindu man and woman who stood in their way. Muslim onlookers joined their frenzy. By the afternoon Hindus and Sikhs had begun to retaliate. By the time soldiers arrived on the second day in sufficient numbers to quell the rioting, the streets were strewn with casualties. The gutters were clogged with blood and hacked corpses; bloated bodies floated in the river and mutilated coolies still hung between the poles of their rickshaws. In 24 hours of appalling ferocity almost 6,000 people had been killed. Jinnah's words suddenly seemed ominous: "We shall have India divided, or we shall have India destroyed."

India was heading towards civil war. The violence soon spread to other cities and then to the countryside, especially in East Bengal, Bihar and the Punjab. For most of the winter, the 77-year-old Gandhi walked barefoot through the three troubled provinces, resting in humble Hindu and Muslim villages alike, pleading

The billowing flames of a funeral pyre consume the body of Mahatma Gandhi, assassinated on the previous day by a Hindu extremist who was opposed to his conciliatory policies towards Muslims. The procession accompanying Gandhi's coffin had taken five hours to travel eight kilometres along streets strewn with rose petals to the site of the cremation, on the banks of Delhi's River Jumna, where one million mourners had gathered. Among them was Prime Minister Nehru *(right)*, who grieved both for a national hero and a personal mentor. In a radio address to the people of India the previous evening, he had declared: "The light has gone out of our lives."

with the different majorities to help the minorities to rebuild their homes, urging the minorities to forget their fears, and reminding them all that they were "leaves of the same tree". As always, the villagers responded to his sincerity and his humility. But their leaders were no longer listening.

Returned to London, Lord Wavell advised Clement Attlee, the Labour prime minister, that the only way to make the League and the Congress come to an agreement would be to prepare for an immediate British withdrawal. Attlee disagreed, and accepted Wavell's resignation. But the man appointed in his place – the forceful, extrovert Lord Mountbatten of Burma, who had been supreme Allied commander in Southeast Asia during the war – insisted that a deadline for withdrawal must be set, and Attlee announced that the British would leave India no later than June 1948. Faced with a deadline, continuing violence and the intransigence of Jinnah, Nehru and the other Congress leaders accepted that they would have to concede the creation of some form of Muslim homeland. Only Gandhi clung to the dream of a united India.

When the new viceroy reached India during March 1947, the violence and the atrocities were reaching new heights in the Punjab and the North-West Frontier provinces. By the end of the following month Mountbatten had seen enough of the horrifying evidence for himself. In the Punjab, he was shown the ruined village of Kahuta, where over 2,000 Hindus and Sikhs had been burnt to death by a Muslim mob. Many of the victims had died in the flames of their homes; those who escaped into the streets were tied together and soaked in petrol before being set alight. "Until I went to Kahuta," said Mountbatten, "I had not appreciated the magnitude of the horrors that are going on."

Lord Mountbatten was convinced that an independent Pakistan could not survive for long, but he also believed that the only way to prevent a cataclysmic blood bath, and at the same time save Britain from the blame of having allowed it to happen, would be to accept partition and grant independence to two separate nations as soon as possible. With advice from Nehru, who had quickly become his friend and confidant, he drew up a plan which seemed to have a chance of being accepted. Then he met Jinnah and warned him that partition would mean the division of Bengal and the Punjab, where there were large populations of both Hindus and Muslims. "I do not care how little you give me," replied Jinnah, "so long as you give it to me completely."

Mountbatten brought forward the deadline for independence to August 15, 1947, and on June 2 his plan was accepted by the Indian leaders. On the appointed day Britain would hand over power to two countries, India and Pakistan; each would be a member of the British Commonwealth, with the right to secede if it wanted, and would elect its own government and appoint its own governor general. It was assumed that those provinces which had elected Congress ministries would wish to be part of India. The people of the Muslim provinces would be allowed to choose which country they wished to join, and the princely states could do the same or else remain independent. New boundaries would be drawn, and the army, the civil service and all resources would be divided.

When the time came to choose, the provinces split as expected, with Muslim East Bengal and West Punjab choosing Pakistan and Hindu East Punjab and West Bengal choosing India. The princes were less predictable, but Mountbatten himself persuaded almost all of them that it was in their own interests to decide before it was too late and surrender their authority in return for compensation.

Deftly, resolutely and just in time, the British Raj had been brought to an end. On August 14 Mountbatten inaugurated the independent Muslim Dominion of Pakistan and installed Jinnah – who was dying of cancer – as governor general. Leaving him to spend his last months as ruler of the country he had devoted his life to create, Mountbatten flew back to Delhi in time to hear Nehru's address to the nation. "Long years ago we made a tryst with destiny, and now the time comes when we shall redeem our pledge, not wholly or in full measure, but very substantially. At the stroke of the midnight hour, while the world sleeps, India will awake . . ."

At midnight Lord Mountbatten transferred sovereignty to the Indian Constituent Assembly. Moments later, in a supreme compliment, the assembly invited him to become free India's first governor general, and as his first official duty he administered the oath of office to his friend, Prime Minister Nehru.

However, while messages of goodwill were exchanged between Indian and British leaders and joyous crowds thronged the public spaces of Delhi in a mood of festive celebration, ominous reports began to emerge from the divided Punjab. On the afternoon of August 15, a group of Muslim women in a town in East Punjab were raped by a Sikh mob and paraded naked in the streets before they were killed and burnt. Across the border on the same day, a Sikh temple was burnt to the ground by Muslims, all the worshippers inside dying in the flames.

As more than 14 million people crossed the new borders of East and West Pakistan, neighbours found themselves divided by nationality as well as religion, and in that division old friends became enemies. Throughout the divided provinces, majorities turned on minorities. Over half a million people were killed in the Punjab alone. Trainloads of refugees travelling in both directions were slaughtered before they could reach safety. The Hindu quarters of Lahore were left as flat and bloodstained as the Muslim quarters of Amritsar. At a textile factory in Lyallpur, Muslim workers massacred all the Sikhs who had been working beside them for years. Desperate men on both sides shot and stabbed their wives and daughters to save them from defilement.

The Boundary Force that had been formed to oversee the peaceable transfer of population proved hopelessly inadequate. British officers entered the ruins of countless villages to be met by sights more terrible than anything they had seen in World War II. One afternoon in late August, an officer was travelling to the town of Hasilpur in Pakistan, just south of the Punjab. In a relaxed and confident mood, pleased to be well away from the worst scenes of violence, he noted what seemed to be heaps of manure scattered near the road. Coming nearer, he realized they were piles of bodies: "Men, women and children, there they were all jumbled up together, their arms and legs akimbo in all sorts of attitudes and postures, some of them so lifelike that one could hardly believe they were really dead."

Gandhi, meanwhile, was in Calcutta, having stayed away from the official ceremonies inaugurating the divided nations. He believed that the violence had

Before the massive basalt arch on Bombay's quayside known as the Gateway to India, a guard of Indian soldiers and sailors prepares to salute the departure of the last British troops from India in February 1948. The gateway had been built to commemorate the visit of King George V and Queen Mary in 1911; once the troops had passed through it to embark for England, it became a monument to a dead empire.

brought dishonour upon India, and that penance, fasting and prayer were the only appropriate methods of celebrating independence. But his personal influence was still powerful: when Hindus began to attack Muslims in Calcutta, he went on a fast, and within five days the city was at peace again. Muslims feared that if he died, they would suffer a new and even more terrible onslaught from the Hindus; Hindus did not want to be held guilty of causing his death.

He then moved to Delhi, where riots, arson and looting had broken out in September, and for the next four months he worked ceaselessly to quell the constant violence. Slowly, as the flow of refugees dried up, the atrocities and retaliations became fewer. At last the antagonisms subsided and the two suspicious new nations stepped back from the brink of suicidal war.

In January 1948, Mahatma Gandhi went on another successful fast to persuade the government to pay a disputed sum to Pakistan and to urge the Hindu citizens of Delhi to allow Muslims to return to their homes. Always the champion of the deprived and the oppressed, Gandhi was proving to be as much an irritation to intolerant Hindus as he had been to the British; and secretly, among a disparate group of men that included a doctor, a municipal councillor and an illiterate youth, a conspiracy began to take shape that aimed to silence Gandhi's voice by means more effective than the British had ever attempted.

On the afternoon of January 30 Gandhi was making his way through a crowd of people towards his daily prayer meeting when a young man stepped up to him and bowed low as if in obeisance. As Gandhi raised his hands in greeting, the young man drew a pistol and shot him three times in the chest at point-blank range. The last word the Mahatma uttered was the name of God.

The assassin was immediately seized by horrified onlookers, and Gandhi's body was carried into a nearby building. Shocked and scarcely believing the news, Nehru and Mountbatten soon arrived to see for themselves. As the latter forced his way through the crowd, he heard someone shout that the assassin was a Muslim. Mountbatten at once responded, "You fool, don't you know it was a Hindu?" Quietly, the press secretary accompanying him asked how he could possibly know this was true. "I don't," said Mountbatten. "But if it really was a Muslim, India is going to have one of the most ghastly massacres the world has ever seen."

It was a Hindu. He was the editor of an extremist Hindu newspaper, an educated man who respected Gandhi's sincerity but who believed that by preaching non-violence and the toleration of Muslims Gandhi was undermining both Hinduism and India. Four months later he was brought to trial together with seven other conspirators; he and his chief accomplice were sentenced to death, five received life imprisonment, and one was acquitted for lack of evidence.

Gandhi had died as he had wished, with the name of God on his lips, but the nation upon which his eyes had now closed was far from the country he had desired it to be. India was free, but at a price – the separation of Pakistan – that he had considered to be too high. Having sought throughout his life to inculcate in his countrymen the ideals of peaceful cooperation, he had witnessed during his last years India's worst ever internecine massacres. And having preached humility and self-sacrifice through his own personal example, he had seen many of the Congress leaders – as soon as independence became a reality – begin jockeying with each other for power and prestige.

But none of the discrepancies between Gandhi's ideals and his actual achievements diminished the force of his legacy to India, and to the wider world. To the often bitter and brutal struggle between Indian subjects and British overlords he had imparted a moral perspective in which the injustices of colonialism were fully exposed. In addition, his beliefs did much to shape the goals towards which his friend and disciple, Jawaharlal Nehru, led India in the decade and a half that followed independence. By a revised constitution inaugurated in 1950, India became a fully fledged republic that was dedicated to socialist principles; and despite overwhelming problems – beginning with vast numbers of refugees and boundary disputes with Pakistan during the early years, and continuing with the frequent domestic conflicts inherent in this vast nation of many religions and many languages – Nehru maintained a system of parliamentary democracy that made the government directly responsible to the people.

Outside India, Gandhi's ideals and methods became an inspiration to numerous other nationalist movements. The independence of India marked the beginning of the end for all the colonial empires. The victory of the Indian people taught other subject peoples that history was on their side.

A DOMESTIC REVOLUTION

"Electricity," claimed its producers in a 1925 pamphlet, "provides the modern housewife with the perfect servant: clean, silent, economical." And the modern housewife seemed to agree. For in the years between the world wars, middle-class homes across America and, later, Europe were transformed by a wave of domestic appliances – refrigerators, irons, cookers, washing machines and many more – driven by the new power source.

This revolution in domestic technology did not happen overnight, however. Most of the "new" products had been invented decades before. But early models were unwieldy, temperamental and expensive, and at a time when electricity was a rather frightening novelty and domestic service was cheap, they had made little commercial impact. After World War I, however, fears of the new technology were allayed by the introduction of electric lighting in streets and homes, and by the advent of home radios, which proved an instant success. With domestic help harder to come by as workers left service for better paid jobs in industry, the market for labour-saving utilities grew.

Led by the electricity suppliers themselves, industry stepped in to satisfy the increased demand. Huge sums of money were invested in research and development, and improved techniques borrowed from the booming automobile industry allowed effective mass production and more elegant design.

In the United States, the household appliance manufacturers quickly began to use the novel medium of commercial radio to sell their products; elsewhere, newspaper and magazine advertisements and door-to-door salesmen soon left the customer in very little doubt that the devices really were indispensable – and, since they were still beyond the reach of most working-class households, they also became coveted status symbols.

But ironically, the amount of time that women devoted to housework actually increased between the years 1930 and 1950. For although the new technology undoubtedly took the drudgery out of many chores, it also set much higher standards of domestic hygiene. In this respect, the "perfect servant" proved to be a demanding taskmaster.

An American family listens to the radio together in Hood County, Oregon, in 1925. Radio built up huge audiences throughout America, and its commercials helped to promote other household appliances far beyond the metropolitan areas.

The cover of a 1929 issue of Italy's *Radiorario* magazine illustrates how radio provides entertainment for all tastes and puts its listeners in touch with events not only in their own land, but also across the globe. In many countries, governments were quick to latch on to the persuasive power of the new medium.

The young Orson Welles broadcasts to America in 1938. That same year, Welles unwittingly demonstrated the power of radio with his adaptation of H.G. Wells's novel, *The War of the Worlds*. Its story of a Martian invasion updated to present-day America was told in a series of "newsflashes", which spread panic across the nation.

Dutch manufacturer Philips achieved sales of over 200,000 during the early Thirties with their Model 930A "Local Station Receiver".

Advertisements present contrasting images to promote the benefits of vacuum cleaners. A 1924 German publicity photo for the AEG "Vampyr" *(top)* implied housework could be the height of sophistication. Western Electric chose a more domestic image for their "Sweeper Vac" in 1930 *(centre)*, while a 1928 Austrian poster *(bottom)* used humour to compare life before and after the suction sweeper.

"I tell you we don't *want* an electric cleaner!" cries the harassed housewife in this Fougasse cartoon from a 1936 issue of London's *Punch* magazine. The persistence of vacuum cleaner salesmen was legendary and a constant source of humour. But their effectiveness as a sales force could not be doubted.

British-made under licence, this mid-Thirties Hoover Model 541 carried the giant U.S. company's distinctive slogan.

This American Kelvinator K.60 refrigerator of the early Thirties was soon superseded by more "streamlined" designs.

Although early refrigerators came in a variety of colours, a glossy white enamelled finish was soon adopted by almost all manufacturers to give an impression of scrupulous hygiene – a quality stressed in this 1934 poster for the "Santo Junior" fridge, made by German manufacturer AEG.

By the standards of the late 1930s, Premier's "Accident-Proof" electric kettle was sophisticated, boasting a cut-out mechanism activated when the appliance boiled dry. Universal's "Automatic Oven" toaster was similarly advanced in having a built-in timer.

Using an electric washing machine outside her Tennessee farmhouse in 1940, this woman would certainly have been envied by her predecessors. Her task was, nevertheless, time-consuming, for although electricity powered the agitator and wringer, it did not heat up the water, and rinsing had to be carried out in a separate tub. Early machines tended to be temperamental, too, and had to be painstakingly oiled before each use.

Small, straightforward and therefore cheap, electric irons were immediately popular. As an Austrian poster of 1928 (*above*) suggests, they were far less unwieldy than the old flatirons, which had to be heated on fires or stoves and which cooled quickly. Dating from the same period, this travelling iron exemplifies the virtues of the new appliances – compact, portable and elegant.

Despite shortcomings, washing machines such as the Beatty "Model F" were hugely popular in the Thirties.

THE STRUGGLE FOR CHINA

4

When the Chinese Nationalist leader Dr. Sun Yat-sen died in March 1925, he was given a funeral fit for an emperor – with two important differences. First, as a member of the Methodist church, he was accorded a Christian funeral as well as a state ceremony; and second, as the inspiration behind the movement to rid China of its foreign Manchu rulers, the Qing dynasty, his death aroused more heartfelt grief than had been shown for any recent emperor of China.

Yet he left behind a nation on the brink of dissolution. At the time of his death, China was divided between a military government in Beijing trying vainly to impose its will on powerful local warlords, and his own Canton-based regime, which enshrined the values of the Guomindang, the revolutionary party he had founded in 1912. Out of the ensuing chaos two other charismatic figures would emerge: Chiang Kai-shek, Sun's successor as head of the Guomindang and the future president of the Republic of China; and the Communist leader Mao Zedong, later chairman of the People's Republic of China. The struggle between these two men would last for nearly a quarter of a century, to end in Communist victory in 1949.

For 30 years, Sun had dedicated his life to what he described as the "overthrow of the Manchus, the restoration of China to the Chinese, and the establishment of a republican government". In the last hundred years of Qing rule – established in the mid-17th century – China had been brought to national ruin. Corruption was rife throughout an administration that proved inadequate at managing the nation.

The population had grown so fast that the economy could not cope. The peasantry – the majority of the population – were crippled by land rents, paid to the landlord gentry. Land was generally measured by the weight of food that it was deemed capable of producing, and rent was levied at an average of 50 per cent of the crop, often more. Since the rent was the same whatever the harvest, the peasantry were never more than one harvest away from destitution or famine. Not surprisingly, autumn riots were commonplace and major rebellions frequent.

These internal crises coincided with the arrival of foreign imperialists. Under pressure from overseas powers, the world's most enduring civilization had been reduced to semi-colonial status – in Sun's words, "not the colony of one nation, but of all". By the so-called unequal treaties, signed by China under the threat of force, foreign powers possessed nearly 100 treaty "ports" – many of them hundreds of kilometres inland – where their nationals could reside, own property and do business outside Chinese jurisdiction. In 16 of these treaty ports, specific areas – called concessions – were set aside exclusively for foreign residents. Shanghai, with more than 36 square kilometres of concessions by 1915, was virtually a European city, complete with fine boulevards, a golf course and a race course.

Mounted on horseback, Mao Zedong, chairman of the Chinese Communist Party, leaves his northern China base in 1947 to lead an offensive during the civil war between the Communists and the Nationalist forces of Chiang Kai-shek. At the beginning of the civil war, a year earlier, the Communists were outnumbered three to one by their better-equipped enemy, but by 1948 the relative strengths of the two sides had been reversed. The next year, following the military defeat of the Nationalists, Mao announced the establishment of the People's Republic of China, which was the first government effectively to unite the country since the overthrow of China's imperial rulers in 1912.

From 1931 to the end of World War II, the struggle between Nationalists and Communists for control of China was complicated by the presence of Japanese forces. At its height early in 1945, the Japanese zone *(yellow)* covered much of the country, from Manchuria to Canton. But the invaders never managed to destroy the Guomindang government, which established its wartime capital at Chongqing, in Sichuan province. And even in the areas nominally under Japanese control, the invaders were harassed by Communist guerrillas operating out of rural bases *(red)*.

The treaty ports were an affront to national pride, but they were also a powerful influence on modernists such as Sun Yat-sen, who could not help but contrast the stability and wealth of the foreign enclaves with the chaotic conditions that were prevalent in most of China. They also contained almost the only modern industries and financial institutions in the country — not just foreign concerns, but Chinese-owned enterprises operating under the protection of alien law. Without the treaty ports, in fact, the modernization of China would have been set back many years.

Sun himself came from a region between the southern ports of Canton and Macao where the foreign presence was particularly strong. Born in 1866, he

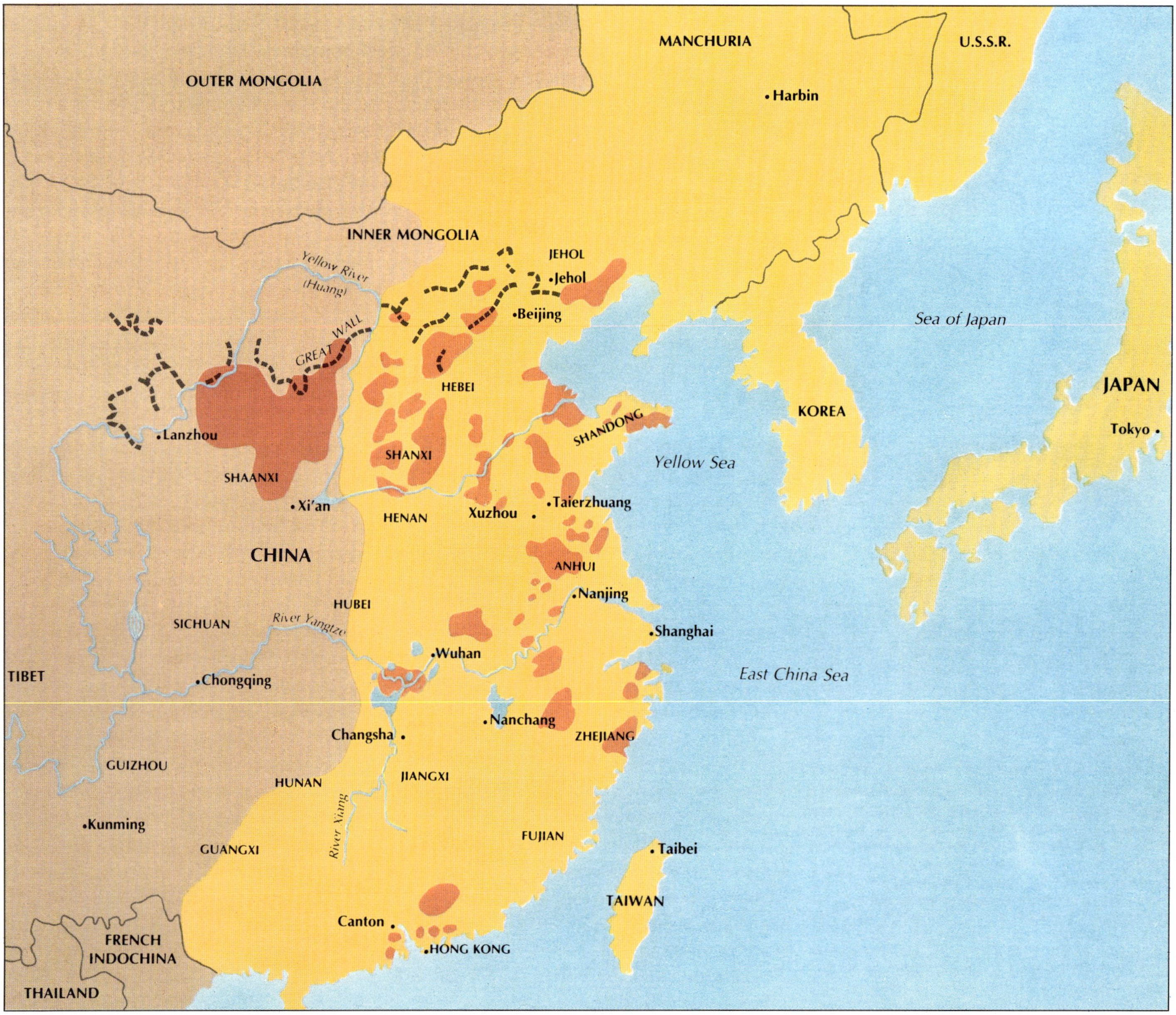

acquired a Western-style education in Hawaii (where his prosperous elder brother had settled), and studied medicine in Hong Kong. Politically active from an early age, he fled abroad in 1895 after organizing the first of 10 unsuccessful revolts against the Manchus. For the next 16 years he travelled the world as a political exile, seeking support for the cause of Chinese nationalism.

He found his strongest backing in Japan, a country that many progressive Chinese regarded as a model for the kind of nation that they wanted to create. Only a generation before, Japan had been apparently as backward and inward-looking as China, but by wholesale borrowing of techniques of government and warfare from the West, it had transformed itself into the strongest and most advanced country in the Far East. Impressed by the country's dynamism, many Chinese reformers turned a blind eye to the fact that Japan had recently inflicted a humiliating military defeat on their country in the Sino-Japanese War of 1894 to 1895, and that some influential Japanese, conscious of their country's limited resources and manpower, had designs on the vast lands and population of their Asian neighbour.

A uniformed Chiang Kai-shek stands respectfully beside his mentor, Dr. Sun Yat-sen, a leading force in the republican revolution that ended imperial rule in China. After serving briefly as the new republic's acting president, Sun was forced into exile in Japan, where he befriended Chiang Kai-shek, a professionally trained soldier and a supporter of Sun's Guomindang, or Nationalist party. In 1923, when Sun succeeded in establishing a government in the southern port of Canton, Chiang was put in charge of the reorganization of the Guomindang army. After Sun died in 1925 leaving no definite successor, Chiang exploited his friendship with the late president to enhance his position as a potential leader of the party, a position that he finally attained in 1928.

Despite this fact, it was in Tokyo in 1905 that the various competing Chinese dissident groups came together in the Revolutionary Alliance, the forerunner of the Guomindang. Sun Yat-sen was recognized as leader of the alliance, but internal divisions prevented him from exploiting the growing weakness of the Qing regime. When the Japanese, concerned at the growing radicalization of his supporters, expelled him in 1907, he resumed his globe-trotting activities, keeping in touch with events in China through a network of spies. In 1911, while he was on a fund-raising mission in the United States, he heard that the Qing dynasty had finally been toppled by a revolutionary uprising backed by the imperial army. When he returned to China at the end of the year, his unflagging opposition to the Manchus earned him election as provisional president of the new Chinese republic.

His tenure was short-lived. Sun's party simply lacked the strength to overcome the problems confronting the nation. Taken unawares by the collapse of the Qing regime, Sun and his colleagues had had no time to work out how they would handle the reins of power; all they had was a vague formula for China's regeneration based on Sun's "Three People's Principles" – nationalism, democracy and "people's livelihood". Their revolutionary movement had few members in China itself; their main backers were Chinese merchants on the Pacific rim. The foreign powers refused to support them, dismissing them as futile visionaries. Worse, they did not command any military force. After only 47 days, Dr. Sun resigned his post in favour of Yuan Shikai, the former war minister of the Qing regime who, by virtue of the control he exercised over the old imperial army, was regarded as the only leader who could make the new republic work.

It was soon evident that Yuan's commitment to Sun's Three Principles was non-existent. When the Guomindang achieved a majority in the elections of 1913, he had its leader assassinated and forced Sun into exile in Japan. Abandoning plans for a constitutional government, he set himself up as a military dictator and embarked on a campaign to have himself crowned emperor. But the bonds that tenuously linked the nation had been broken, and he found that his authority extended only to those places where troops loyal to him could impose his will. Elsewhere, power passed into the hands of local military commanders. The warlord era had begun.

Until his death in 1916, Yuan was fully occupied trying to control these freebooters; but the warlords invariably combined against any of their number who looked set to gain supremacy, including Yuan himself. While he was alive, foreign powers preserved the fiction that he represented an effective central government, if only because they needed someone to negotiate treaty rights and debt repayments with. But when they became embroiled in what one Chinese called "the European civil war" – World War I – one of the powers extended its influence in China: in 1915, Japan seized the German concessions in Shandong province and presented a set of demands that would have made China a Japanese protectorate. Yuan temporized, eventually making concessions that gave Japan a sphere of influence in Manchuria. At the Versailles peace conference after the war, the victorious allies confirmed Japan's holdings in China.

The commander of a warlord's execution squad signals that his men have performed their duty. Taking advantage of the anarchic conditions following the collapse of imperial rule in 1912, local military leaders set up personal power bases over huge tracts of China. Taxes levied to support petty conflicts caused hardship and deprived the national government of vital revenues. In the turmoil of the warlord era, millions of peasants fled their homes, leaving flood control and irrigation works in decay. Though Chiang's first mission as military leader of the Guomindang was to destroy the warlords, the last of them were not deposed until the civil war ended in 1949.

This example of European jobbery inflamed anti-imperialist sentiment, producing a wave of patriotic fervour in all sections of Chinese society, particularly among the young. On May 4, 1919, 3,000 students staged a demonstration in Beijing. "China's territory may be conquered," they declared, "but it cannot be given away. The Chinese people may be massacred but they will not surrender. Our country is about to be annihilated. Rise up, brethren!" A third of them were jailed after wrecking the house of the Chinese minister they blamed for the humiliation, but, under pressure of public opinion, the warlords who controlled the capital released them.

Short-lived as the incident was, its impact was huge. Besides forcing the government to reject the Treaty of Versailles, it triggered a reformist movement whose aims, besides resisting imperialism, included the replacement of Confucian ethics by more modern concepts and the use of phonetic spelling for written Chinese. Among the exponents of reform were China's handful of Communists.

Sun Yat-sen was too busy struggling to retain a place in the political arena to participate in the May Fourth movement. After Yuan's death, he made several comebacks, establishing with the help of local warlords two short-lived revolutionary governments in Canton. Each time he squabbled with his backers and was ousted; but he refused to give up the cause of national unification and in January 1923, after militarists loyal to him expelled rival warlords from Canton, he returned to install himself as leader of a new regime dedicated to the reconstruction of China.

This time, however, he determined to approach his goal by a different path. Trying to make an accommodation with local warlords had proved disastrous. The foreign democracies he so much admired had consistently turned down his pleas for assistance. Nevertheless, in February 1923 he made another desperate attempt to enlist Western aid, going so far as to invite the United States to lead an international occupation force with authority over the Chinese army and police, and the right to appoint key administrators. Rebuffed yet again, he announced that he had lost "hope of help from America, Britain and France . . . the only country which showed signs of helping us is Soviet Russia".

In fact, he had been in contact with the Soviet government almost from the beginning of its existence in November 1917. He also had meetings with members of the Chinese Communist Party (CCP), which had been officially founded in July 1921 by 12 Chinese officials and a Dutch and Soviet representative of Communist International (Comintern). A pledge by the Soviets to renounce their concessions in China (a promise that was not to be fulfilled) helped transform Sun's view of the Soviet Union from that of a menacing foreign aggressor to that of a fellow Asiatic power also struggling to throw off the chains of imperialist domination. Late in the year 1922, Sun engaged in talks with a Soviet emissary which culminated in a joint manifesto that was designed to pave the way for collaboration between the Guomindang and the Chinese Communist Party.

Many members on both sides disliked the idea of an alliance, but Sun dragooned his party into accepting it, while the CCP, under pressure from Moscow, reluctantly conceded that "the Guomindang must be the central force of the revolution, and assume the leadership of it". The fact was, the Communists' Soviet backers did not believe that the CCP – which had only 432 members by June 1923 – could bring about a true socialist revolution in an agrarian society. The peasants, according to orthodox Communists, were too scattered, too innately conservative, and too wedded to the ambition of becoming landlords themselves. In Marxist-Leninist theory, the revolution could be achieved only by an uprising of the disaffected urban working classes – or, in Lenin's own words, "as the number of Shanghais increases". But as a first step along this revolutionary path, so the Soviet theorists insisted, left-wing and "bourgeois democratic" elements must form a united front to liberate China from imperialists and their warlord lackeys.

Sun reaped the first benefits of the alliance in August, when a Guomindang delegation visited Moscow on a mission to obtain Soviet military aid. Two months later, Moscow sent an experienced Comintern revolutionary, Mikhail Borodin, to reorganize the Guomindang along the lines of a centralized party dictatorship. The veteran of a dozen Comintern missions, this Latvian-born, Russian-trained, former Chicago language school owner soon became Sun's closest adviser. Over the next few months he turned his organizing talents to restructuring the party, developing trade unions, taking propaganda to the peasants, and constructing a reliable army.

On Borodin's recommendation, Russian funds were used to establish a military academy on the island of Huang Pu, off Canton. Its first director was the 37-year-old leader of the delegation recently returned from Moscow, Chiang Kai-shek. An austere man with grey eyes, unusual in a Chinese, Chiang held himself with the formal rigidity that he had learnt at a Japanese military academy. During the 1911 revolutionary period, he had led a regiment partly financed by a Japanese secret society which gave backing to Sun Yat-sen. The two became friends when Chiang, an opponent of Yuan Shikai, was forced to flee to Japan. After the President's death, he returned to Shanghai, where he enriched himself by speculating on the Shanghai stock exchange. He also formed strong links with the city's criminal underworld, possibly joining the inner circle of the notorious Green Gang, which controlled much of Shanghai's opium trade, gambling, prostitution and protection rackets. In the jockeying for power following Yuan's death, Chiang risked his life by allying himself with Sun; his support enhanced his standing in the Guomindang when Sun finally came to power. His wealth and influence would be increased in 1927, when he married a sister of China's richest banker, T.V. Soong (another sister was the widow of Sun Yat-sen), converting to Methodism on his wife's account.

These were not the credentials of a committed socialist, and in truth, Chiang nurtured a pathological hatred of his Communist colleagues. But at this stage of his career, he cultivated the image of a revolutionary nationalist, and he was highly respected by Borodin and the Soviet military adviser, General Blücher, who was a hero of the Russian Revolution. Among Chiang's closest associates at Huang Pu was his elegant and cultivated senior political commissar, Zhou Enlai, who had recently returned from Paris, where he had helped set up the European headquarters of the CCP. Only 26 in 1924, Zhou was destined to play a leading role in the foundation of the People's Republic of China, as was his deputy, Chen Yi.

In this phase of cooperation between right and left, Chiang's apparent support for the revolutionary union was reciprocated by Mao, a diligent member of the Guomindang's Central Committee. Aged 30 in 1924, Mao was the son of a grasping peasant in Hunan province, which he had represented at the formal establishment of the CCP. His revolutionary consciousness had been developed during a spell as a librarian at Beijing University, where he met the first of his three wives, the daughter of a radical professor. Tall and thin, with dark good looks in early adulthood, he was an accomplished poet and pamphleteer whose political ideology was inspired as much by the Chinese classics as by the text books of Karl Marx. Although he was not an orthodox communist, his rural upbringing had given him an understanding of the Chinese peasantry unrivalled by his colleagues. His combination of romantic idealism and practical knowledge would prove vital to the Communists' survival in the years after Dr. Sun's death.

A poster bearing idealized likenesses of Sun Yat-sen *(top)* and Chiang Kai-shek *(bottom, on a white horse)* commemorates Guomindang victories over warlords during the Northern Expedition of 1926 to 1928. During the first year of this campaign, a united front of Nationalist and Communist forces managed to defeat some 30 separate warlord armies. Chiang Kai-shek, who commanded the joint forces, subsequently emerged as the most powerful figure in China. The military was backed by a well-organized propaganda machine that was staffed by more than 3,000 student volunteers. Covering large parts of the country in trains equipped with printing presses, they were highly successful in broadcasting the Guomindang goal of a republican China unified under the Nationalist flag.

Chiang was under no illusions about the aims of the CCP – to use the Guomindang as a tool to bring about a Marxist revolution. But he was obliged to maintain a façade of cooperation because he needed Soviet aid to build up a strong army around Huang Pu's graduate officers. Once this had been formed, his intention was to break the northern warlords and take Beijing. International recognition would be his reward, together with control of all customs revenue and access to the foreign monies that were required for China's modernization. Only then would he be in a position to crush his Communist colleagues.

With these aims in mind, Chiang set about cultivating allies, embarking on a masterly campaign to make himself indispensable to all factions. For the benefit of Sun Yat-sen's admirers, he presented an attitude of filial veneration, the better to demonstrate his right to inherit the mantle of leadership. From the Russians he received aid to counter the Japanese, who were developing Manchuria as a major source of food and raw materials. For their part, the Japanese offered assistance in return for a pledge to limit Soviet influence in the region. In addition, Shanghai's business community promised financial support on condition that he eradicate the left-wing organizers of the new unions in the rapidly industrializing city. At the same time, Chiang continued to encourage the Communists in their task of building up the Guomindang. To the warlords, Chiang promised rank or money provided that they joined his side.

By the spring of 1925, Chiang was quite confident that he had assembled enough support to launch the much-heralded Northern Expedition against the warlords. The ultimate aim was to take Beijing and unify the whole country, first consolidating Nationalist control in the south. On June 5, 1925, the Guomindang government named Chiang as commander-in-chief of the National Revolutionary Army (NRA); its first, and only, revolutionary campaign began the following month.

Although outnumbered by the opposing forces, the NRA — advancing north from Canton — was in a position to exploit the chronic disunity of the warlords. And it was well led by graduates of Huang Pu and their Soviet military advisers. Moreover, it reaped the benefits

A Nationalist picket searches a man suspected of carrying left-wing pamphlets during the Shanghai Purge of April 1927, which ended the fragile union of conservative and Communist elements in the Guomindang. Chiang's army had entered Shanghai a few days earlier, after pro-Communist trade unions had seized control of the city. With the help of underworld thugs and right-wing trade unionists, Chiang crushed the opposition. About 5,000 Communists and their sympathizers — including this suspect — were killed, while their leaders were forced to go underground.

of a massive campaign of propaganda and subversion. A new labour organization called strikes at strategic times and places to stop the movement of warlord troops and their supplies. Members of the recently formed farmers' unions impeded the passage of enemy forces while helping the NRA with supplies and information. Bribes brought many warlords and their generals over to the Nationalist side. By the end of the year, the Guomindang controlled the seven southern provinces and close to half of China's population. During the advance, membership of the Guomindang and its unions had soared. The majority of the unions were under the leadership of the Chinese Communist Party, which saw its membership rise to a total of 70,000 by the beginning of 1927.

But even as the army was rolling north, another battle was raging within the Guomindang itself. A majority of its members, which included the left wing, wanted to set up a new capital at Wuhan, a Communist stronghold in the central province of Hubei; Chiang and his right-wing supporters favoured Nanchang, provincial capital of neighbouring Jiangxi, as the new seat. The leftists were the first to act, proclaiming Wuhan the capital on January 1. Conscious of the very real threat to his own position, Chiang abandoned his revolutionary goals together with

In 1933, two years after Japan occupied and set up a puppet state in Manchuria, Japanese soldiers advance to take the northern Chinese province of Jehol. Japanese expansionist fervour had swelled at the end of the 1920s, when the world depression impoverished the country by crippling its export markets. An authoritarian philosophy took hold among Japan's military, who disregarded civil government in their determination both to check Soviet influence in East Asia, and to acquire territory that would provide resources and living space for the large Japanese population. China, embroiled in conflicts between Nationalists, Communists and warlords, could put up only limited resistance to Japan's imperialist designs.

his drive to the north. Instead, while stressing the need for the continuance of the Guomindang-CCP alliance, he turned his attention to Shanghai.

Several factors influenced his decision. Having succeeded in establishing excellent relations with Shanghai's business community and gangs, he could count on them to give him the financial support that would make him independent of the Wuhan government and Soviet aid. Equally important, Shanghai was China's window on the world, and therefore it was the best place to demonstrate to foreign powers that the kind of Nationalist government he envisaged posed no threat whatsoever to their interests. Shanghai, however, was also China's biggest industrial city and the stronghold of the Chinese labour movement; it was the workers, organized by Zhou Enlai among others, who took control on March 21, 1927. Five days later, Chiang Kai-shek entered the city.

Now he fulfilled the bargain he had made with the city's merchants and bankers; even while Stalin and other Communist leaders were hailing Chiang's military successes, the General was plotting a purge of the left. To that end, the first person he received was the boss of the Green Gang. On April 12, Green Gang bands attacked the headquarters of the Shanghai Trade Union Federation and other union offices, massacring many of their members. A protest demonstration held the next day was machine-gunned down by Chiang's army, and during the week that followed an estimated 5,000 leftists were hunted down and then killed, their dripping heads displayed on bamboo poles or platters for all to see.

In other cities held by the Guomindang, fierce fighting broke out between Chiang's supporters and the Communists. It was the right wing who had the initiative, and it was they who generally proved succesful. On April 18, at a banquet attended by his Soviet advisers, Chiang ended a long speech by raising his glass and shouting: "Down with the Communist party."

At this point, Stalin reversed his policy and ordered the CCP to take power by force. But party membership had fallen drastically as a result of persecution, and many of its leaders were dead or in hiding. A Communist rising in Canton was easily and brutally suppressed with the destruction of much of the city. In Wuhan, the left wing of the Guomindang decided to break with their CCP colleagues, leaving them defenceless against Chiang's forces, which slaughtered some 100,000 party members and their sympathizers in a massacre that raged until the summer of 1928. Borodin and Blücher managed to escape to Moscow, where both eventually fell victim to Stalin's purges. The few survivors of the Central Committee of the CCP went underground in Shanghai. By 1928, when the party held its Sixth Congress, in a Moscow suburb, it had fewer than 10,000 members.

Meanwhile, the Nationalists had continued the Northern Expedition, successfully capturing Beijing from the warlords and establishing a national government in Nanjing headed by Chiang Kai-shek, who also retained his previous position as commander-in-chief of the National Revolutionary Army. As he had anticipated, foreign countries accorded China a new degree of respect. Although Japan remained determined to retain its influence in Manchuria, Britain, which had the largest interests in China, relinquished two of its treaty ports, and the United States, which had a strong missionary presence in China, was sympathetic to the new government and its Christian leader. It was a period of great optimism and idealism for the Chinese. "Something new has come to China," declared a Nationalist commander, "the birth of patriotism and public spirit."

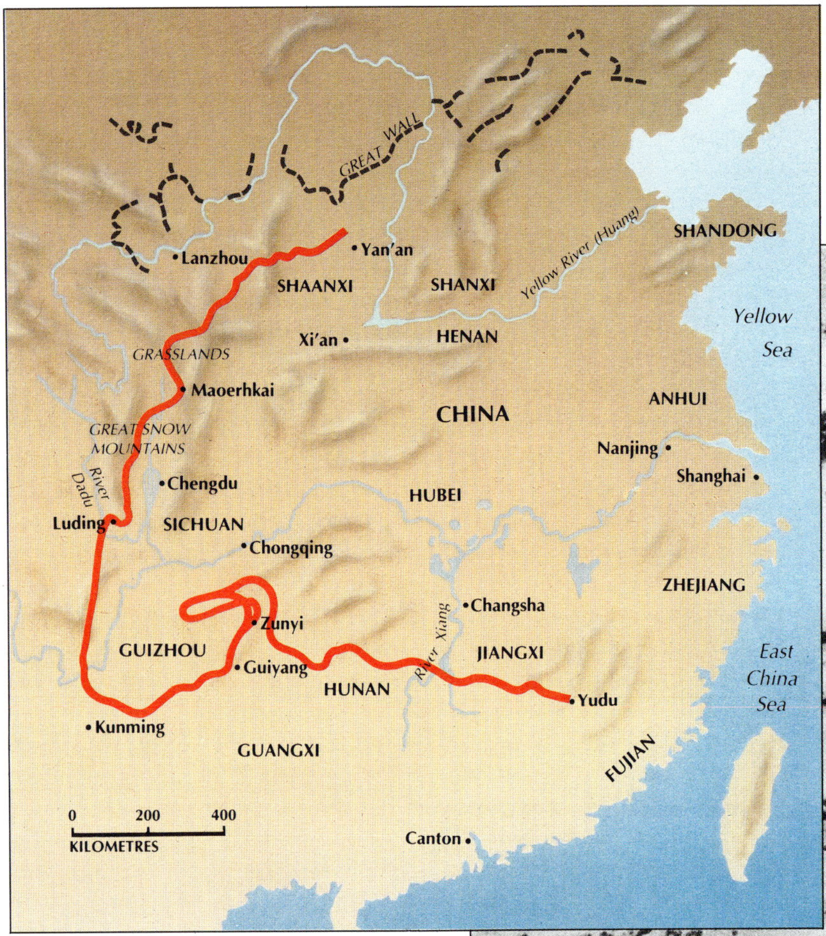

In 1935, towards the end of the 10,000-kilometre trek that became known as the Long March, Communist troops clad in quilted cotton tunics and cloth shoes brave the Great Snow Mountains. The march had begun in October 1934, when Nationalist pressure forced some 85,000 Communists to abandon their base in southern China. Over the next year, they followed a circuitous course *(above)* that took them across 18 mountain ranges and 24 major rivers before they reached the relative safety of Shaanxi province in the north. Less than one in four of the Long Marchers completed the journey. At a conference held at Zunyi during the march, Mao Zedong emerged as the supreme leader of the Communist party, and, after the founding of the People's Republic, most of the highest positions in the party and government were held by survivors of the odyssey.

And yet the country's basic problems had not changed. The Guomindang was a collection of competing factions whose allegiance to Chiang was uncertain. The warlords had been tamed rather than defeated, and Chiang's sphere of control was still confined to the lower Yangtze valley; in the rest of the country the writ of the Nanjing government ran only on sufferance. The lives of the peasantry were still subject to the vicissitudes of the weather and the greed of their landlords. Between 1929 and 1930, an estimated six million Chinese died in a famine that went virtually unreported by the world press. Dr. Sun's widow left the Guomindang and went into exile, accusing her husband's successors of organizing the party as "a tool for the rich to get still richer and suck the blood of the starving millions". During the early 1930s, Chiang made efforts to stem the corruption within his party. Disillusioned with democracy, he flirted with fascism and established the Blue Shirts, a body devoted to building him up as a dictator and to promoting his semi-religious New Life Movement for the moral regeneration of the nation. And all the time, he continued his efforts to eradicate communism from China.

Tied to communist orthodoxy and bound to obey the Comintern, the surviving remnants of the CCP continued to pin their hopes on the urban proletariat; but cities were few in China, and even the warlord armies were better trained and equipped than the workers' militias. Mao, however, was beginning to move away from Marxist-Leninist doctrine. After spending much of 1925 organizing peasant associations in his native Hunan, he had written a report in which he identified the revolutionary potential of the rural masses. Oppressed by heavy rents and interest rates as high as 80 per cent, and exploited by corrupt officials, they were ripe for revolution, he claimed. He also believed they could provide what the CCP lacked, a large and effective military force.

Although his theories were rejected out of hand by the CCP's political office, or Politburo, he had been given a chance to test them in Hunan as one of the leaders of a movement called the Autumn Harvest Uprising, staged in 1927. It was a disaster. The peasantry responded with apathy to his calls for insurrection, and the few who did join the rising were poorly armed and badly coordinated. They were brutally suppressed and Mao himself narrowly escaped with his life after being captured by Nationalist troops. For this failure, Mao was dismissed from the Politburo. Unaware of this, he retreated with the remnants of his force, finding refuge in the notorious bandit lair of Jinggangshan, on the Hunan-Jiangxi border. There he was joined in April 1928 by a professional officer, Zhu De, and 600 survivors of a Communist uprising in Nanchang. Among them was Chen Yi, the former deputy of Zhou Enlai (who remained in Shanghai), and a brilliant 21-year-old soldier called Lin Biao, who would eventually become Mao's heir apparent.

In defiance of his Shanghai colleagues, who accused him of being a military adventurer and deviationist, Mao began the long procedure of building up a guerrilla army, gaining the support of the peasants by taking action against what he described as "local bullies and bad gentry, corrupt officials, militarists and all counter-revolutionary elements".

While Zhu and Lin directed their efforts to turning peasants into soldiers, Mao concentrated on their political training, using sets of slogans easily learnt by the mainly illiterate recruits. The Communists' Three Principles summed up the behaviour demanded of the troops: obey orders at all times; do not take even a

MAO'S SOCIAL EXPERIMENT

In 1936 Mao established a Communist capital at the small town of Yan'an, in Shaanxi province. Poor and remote, plagued alternately by flood and drought, it seemed an unpromising place to test Communist theories of social organization and economic development. Even finding sufficient food would present a problem; between 1927 and 1930, more than a quarter of the local population had died of plague and starvation.

Since the production of food was considered to be everyone's concern, the army played a significant and leading part in reclaiming the powdery loess soil surrounding Yan'an. All soldiers assisted with the digging, planting, hoeing and harvest. By 1944, the Communists claimed that more than one million hectares of land had been opened up, and that production of cereal had doubled.

Mao also introduced a large-scale programme of indoctrination, designed to instil what he called a "firm and correct political orientation". To this end, the Party Politburo established the Kangda military and political institute, which attracted left-wing sympathizers from all over China. In addition, the Communists launched a literacy programme; waged campaigns against superstition and unhygienic habits; and set up newspapers, technical colleges, a medical school, and an arts and literature academy.

From the very beginning, economic development was severely disrupted – first of all by a Guomindang blockade and later by Japanese bombing. And yet the base survived, becoming in some ways a prototype for the kind of self-sufficient society which the Communists imposed on China after they came to power.

A lecturer instructs his class in the open air. The Communists set great store by verbal teaching, for books were in short supply and most recruits, like the overwhelming majority of Chinese, were illiterate.

Soldiers join the women of Yan'an at spinning. As part of their quest for self-sufficiency, the Communists introduced cotton to the region.

Yan'an shows the effects of Japanese bombing. For their protection, the Communists dug a gallery of caves into the loess hills surrounding the town.

Cavalry troops at Yan'an practise using their horses as shields. The military and political institute was initially headed by Lin Biao, the Red Army's leading exponent of guerrilla warfare.

Red Army troops help prepare the land for tillage. Mao taught that a soldier should be "three in one": a worker, a soldier and a peasant. On average, each recruit cultivated about six hectares of land.

needle or a piece of thread from the people; turn in all confiscated property to headquarters. Tactics were governed by rhymed Chinese verses:

When the enemy advances, we retreat.
When he escapes, we harass.
When he retreats, we pursue.
When he is tired, we attack.

When Mao's army grew too large for the local food supply, he led it into an upland region on Jiangxi's southern border, where a series of corrupt governors had created an area of seething discontent. In this ripe soil, Mao set up the largest of the dozen or so Communist base areas scattered in remote areas of China.

It was not easily done. Chiang, not a man to underestimate the Communist threat, launched the First Annihilation Campaign in 1930, sending 100,000 troops – supplied mainly by warlord allies – against Mao's 30,000-strong Red Army. By adhering to guerrilla tactics, for which Jiangxi's rugged hills and narrow valleys were ideally suited, Mao's commanders lured the Nationalist forces deep into Red territory and then, by hard marching, isolated enemy divisions and dealt with them piecemeal. The result of the first battle exceeded all expectations, the Red Army taking 9,000 prisoners, 8,000 rifles and machine guns, and two radios which greatly improved the Communist army's communications. The capture of the payroll for three Nationalist divisions was a welcome bonus.

At this juncture, the Japanese threw a spanner into the works by seizing several cities in Manchuria. Chiang was placed in an impossible situation. He was indebted to the Japanese for the aid they had given him, and as an accomplished soldier he knew that the Nationalist army, with or without its warlord allies, was no match for the Japanese armed forces. He was therefore obliged to make certain concessions to the invaders, hoping that their ultimate aim was not the conquest of China but a war against the Soviet Union – a policy that was favoured by Japan's influential Strike North faction. In 1932, Japan took the rest of Manchuria, setting up the last of the Manchus as puppet emperor of the state of Manchuguo, and the following year it picked off the northern province of Jehol. Public opinion was outraged, but Chiang felt that the loss of these territories on the periphery of China was a worthwhile price to pay in return for Japan's continuing support in quelling the Communists. "The Japanese are a disease of the skin," he said later. "The Communists are a disease of the heart."

Mao's tactics against Chiang's first campaign proved a model for the next three. The Communists used their superior knowledge of the terrain, greater mobility, and ruses such as wearing enemy uniforms, to confuse the opposing, mainly warlord, forces and pick them off one at a time. Their greatest advantage was the support of the peasants. As a Nationalist general ruefully confessed: "Wherever we go we are in darkness; wherever the Reds go they are in light." Another disadvantage that Chiang was never quite able to surmount was the reluctance of his warlord commanders to go to each other's assistance. They believed, with justice, that their forces were being used as cannon fodder while the Generalissimo kept the Nationalist army intact, the better to coerce them.

After the Red Army's success against the first three Guomindang expeditions, the Jiangxi base area had been declared a soviet – a region governed by a Communist committee. Covering several thousand square kilometres, it had a population of between eight and nine million and was the largest in the world outside the U.S.S.R. Mao was elected its first chairman, but soon his position was seriously weakened by an influx of Comintern-dominated officials fleeing intense Nationalist repression in the cities. Among them was Zhou Enlai, at that period a follower of the Moscow party line. By the time Chiang launched his Fifth Annihilation Campaign in 1933, Mao no longer had a voice in Communist military operations or political decisions.

For the Fifth Campaign, Chiang's strategy was different. His plans, drawn up with a large team of German advisers, aimed at the slow strangulation of the Jiangxi soviet. Lines of blockhouses connected with barbed wire were built around the Red Army's base area, and the Communist strongholds were isolated by a "fiery wall" — areas where crops and villages were burnt. Nearly one million Nationalist troops, including Chiang's best divisions, were thrown into action against the 180,000-strong Red Army. For the first time, the Jiangxi army found itself facing a well-trained and mobile enemy, backed up with armour, artillery and aircraft, and directed by a purposeful central command with good communications.

As the ring tightened, Mao and Zhu De advocated that the Red Army break through the circle and then split into small guerrilla units. But the party leadership,

In December 1937, five months after the outbreak of the Sino-Japanese War, a Japanese tank joins the assault on Nanjing, the Nationalist capital. When the city fell, the invaders immediately engaged in an orgy of rape and massacre that claimed the lives of an estimated 200,000 civilians. The "Rape of Nanjing" was calculated to destroy the Chinese armies' will to resist, but in fact it achieved the opposite effect and aroused worldwide revulsion.

mainly city-bred and Comintern-dominated, seemed, in the words of one observer, "to be seized with paralysis". Having been forced out of Shanghai, they could not bear to give up their peasant soviet. Instead, they sought the illusory security of fixed positions, ordering the building of fortifications and exhorting their troops with the slogan: "Don't give up an inch of soviet territory."

For the duration of the winter, the Red Army continued to batter itself against Chiang's strategically placed ring of steel and concrete. As the blockade intensified, the soviet grew desperately short of salt, cloth, kerosene and other goods. A shattering military defeat in April 1934 cost the defenders 4,000 dead and 20,000 wounded. Men began to slip away; desertion, said the party newspaper, was "an enemy more fearful than Chiang Kai-shek".

As the Communists' situation worsened, the arguments in favour of a complete evacuation gained weight. On the night of October 2, plans for the abandonment of the Jiangxi base were agreed by a military council that included Mao and Zhou Enlai. Over a decade later, when he was asked about the Communists' goal, Mao replied: "If you mean, did we have any exact plans, the answer is that we had none. We intended to break out of the encirclement and join up with the other

Nationalist soldiers – apparently younger than the official conscription age of 18 – take a break from training. Conditions for Guomindang conscripts were generally appalling; on average, ordinary soldiers received meat only once or twice a month, and the poverty of their diet left them anaemic and susceptible to eye and skin diseases and parasites. This, combined with a shortage of both doctors and medicines, meant that fewer than a third of the men were, according to American standards, fit to fight.

soviets. Beyond that, there was only a very deliberate desire to put ourselves in a position where we could fight the Japanese."

Towards dusk on October 18, 1934, the main body of the Red Army left the town of Yudu, heading south where, they thought, they would find the weakest link in the forces surrounding them. This was the start of the Long March – the forge of hardship and heroism that was the making of the Chinese Communist Party. About 85,000 men and 35 women – senior party leaders – set out on the epic journey, with food, weapons and printing presses. Twenty thousand noncombatants and 6,000 soldiers were left behind. Among them were many of Mao's supporters, reflecting his poor standing in the party hierarchy. Most were later executed by the Guomindang. Mao left three of his children behind; he never saw them again.

The Communists' guess about the weakness of the southern perimeter was correct. After heavy skirmishing, they forced their way past the lines of blockhouses and moved southwest in the mountains marking the provincial boundaries. The warlord generals in the region cherished dreams of an autonomous, non-Mandarin-speaking south. They decided not to risk their forces on behalf of the Guomindang.

When the Red Army reached the Xiang River farther west, it found that Chiang had anticipated their plan and assembled far larger forces than the Communists had expected. The battle to cross the Xiang lasted a week and cost 30,000 casualties. Once across, the Communists had the choice of making for either of two Red base areas: Sichuan, on the Tibetan border, or Hunan, Mao's home province.

Chiang had taken steps to close both options, and the Communists ran into new lines of fortifications. For weeks they marched and countermarched through the mountains of Guizhou province, unable to break through the Guomindang lines. Once again, Chiang's generals claimed that they had the Red forces bottled up. But the low cloud which covers the province for much of the year hid the fugitives from the Nationalists' spotter planes, and by ruse and clever manoeuvring, the Communists eluded their pursuers. Then they captured the provincial centre of Zunyi, and the party's political and military leaders debated their next move.

This was to be a major turning point for the Chinese Communist Party. Before the conference at Zunyi, the ruling Politburo had been controlled by the Soviet-sponsored faction, and military strategy had been largely determined by foreign Comintern agents. But after an exhaustive review of policy and tactics, it was recognized that Moscow's doctrinaire approach to China was unproductive, and that the Comintern ideologists' reliance on positional warfare was impractical. With the support of Red Army commanders such as the young Lin Biao, who favoured unorthodox mobile warfare, Mao was elected chairman of the Politburo, while Zhu De was made commander of the Red Army, with Zhou Enlai – now and henceforth a firm ally of the Chairman – as his chief political officer.

To escape Chiang's armies, Mao determined to head south and then begin a large flanking movement – first west, then north – to link with other Red Army forces in Sichuan. He reasoned that the mountainous terrain of China's western border regions would prevent Chiang from massing troops in force; but he was also aware that even small Guomindang garrisons could hold his men up in the many gorges and valleys they would have to cross.

By the time the Red Army emerged from the highlands of Guizhou, it had shed its printing presses and other heavy equipment and was travelling light, with only food, ammunition and weapons. Each man carried a rice ration of about two kilograms, plus a load of ammunition or grenades or tools and machinery slung from a shoulder pole. In addition, each man started out with a pack containing a blanket, a quilted winter uniform and three pairs of cloth shoes. Alfred Bosshardt, a Swiss missionary who was captured by the Communists and later released, recalled the shoes. They were bound on to the feet with string or straw, and in wet weather they would disintegrate within a day. After a long stage, the footsore soldiers would literally weep with pain. Troops unable to continue on the journey were left behind with their rifles, ammunition and some money; their task was to organize and lead the local peasants in partisan warfare.

Although there was rarely enough food for the marchers, Mao's injunctions about respecting peasants' property were usually obeyed. Bosshardt remembered resting in a fruit grove at a time when everyone was desperate with hunger. But the troops would not touch the ripe fruit because no-one could be sure whether it belonged to a peasant or a landlord. The property of landlords and officials could be confiscated only on party orders; the property of the peasants could be purchased only with the owner's consent. In this particular case, a woman finally came out and offered to sell the fruit to the marchers.

Despite the constant hardship, there were also moments of beauty. The chief engineer of the force recalled later that "Night marching is wonderful if there is a moon and a gentle wind blowing. When no enemy troops were near, whole companies would sing and others would answer. If it was a black night and the enemy was far away, we made torches from pine branches or frayed bamboo, and then it was truly beautiful. When at the foot of a mountain, we could look up and see a long column of lights coiling like a fiery dragon up the mountain side."

Such moments were rare. Ten years after the event, Peng Dehuai, an army corps commander, claimed that there were so many battles, he could not accurately recall the sequence of events. "Now when I look back, it seems to be one enormous battle going on all the time."

Among the many incidents that passed into Chinese legend, a few stood out with crystal clarity. At the crossing of the Dadu River in the borderlands of Sichuan, the fate of the Long March hung in the balance. It was the Guomindang's last chance to destroy Mao's army before it joined up with the Communist force in Sichuan, and the local warlord, goaded by Chiang, was moving troops to prevent the crossing and surround the army. On the face of it, he and the Guomindang had an easy task. Here, high in the mountains close to Tibet, the river falls through steep gorges. Within a stretch of 150 kilometres, there were only two bridges and a single ferry.

The Sichuanese commander had garrisoned the northernmost bridge, at Luding, with two regiments. Another regiment held the north bank of the ferry crossing situated 80 kilometres downriver, while two more waited for the arrival of government reinforcements at the southern bridge. Zhu De made a feint to tie down the forces advancing from the south, and sent one regiment on a forced march to take the south bank of the ferry. The regiment crossed 80 kilometres of rugged country in 24 hours, surprising the Sichuanese commander and his officers playing mahjong at a relative's feast. A native of the region, he had not believed that troops could cover the distance in such a short time.

Contrary to Chiang's orders, the local troops had left one of the ferry boats moored on the south side of the river. Using this, and supported by light artillery

In 1944, during the last major Japanese offensive in China, Nationalist troops beat a retreat through a southern Chinese village. The extent of Japanese-occupied China had not grown much since the massive campaigns of 1937 and 1938, but as the war in the Pacific intensified, the invaders became increasingly concerned by U.S. air attacks that were delivered by warplanes flying from Chinese bases. Fearing the arrival of American bombers with sufficient range to launch raids on Japan itself, the Japanese directed 15 divisions to capture strategic targets in south and east China, including the airfields. The Nationalist army was quite unable to hold back the advance, and, as city after city fell, millions of Chinese troops and civilians alike fled for their lives.

and machine guns, a squad of 16 volunteers crossed the river under fire. They maintained and enlarged this toehold until most of a division had crossed. But by this time Chiang's air force was bombing the crossing and his reinforcements were drawing closer. With the river flooding and the rest of the army piling up on the south bank, it became obvious that it would take weeks to get all the Long Marchers across. The commanders decided to try to capture the Luding bridge.

In two days the leading regiment made a march of more than 150 kilometres, taking two passes by assault and repairing a bridge on the way. During the last 24 hours, they had only 10-minute rests every two hours and were falling asleep

as they marched. They found the bridge intact. Famed throughout the province, it had been built at enormous expense in 1701 by the emperor Kang Xi, and the Sichuanese troops in the walled town of Luding could not bring themselves to destroy it. Swaying high above the tumbling river, it consisted of 13 iron chains, each link "as thick as a rice bowl", with two chains as guard rails and the rest carrying wooden planks. A number of the warlord's troops had removed the planks from the Communist side of the bridge.

A force of 22 soldiers attempted to fight their way across. An eyewitness later described the assault to Agnes Smedley, a radical American writer: "The army watched breathlessly as the men swung along the bridge chains. Ma Dajiu was the first to be shot into the wild torrent below. Then another man and another. The others pushed along but just before they reached the flooring at the north bridgehead they saw enemy soldiers dumping cans of kerosene on the planks and setting them on fire. Watching the sheet of flame spread, some men hesitated, but the platoon political leader at last sprang down on the flooring before the flames reached his feet, calling the men to follow. They ran through the flames and threw their hand grenades in the midst of the enemy. More and more men followed, the flames lapping at their clothing." Within the space of two hours the town was carried by assault and the way for the army was clear.

At their first meeting for 18 years, Mao Zedong and Chiang Kai-shek toast each other during conciliatory talks in 1945. The talks were arranged by an American emissary, General Patrick J. Hurley, who had been dispatched by President Roosevelt to help bring about a coalition government of Nationalists and Communists. Although each side was determined to create a one-party state, both found it advantageous briefly to feign support for the initiative. Chiang pretended that he was willing to work towards a peaceful accommodation with the Communists in order not to jeopardize the American aid on which his regime depended. For his part, Mao reckoned that it would take 10 years to defeat the Nationalists, and he believed that even a short-lived treaty would give the Communists time to increase their strength.

Other well-remembered incidents were triumphs of endurance. After the capture of the Luding bridge, the Long Marchers were only 160 kilometres as the crow flies from their comrades in the Sichuan Red Army base, but between them lay seven distinct ranges of high mountains. The first and most formidable obstacle was the Great Snow Mountains. Crossing it took the marchers up to 5,000 metres, and since most of them were from low-lying provinces, they suffered terribly from altitude sickness. They also endured the agonies of cold, for their clothing was quite inadequate. One marcher recalled: "All along the route we kept reaching down to pull men to their feet only to find that they were already dead."

After the two Red Army forces met, their leaders argued about goals and eventually split, with the Sichuan contingent moving farther west into Tibet, and Mao's force marching north to the Shaanxi base area in the shadow of the Great Wall, close to possible Russian aid. The Long Marchers moved off to tackle the last great obstacle, the grasslands, a trackless wilderness stretching for hundreds of kilometres. No trees grew there, only clumps of grass that often disguised treacherous bogs. Sometimes the soldiers had to sleep kneeling back to back because there was nowhere to lie down. In the mists that blanketed the area, many marchers lost their way and perished. Because it was impossible to carry litters, the sick had to be abandoned. As many as a third of the force died on the crossing.

Finally, in October 1935, the surviving 20,000 men straggled into the Shaanxi base area. Even this figure does not truly reflect the losses suffered en route, for most of the survivors had been recruited during the march. Two months later, Mao summarized what they had endured. "For 12 months we were under daily reconnaissance and bombing from the air by scores of planes; we were encircled, pursued, obstructed and intercepted on the ground by a big force of several hundred thousand men; we encountered untold difficulties and great obstacles on the way, but by keeping our two feet going we swept across a distance of more than 20,000 *li* (10,000 kilometres) . . . Has there ever been a long march like ours?"

Mao's claim to have won a great victory was less easy to believe. Membership of the Chinese Communist Party had fallen and the party's armed force had shrunk to less than 50,000. But the Communists had acquired intangible assets far more valuable in the long term than battle honours. Within the party, the marchers' discipline, self-sacrifice and military skills were to provide an inspiration and a pattern for the future. Among the populace, the legend of the indestructible army dedicated to repelling the Japanese was to grow (with the help of Communist propaganda) through the years. The peasants were to remember the army that did not loot, and whose officers and men, sharing the same uniforms and rations and dangers, preached an end to the iniquities of high taxation and rent.

Chiang's determination to crush the Communists remained unabated, but he had badly misjudged the temper of his military allies, who were more anxious to fight the Japanese than to kill their own countrymen. In December 1936, when the Generalissimo flew to Xi'an, capital of Shaanxi province, to announce a new anti-Communist campaign, he was arrested by Manchurian warlords who demanded the formation of a united national army to liberate their homeland. The Communists, represented by Zhou Enlai, were invited to join the negotiations that followed. Many of Zhou's colleagues were in favour of putting Chiang on trial, but under pressure from Stalin, who believed that Chiang was the only leader capable of uniting China against the Japanese, Zhou was obliged to recommend the release of his party's sworn enemy. In return, Chiang agreed to abandon his blockade of the Shaanxi soviet. The following year, the Russians pressed Chiang into a formal alliance with the CCP. His reward was a considerable amount of military aid, including 1,000 planes and 2,000 pilots.

For some time, Chiang's Strike North allies in Japan had been losing the struggle for influence with the Strike South faction, which advocated war with China as a means of opening up a path to the oil and rubber resources of Southeast Asia. Now, alarmed by the prospect of a united Nationalist and Communist front, Japan's imperialists decided to strike the first blow while there was still time. On July 7, 1937, Japanese troops apparently provoked a clash with Chinese troops at the Marco Polo bridge, near Beijing. When Chiang made it plain that he intended to resist aggression, the Japanese poured troops into north China. Beijing fell at the end of July, and by the close of the year Shanghai, and Nanjing, the Nationalist capital, were in Japanese hands. The invaders wanted a short war and decided that terror tactics were the way to achieve it. When the imperial army entered Nanjing, it was ordered to make an example of the city to break the Nationalists' morale. For two months, under the eyes of Nanjing's foreign community, the occupying troops indulged in an orgy of rape and murder. An international tribunal later found that 20,000 women had been raped and over 200,000 men killed.

Before Nanjing fell, Chiang had removed his government to Wuhan, cutting the dykes of the Yellow River as he retreated, causing floods. The Japanese advance was briefly halted, but hundreds of thousands of Chinese peasants drowned or died in the ensuing famine. In March 1938, the Nationalist army achieved one major military success, inflicting 16,000 Japanese casualties at Taierzhuang. But the setback was temporary. In late October 1938, the Japanese took Wuhan, forcing Chiang to flee west to Sichuan; as one of his commanders put it, he was trading space for time. Behind the mountain barrier of Sichuan, the Nationalists established a temporary capital at Chongqing, the most important town of the province. Thereafter, they made little effort to recapture lost territory. By the end of the year, the Japanese occupied most of China's major cities, including all its ports, all the principal industrial areas and most of the main lines of communication.

In the huge areas of north China that the Japanese had overrun but not fully occupied, the Communists began organizing resistance. The railway system, secured by blockhouses every few kilometres, made an ideal target for the guerrilla tactics of the Red Army, which shredded the Japanese defenders in a week of battle. The Japanese responded by bringing in more troops and launching what they called the "Three Alls" campaign: kill all, loot all, burn all. The Communist army then avoided pitched battles, restricting itself to harassment behind enemy lines. "The people are the sea," declared Zhu De's deputy, "while the guerrillas are the fish swimming in it." As well as mobilizing the populace against the Japanese, Mao carried on the social revolution, winning local support by introducing reductions in rent and tax that significantly improved living conditions for the peasantry. Yan'an, the small dreary town in Shaanxi where the Communists established their capital, became a magnet for tens of thousands of active young people from all over the country. This influx helped swell the ranks of the party to 400,000 by 1940.

While the Communist movement grew and spread in north China, Chiang sat in his fortress at Chongqing, biding his time. He was convinced that Japan's expansionist policies in the Pacific would eventually bring it into conflict with the United States, and that the United States would win. Until then, he would fight the Japanese only as much as he must, keeping his government and army intact so that he would be in a position to take over the whole country at war's end.

The inevitable result of this enforced idleness was a slow corrosion of morale among the Guomindang establishment and an increasing sense of disillusionment

Guomindang soldiers bombard Communist positions outside Nanjing, the Nationalist capital, in the autumn of 1948. During the latter stages of the civil war, the Nationalists incurred heavy losses of men and arms by attempting to defend isolated city strongholds. By 1948 casualties and desertions had reduced their army to a fraction of its former size, but its commanders refused to relinquish their capital without a fight. After Communist troops encircled the defensive forces outside the city, severing all lines of supply and communication, Nanjing was lost, and with it all hope of a Guomindang government in mainland China.

among the many patriots who had joined the government in exile. Deprived of trade and customs revenues, the Nationalists financed their administration and lined their own pockets by printing money, producing an inflationary surge that saw prices rise 250-fold between 1942 and 1944. Local governors also introduced a range of special taxes, including such imaginatively named levies as the "contribute-straw-sandals-to-recruits" tax, a "comfort-recruits'-families" tax, and the "train-anti-aircraft-cadres" tax. Relations between the Nationalists and the local population deteriorated steadily: "downriver gangsters" was the term used for Guomindang officials by the Sichuanese people. Dissent was crushed by the strong-arm tactics of Chiang's secret police. Because of the fear that the populace

In December 1948, with inflation out of control, a crowd rushes a Shanghai bank to exchange their devalued currency for gold. The raging inflation in Guomindang-controlled China meant that the city dwellers in particular had difficulty maintaining even a minimal standard of living. On receiving their wages, workers would hurry to exchange sackfuls of notes for food or fuel, knowing that only a few hours later prices would have doubled. In a desperate attempt to halt inflation, Chiang replaced the Chinese dollar with a new currency, the *yuan*; nevertheless, over the next six months, prices rose 85,000-fold.

would turn against them in armed revolt, the Guomindang made no effort at all to mobilize the peasantry as the Communists were doing.

From 1939, the U.S. gave Chiang financial aid, which was increased when the Guomindang threatened to make an accommodation with the Japanese. Although Chiang did not intend to carry out the threat, it was given substance by the defection of his deputy and chief political rival, who the Japanese made head of a puppet government in Nanjing. Elsewhere, warlords and provincial commanders made alliances with the Japanese, sometimes fighting with them against the Communists.

When the United States entered the war, the government appointed the abrasive General Joseph Stilwell as Chiang's chief of staff — a position he held in addition to

his role as commander of the U.S. China-Burma-India theatre. At one of their first strategy meetings, Chiang stunned Stilwell by telling him that Chinese divisions should not be deployed even in defensive positions unless they outnumbered the Japanese by five to one. In fact, the Generalissimo continued, Chinese forces should never be massed, because they would simply be destroyed wholesale. "What a directive," Stilwell wrote in his diary. "What a mess."

Given the generally poor state of the Nationalist forces, Chiang was probably right. He did have some good troops, who served with distinction in Burma, but after 1941, when the shaky alliance between the Guomindang and the Communists broke down, many of his best divisions were used to contain the Red Army in the north. The bulk of his army was made up of male conscripts aged between 18 and 45. In theory, conscription was by ballot, but the process was warped by corruption, which spared the rich and filled the ranks with disaffected, illiterate peasants, who were often treated as coolies rather than fighting men. Many conscripts had to walk hundreds of kilometres to their units. Stilwell found in 1943 that only 56 per cent of all recruits reached their assigned destinations; the rest deserted or died of disease or malnutrition on the way. Food was short anyway, and what little there was was often withheld by officers who sold it on the black market.

During the eight years of what the Chinese call the War of Resistance, the Nationalists mobilized some 14 million troops. An estimated three million of these became combat casualties, many dying of infection as a result of relatively minor wounds that went untreated. About half a million men, including 700 generals, went over to the Japanese puppet forces. Most of the other 10-million-plus men are simply unaccounted for; many must have deserted, but even more probably died of starvation. One American officer reported seeing famished Nationalist soldiers toppling over and dying after marching a distance of less than two kilometres; the Nationalist army's lines of march could be followed simply by the trail of dead soldiers. Some recruits fell victim to their own countrymen, enraged by the excesses of the soldiery. In Hunan province, suffering under a long-predicted famine that no-one tried to alleviate, the peasants disarmed retreating Nationalist troops, shot them and welcomed the Japanese.

When the Americans made their first official contact with Mao's soviet government, in July 1944, they found a striking contrast to conditions in the Nationalist-occupied areas. "We have come into a different country," one of the American delegation reported, "and are meeting a different people." In north and central China, the Communists exerted both military and political control over some 95 million people in a total area of 800,000 square kilometres. Their administration enjoyed widespread popular support, and their troops were loyal, well disciplined, respectful of civilian rights and highly motivated.

Many Americans questioned the Guomindang's fitness to govern a liberated China, but their warnings were drowned by the voice of Patrick Hurley, President Roosevelt's flamboyant representative, whom Mao Zedong regarded – with some justification – as little more than the Generalissimo's mouthpiece. When Hurley's clumsy efforts to arrange a democratic coalition of Nationalists and Communists broke down, the Ambassador urged Washington to give full and unequivocal support to the Chongqing government. In fairness, the United States had little room for manoeuvre; having recognized its ally Chiang as the rightful head of China, it was legally obliged to support his regime. In this respect, American policy on China differed little from the stance adopted by Stalin, who also regarded Chiang as the legitimate head of state, and who was increasingly displeased by the Chinese style of communism – "two peasants wearing the same pair of pants," as Soviet wags put it. On a stopover in Moscow, Hurley was told by Stalin that Mao's supporters were nothing more than "radish communists – red on the outside, white inside".

Chiang, however, did not underestimate the task that lay before him when the Japanese were finally driven out. Aware of the weaknesses of his own military, he hoped to take over China on the coat-tails of an American invasion force. But the dropping of the atom bomb – a weapon that neither the Chinese nor the Soviets were told about in advance – meant that there was no large-scale American invasion. Instead, it was the Soviet Red Army that entered Chinese territory, occupying Manchuria in a lightning advance. The Americans diverted 53,000 marines to Beijing in case the Russians advanced too enthusiastically, but Stalin honoured his pledge to restore China to Chiang, who asked the Soviet Union to extend its occupation of Manchuria until his own troops could take control. Now that the United States no longer needed its vast arsenal, it handed over much of its surplus to the Nationalist army, and American pilots flew Chiang's representatives to take surrenders from the Japanese, even where the CCP was closest to the former enemy. As both sides raced to take over liberated territory, Chiang ordered Japanese commanders and their troops to resist the Red Army.

Even before the Japanese surrender, Chiang had announced his next goal. "Now at last the time has come to destroy the Communists root and branch," he told his army commanders in August 1945. Unprepared for this struggle for the heart of its ally, the United States tried every expedient to bring the two sides together. It patched up local and national truces between the two sides and even induced Chiang and Mao to meet. General George Marshall, U.S. wartime chief of staff and shortly to be the author of the Marshall Plan which revitalized war-ravaged Europe, was sent to prevent civil war. Teams of American officers were sent round the country to try to stop outbreaks of fighting between the two sides. But a year later Marshall returned to the United States, confessing his mission a failure. "The greatest obstacle to peace," he reported, "has been the complete, almost overwhelming, suspicion with which the CCP and Guomindang regard each other."

On paper, the Communists in 1945 were very much weaker than the Nationalists. Chiang had more than three million men under arms, many of them trained and supplied by the British or the Americans. With a thousand American planes, his air force was the unchallenged master of the skies. Most of the major population centres were under his control, and he commanded all the organizational and financial resources of the government. Through eight years of war he had kept his administration more or less intact, and his forces had made a significant contribution to the Allied campaign in Burma. Recognized as one of the four major powers in the war against Japan, he enjoyed the security of alliances with the Big Three of Russia, Britain and the United States.

In contrast, the Red Army – renamed the People's Liberation Army (PLA) after the defeat of Japan – had fewer than a million soldiers, of whom only half were armed. Although membership of the CCP had grown to some 1,200,000, its leader's name was still little known outside China. The Soviet Union's support was equivocal. It made no attempt to extend Communist influence in Manchuria, returning the cities to the Guomindang and seizing the industrial plants as war booty for itself. Stalin even tried to discourage Mao from engaging in civil war with Chiang, urging him to accept a subordinate role in a coalition government. Mao seems to have been persuaded, for at his meeting with the President he gave the toast "Long live Chiang Kai-shek", and in at least one official document of the period, he accorded Chiang the respectful title of "uncle".

Chiang, however, was so certain of his strength that no amount of persuasion or coercion would make him pay more than lip service to the truces painfully hammered out by United States representatives. In June 1946, he started to move in force against the People's Liberation Army. During this first phase, his armoured divisions were everywhere successful against the lightly armed PLA. Lin Biao, commander of the Communist army in Manchuria, used human wave tactics to try to

Riding on American trucks seized from the Nationalists, Communist soldiers enter Beijing in triumph on February 3, 1949. Demoralized by Chiang Kai-shek's failure to send sufficient arms, the city's Nationalist defenders had attempted to negotiate an armistice with the Communists. At the very last moment, the long-awaited weapons were dispatched – and were promptly intercepted by the Communists, who then abandoned the negotiations. The Nationalist forces withdrew into Beijing's medieval walled city, and finally surrendered six weeks later.

neutralize the enemy's advantages in weapons, but after a month of bloody fighting he was forced to retreat. By late in the year 1947, the Guomindang controlled every provincial capital and most other important cities, in addition to China's major transportation routes. Even Yan'an had fallen into its hands.

But Chiang's chosen tools of control were not altogether reliable. The Nationalist officials he had brought with him from Sichuan had lived for a period of eight years on a combination of inflation, graft and American aid. Far from altering their habits, they descended on their nominal posts like robber barons. Loyalty to Chiang himself rather than competence was the principal criterion for office, and indeed it can be said that his subordinates were loyal to him precisely because they were so incompetent. But their personal allegiance to Chiang was outweighed by their dedication to enriching themselves; corruption at every single level of the administration ensured that the Generalissimo could never count on getting his orders obeyed. He was also fast losing the support of the middle class, which had hoped for the introduction of a liberal, democratic regime, and instead found itself living under an authoritarian military dictatorship which employed force to stifle even the mildest demands for reform.

Like the Japanese conquests in China, the Nationalists' advances gained little except territory, for, in keeping with Communist strategy, the PLA conserved its strength by avoiding disadvantageous actions and abandoning indefensible positions. Meanwhile, Mao Zedong set his cadres to winning over the support of the people by replacing the policy of rent reductions with the confiscation and redistribution of landlord property. The implementation of this land reform programme helped consolidate the Communists' support in the countryside and proved to be of considerable value in the struggle.

Chiang, meanwhile, faced a serious problem in his main political base – the cities. Inflation, which had been growing throughout the war, was to sweep out of control by 1948, bringing famine in its wake. By the middle of that year, 500 grams of rice cost a quarter of a million Chinese dollars. Each night, hundreds of people died in the streets, their bodies collected by the municipal dust carts in the morning. In the Communist-controlled areas, by contrast, there was little starvation, for the Communists lived in effect outside the cash economy. Nor was there any hoarding of food; rations were about the same for all ranks.

Support for Chiang eroded to the point where it could only be enforced at the point of a bayonet. Demoralized and hungry, Nationalist troops began defecting to the People's Liberation Army, only too happy to exchange their rifles for a square meal. At the beginning of 1947, an entire Nationalist division went over to the PLA. Ignoring all American warnings that his troops were dangerously overextended, Chiang adamantly refused to give ground.

In September 1947, Lin Biao renewed his offensive. By the end of the year his men had shut down the railway system in Manchuria, isolating 250,000 of Chiang's best troops in the cities and effectively cutting communications with the south, where units of the PLA had reached the Yangtze River, China's great east-west highway. Defections now began in earnest; indeed, of all the Nationalists who fell into Communist hands, three quarters simply surrendered. By the autumn of 1948, the relative strengths of the two sides had been reversed.

The last great campaign of the civil war was the battle for Nanjing, the Guomindang capital. Half a million men were committed on each side for a total of 65 days. The PLA severed the Nationalists' communications and picked off Chiang's divisions one by one. Entire units went over to the Communists, taking with them all their military equipment. By the end of the year, the Nationalist regime was on the brink of total collapse. At the end of January 1949, the PLA entered Beijing, encountering no resistance at all. The same month, the Nanjing government sued for peace, but when negotiations broke down, Mao ordered his troops to cross the Yangtze River and achieve final victory.

After the fall of his capital in April 1949, Chiang retreated, first to Sichuan, then later to Taiwan where, vowing that one day he would return to the mainland, he set up the government of the Republic of China in opposition to the Communists. On October 1, 1949, Mao appeared at the Gate of Heavenly Peace in Beijing and proclaimed the People's Republic of China. "Ours will no longer be a nation subject to insult and humiliation," he declared. "We have stood up." But he also had words of warning for his countrymen. "The victory of the Chinese people's democratic revolution, viewed in retrospect, will seem like only a brief prologue to a long drama. A drama begins with a prologue, but the prologue is not the climax."

Wearing the plain cotton uniform that would become one of the symbols of Communist China, Mao announces the establishment of the People's Republic on October 1, 1949. His proclamation was delivered from the Gate of Heavenly Peace in Beijing, a rostrum for the announcement of new dynasties during China's imperial era. Three months after the founding of Communist China, what was left of the Nationalist government left its last base on the mainland and established the Republic of China on the island of Taiwan. Though Chiang Kai-shek's Guomindang was still recognized by the U.S. as the legitimate government of China, the Communists' control of the mainland was unassailable, and within a year they had extended their power still farther by occupying Tibet.

None of his listeners could have foreseen the nature of the drama yet to unfold: the Korean war, the economic lunacy of the Great Leap Forward, the turmoil of the Cultural Revolution, armed conflict with India and then with the Soviet Union, the Sino-American rapprochement five years before Mao's death in 1976. It had been a long journey for the peasant boy from Hunan and for the Chinese people it was far from over. "Our past work," Mao had said, "is only the first step in a long march."

THE COMING OF THE COLD WAR

The winter of 1947 was the coldest most people in Europe could remember, and the freezing weather matched the continent's political temperature. World War II had been over for a year and a half, but a mounting tide of fear and distrust was eroding the longed-for consolations of peace. To everyone suffering the hardship of that bleak winter, "Cold War" – a phrase popularized by U.S. commentator Walter Lippmann – was a cruelly apposite description of the deteriorating relations between the Soviet Union on the one side and the United States and Great Britain on the other – nations that had so recently been allies against Nazi Germany. When, in the summer of 1948, Soviet occupation forces in Germany suddenly closed the borders of Berlin to all traffic with the West, confrontation teetered on the brink of outright hostilities. An apparently irrevocable split had opened between the Eastern and Western blocs, and the postwar world had taken on the threatening aspect it was to wear for a generation.

The reversal from victorious alliance to embattled enmity, accomplished within such a short period, had deep roots. The wartime alliance of 1941 between the Soviet Union and the Western powers had masked deep ideological differences that went back at least as far as the Russian Revolution of 1917, when Western governments had actively sought to defeat the rise of Bolshevism. Outside the League of Nations until 1934, struggling throughout the interwar years with huge economic and political problems, the Soviet leader Joseph Stalin was well aware of the West's hostility – manifested by its reluctance in the 1930s to offer Russia support against a hostile Germany. Stalin felt that he had been driven into the nonaggression pact he signed with Hitler in 1939.

Western governments in their turn felt threatened by a communist government that was still officially committed to exporting revolution – a threat given force by the Soviet Union's growing economic and military strength. In Moscow, the brutal excesses of Stalin towards his own people were observed by U.S. diplomats whose opinions were later to be decisive in moulding American policy.

Stalin's alliance with the United States and Great Britain came about only when Hitler betrayed his pact by invading Russia in 1941, and the strains between the wartime partners began to appear almost immediately. From the start, Stalin was determined to safeguard the postwar security of the Soviet Union by creating a defensive buffer round the nation's borders, while President Franklin Roosevelt and, to a greater extent, Prime Minister Winston Churchill were intent on curbing communist expansion after the war.

As early as 1943, when Churchill, Stalin and Roosevelt met in the Iranian capital, Tehran, Churchill confided to one of his personal staff that he considered Germany already finished and that "the real problem now is Russia". Believing that postwar cooperation with Stalin would be difficult, but not impossible, Churchill decided on a pragmatic course designed to determine the political future of Europe. In 1944, during a visit to Moscow, he privately proposed a division of the continent into spheres of influence. He was prepared to resign eastern Europe to Soviet influence provided that the West was able to retain a controlling role in Greece, effectively excluding Stalin from the Mediterranean.

Whereas Churchill was ready to frame policies that took account of the conflict of interests between East and West, Roosevelt was more reluctant to make hard decisions. He was anxious not to forfeit Stalin's cooperation, both for the final defeat of Japan and for the setting up of the United Nations, which he hoped would resolve international disputes. By his efforts to woo Stalin, he managed to postpone the impending split between the Allies. When the Big Three met at Yalta in the Crimea in February 1945, the public appearance of concord remained; but the conference pledge to provide governments responsive to the will of the people of liberated Europe merely disguised Stalin's intention to impose his own brand of government on Poland, Bulgaria and Romania – the eastern European states he regarded as crucial to Soviet security.

By the time Germany surrendered in May, Roosevelt was dead. In Poland, where elections for a provisional government had been held in March 1945, after the liberation of the country, Russian pressure to secure a pro-Soviet government had been quite undisguised. To the United States, this blatantly contravened the Yalta pledge. It fell to Harry Truman in the first few days of his presidency to point that out to the Soviet foreign minister, Vyacheslav Molotov, whom Stalin had reluctantly dispatched to America for the opening of the United Nations. Molotov protested that he had never been talked to like that in his life. "Carry out your agreements," Truman retorted, "and you won't get talked to like that."

But American protests about coercion ıad little effect on Stalin, who felt that Vestern scruples about Poland were an ıttempt to stir up anti-Russian sentiment ɔn his doorstep. As he and Churchill had oreseen, the military dispositions at the ɜnd of the war were the decisive factor in letermining the political map of Europe.

Even in defeat, Germany was the main source of tension. The country was split nto British, American, Soviet and French zones prior to an Allied agreement on a peace treaty. At Potsdam in July 1945, a conference that was held to decide the ate of the country ended inconclusively. The Soviets insisted on imposing crushing eparations on their former enemy; the 3ritish and Americans, fearing that the eduction of Germany to an industrial lesert would promote a communist revolıtion, proposed less punitive measures. Such disagreements paved the way for the livision of Germany into two states – one ɔuilt into the structure of the Western ɔloc, the other belonging to the East. By April 1946, Stalin had imposed a oneɔarty government in the Soviet zone, and 3ritain and the United States had merged heir zones into a single economic unit.

Discord over Germany's future soon grew into a confrontation that included most aspects of global politics. At first Great Britain took the lead in trying to counterbalance Russia, but the country was exhausted – militarily and economically. With the collapse of war-torn Europe's political structure, the United States and the Soviet Union had emerged as "superpowers", and the two rivals soon bore the brunt of the contest.

For both sides, ideology was recruited in order to supply a rationale for growing hostility, and to mobilize the support

Jntil the Korean War began in 1950, Europe was the rena for the Cold War between East and West. From 945 to 1950, communist parties loyal to Moscow set ıp Soviet-style regimes in Poland, Czechoslovakia, 3ulgaria, Hungary, Romania and the German Democratic Republic *(countries shaded red)*. But Stalin ailed to take over Berlin or impose the Moscow party ine on Yugoslavia's independent-minded communist eader Marshal Tito. Albania, which had set up a communist regime without outside help, entered into a hort-lived alliance with the Soviet Union in 1948.

of their peoples for the efforts required to compete on a global scale. In Marxist-Leninist theory, the march of the revolution was a historical necessity, and the Americans were ready to read signs of Stalin's global ambitions in many situations that were perhaps only the results of defensive paranoia – quite understandable in a nation that had suffered so many casualties in the war. By considering all contact with the West as a threat, the Soviets chose a path of self-isolation and entrenchment that led to a spiral of repression at home and in eastern Europe.

In February 1946, George Kennan, a veteran U.S. diplomat in Moscow, sent Washington an influential analysis of Soviet intentions. Russia, he argued, was committed to the belief that there could be no permanent accommodation with the United States. The Communists could, however, be contained without recourse to war provided that the U.S. ensured the "cohesion, firmness and vigour" of the West. A month later, Churchill – now out of office – added the full weight of his rhetoric to Kennan's view. On a visit to Westminster College, Fulton, in Truman's home state of Missouri, he evoked for the first time in public the image of an "Iron Curtain" descending across the continent. The Soviets did not desire another war, he said, but he was "convinced that there is nothing they admire so much as strength".

Friction points arose outside Europe, in Turkey and Iran, where the Soviets proposed to establish advance defences. In the end, United Nations' pressure forced Stalin to withdraw his troops from Iran and to stop leaning on Turkey, but many Western diplomats, mindful of Hitler's step-by-step expansion in the 1930s, interpreted his actions as signs of the Soviet Union's global ambitions. Stalin, however, saw the West's activities as interference in territories adjacent to the Soviet border.

The rift widened fast, but it was not until 1947 that the point of no return was reached. In February, as blizzards swept western Europe, the Labour government of Prime Minister Clement Attlee told Truman that Britain could no longer provide economic support for Greece, where British troops had helped return a royal government-in-exile to power by overcoming communist-led resistance forces in 1945. Since then, a new guerrilla movement, supported by the communist governments of Yugoslavia and Albania, was threatening what it described as Greece's "monarcho-fascist regime".

That March, Truman replied. In terms designed to accentuate public fear of a communist terror stalking the world, he persuaded Congress to grant military aid to Greece and Turkey. His administration did not know, or would not acknowledge, that Stalin had tried and failed to prevent Yugoslavia from helping the rebels, precisely because he knew it would be impossible for the West to allow their only base in the Balkans to be taken.

In the course of his address to Congress, the President enunciated what came to be known as the Truman Doctrine: "that it must be the policy of the United States to support free peoples who are resisting attempted subjugation by armed minorities or by outside pressures."

Believing that the economic chaos crippling western Europe was giving the Communists a chance to advance their cause, Truman's advisers were convinced that massive American aid was the only way to forestall the danger. In March 1947, Secretary of State George Marshall presented the European Recovery Plan, better known as the Marshall Plan, as a package of economic aid offered equally to all states that applied for it. But applicants had to open their doors to outside scrutiny to determine the extent of their needs, and Stalin, who condemned the plan as an attack upon national sovereignty, refused to allow any Eastern bloc countries to participate. Czechoslovakia was warned not to apply for Marshall Plan aid, and when it did, Stalin exploited a Czech communist coup in February 1948 to put an end to its existing coalition government, which was replaced by a solidly pro-Soviet regime. Pointing to the coup as one more proof of Soviet plans to swallow the remaining free nations of Europe, Truman succeeded in getting Congress to reintroduce conscription, and moves were undertaken for organizing the collective defence of the West.

Faced with the prospect of a unified Western front, Stalin felt nothing was to be gained by prolonging any illusion of cooperation between the blocs. In a bid to compel the U.S., Britain and France to abandon their aim to create a prosperous West German state out of their zones of occupation, he decided to blockade Berlin. The city was divided into four sectors administered by the wartime Allies and France, but it was located at the end of a 150-kilometre-long road and rail corridor deep within the Soviet zone. In June 1948, five days after the Western powers announced currency reforms to help revive

Germany's shattered economy, the Sov-ets declared that all traffic in and out of West Berlin was to be suspended.

The city was saved by a 10-month air-lift of supplies, during which British and American aircraft flew in everything from coal to new-fangled antibiotics. Stalin's efforts to halt the revival of Germany had failed, but the polarization of Europe was now formally acknowledged. In May 1949, the month the blockade ended, the West German state was founded, and in October the German Democratic Repub-lic (East Germany) came into being. The acute threat of war had already, in April 1949, brought Canada and most of the western European countries into a com-mon defensive policy – the North Atlantic Treaty Organization, NATO – under U.S. leadership. Even before then, during the Berlin crisis, American B-29s reportedly capable of delivering atomic bombs had flown into Britain, and a year later the United States asked for permission to es-tablish permanent bases of their own on British soil – a request that the British government granted without first seeking parliamentary approval.

In his dealings with the Soviet Union, Truman had been emboldened by the United States' monopoly of the nuclear bomb, but on September 23, 1949, he was obliged to announce that the Soviets had successfully performed their first nuclear test explosion. In Europe, the Cold War had reached an equilibrium of sorts, but the conflict shifted elsewhere – to China, where the Chinese Communists had suc-cessfully ousted the Nationalist govern-ment of Chiang Kai-shek, and to Korea where, in June 1950, the smouldering ani-mosity between Western democracy and communism finally ignited in open war.

West Berliners watch a C-54 transporter coming in to land with supplies for their city. In an attempt to drive the Western powers out of the German capital, the Soviets mounted a blockade, cutting off supplies for two million citizens. Rather than abandon the city, which lay 150 kilometres inside the Soviet zone, the Western Allies mounted a relief operation by air. Start-ing on June 25, 1948, they had airlifted over 1.5 million tonnes of goods into Berlin by May 12, 1949, when the Soviets, acknowledging that their siege had failed, reopened rail and road links to the West.

	1925-1930	1930-1935	1935-1940
EUROPE	Adolf Hitler reorganizes the German Nazi party and publishes the first volume of *Mein Kampf* (1925). Nazis win their first seats in the Reichstag, Germany's Parliament (1928). Joseph Stalin launches the first Five-Year Plan in the Soviet Union and orders the collectivization of Soviet agriculture (1928). Leon Trotsky, a leader of the Russian Revolution and an opponent of Stalin's policies, is expelled from the Soviet Union (1929).	Unemployment in Germany rises to four million. In elections, Nazis win 107 seats from the centre parties (1930). Field Marshal Paul von Hindenburg beats Hitler in German presidential elections, but in the Reichstag elections Nazis become the largest party with 230 seats (1932). Hitler is appointed German chancellor and is later granted dictatorial powers through the Enabling Law (1933). Italy's dictator, Benito Mussolini, meets Hitler in Venice (1934). Stalin uses the assassination of Leningrad Communist party chief Sergei Kirov as a pretext to instigate a purge of political rivals (1934).	Hitler defies the Versailles Treaty by reintroducing compulsory military service (1935). The Nazi government introduces the Nuremberg Laws depriving German Jews of their citizenship (1935). Italian troops invade Ethiopia (1935). German troops occupy the Rhineland (1936). The Spanish Civil War begins (1936). Six months after annexing Austria to the German Reich, Hitler occupies Czech border regions (1938). Hitler and Stalin sign a nonaggression pact (1939). Britain and France declare war on Germany, two days after the German invasion of Poland (1939).
CHINA, JAPAN AND THE PACIFIC	Sun Yat-sen, republican revolutionary and leader of the Guomindang, or Nationalist party, dies (1925). Chiang Kai-shek is named commander in chief of the National Revolutionary Army, a joint Guomindang and Chinese Communist force formed to defeat China's warlords (1925). Guomindang troops and right-wing sympathizers turn on Communists in Shanghai, beginning a wholesale purge of the Left in China (1927). Chiang Kai-shek is elected president of China (1928).	Chiang Kai-shek attacks Communist bases in southern China (1930). Japanese forces set up a puppet state in Manchuria (1932). Japan, criticized for its expansionist policies in China, leaves the League of Nations (1933). Threatened by Chiang Kai-shek's Nationalist forces, the main body of Chinese Communists breaks out of their base in southern China, beginning the Long March to the province of Shaanxi. During the year-long trek, Mao Zedong is established as chairman of the party (1934).	A shooting incident near Beijing leads to the Sino-Japanese War. The Japanese seize Beijing, Shanghai and the Nationalist capital, Nanjing (1937). Chiang establishes a wartime capital at Chongqing, in Sichuan province (1937).
THE UNITED STATES	Herbert Hoover, Republican, is elected U.S. president (1928). New York's Wall Street stock market crashes, triggering a collapse of confidence in the financial market and an economic slump that gradually deepens into a global depression (1929).	President Hoover approves the imposition of high tariff barriers intended to shield the U.S. economy from foreign competition (1930). Franklin D. Roosevelt wins the U.S. presidential election in a Democratic landslide (1932). America protests against Japanese aggression in Manchuria (1932). With unemployment at 13 million, President Roosevelt approves a programme of public works known as the "New Deal" (1933).	President Roosevelt signs the U.S. Social Security Act (1935). Roosevelt is re-elected president on a "no war" ticket (1936). Roosevelt boosts the defence budget, and demands assurances from Hitler and Mussolini that they will not attack 31 named states (1939). After Britain and France declare war on Germany, Roosevelt declares the U.S. officially neutral while making it clear that American sympathies are with the Allies (1939).
INDIA, NORTH AFRICA AND THE MIDDLE EAST	Great Britain appoints an all-British commission to recommend steps towards Indian self-government (1927). Arabs attack Jews in Palestine following sectarian disputes in Jerusalem (1929).	Mahatma Gandhi pledges the Indian National Congress to complete Indian independence and launches a campaign of civil disobedience intended to make the country ungovernable (1930).	Muslims in Palestine stage an Arab revolt against the British authorities' refusal to end Jewish immigration (1936). The British government publishes a white paper – a policy statement – suggesting an independent Palestine with an Arab majority and proposing limitations on continued Jewish immigration (1939).

A Chronology of Major Events: AD 1925-1950

1940-1945

1945-1950

In a three-month period, Germany conquers Denmark, Norway, the Low Countries and France, but abandons its planned invasion of Britain after the German Luftwaffe fails to destroy the Royal Air Force (1940).

In contravention of Hitler's pact with Stalin, German troops invade the Soviet Union, approaching Moscow before Soviet counterattacks halt the German advance (1941).

Germany and Italy declare war on the United States (1941).

Regular British bomber raids on Germany begin (1942).

The survivors of the German Sixth Army surrender after a five-month battle for Stalingrad (1943).

The battle for Kursk, the largest armoured clash in history, ends with a German withdrawal and a massive Soviet offensive (1943).

An invasion of Sicily is followed by Allied landings in mainland Italy (1943).

Operation *Overlord*, the Western Allies' campaign for the liberation of Europe, begins with a full-scale invasion of Normandy (1944).

German officers who want to end the war make an unsuccessful attempt on Hitler's life (1944).

Paris and Brussels are liberated (1944).

A week after Hitler commits suicide in Berlin, the Germans sign an unconditional surrender (1945).

Winston Churchill makes the first public reference to the Iron Curtain (1946).

General George Marshall, appointed U.S. secretary of state, calls for a European economic recovery programme – the Marshall Plan – as a means of countering Soviet influence in Europe (1947).

Stalin lifts a 10-month Soviet blockade of Berlin intended to thwart Western plans for the economic recovery of Germany. The country is then divided into democratic West Germany and communist East Germany (1949).

The Soviet Union successfully detonates its first atomic weapon (1949).

The Japanese set up a Chinese puppet government at Nanjing (1940).

Japan signs a tripartite pact with Germany and Italy (1940).

Japan attacks the American Pacific naval base at Pearl Harbor, Hawaii, and simultaneously attacks the Philippines, Hong Kong and Malaya (1941).

In a campaign lasting only 100 days, Japan captures Singapore, the Burmese capital Rangoon, and the Dutch East Indies (1942).

At the battles of the Coral Sea and Midway, American naval forces break Japan's run of successes (1942).

U.S. landings in the Solomon Islands mark the beginning of an island-hopping offensive against Japan (1942).

Japan renews its offensive in China. The U.S. launches the first bombing raids on Japan from China (1944).

U.S. landings in the Philippines are followed by the Battle of Leyte Gulf, in which much of the Japanese navy is destroyed (1944).

In the space of four days, the U.S. drop atomic bombs on Hiroshima and Nagasaki, and the Soviet Union declares war on Japan, which capitulates one week later (1945).

Civil war breaks out between Chinese Nationalists and Communists (1946).

After the Chinese Communist defeat of the Nationalists, Mao Zedong announces the establishment of the People's Republic of China, and the remnants of Chiang Kai-shek's Guomindang government retreat to the island of Taiwan (1949).

The U.S. places an embargo on sales of scrap iron and war materials to Japan (1940).

President Roosevelt, re-elected for a third term, signs the Lend-Lease Bill, enabling Great Britain to obtain American war materials in return for a promise of payment after the war (1941).

A day after the Japanese raid on Pearl Harbor, the United States declares war on Japan (1941).

The "Manhattan Project" of intensive atomic research begins (1941).

As the "arsenal of democracy", the United States produces 40 per cent of the world's armaments (1944).

Roosevelt is elected for a fourth term as president of the United States, with Harry Truman as vice president (1944).

At a conference in Washington, discussions are held on the establishment of the United Nations, to take the place of the League of Nations (1944).

President Roosevelt dies and is succeeded as U.S. president by Harry Truman (1945).

Scientists of the Manhattan Project carry out a successful atomic test explosion (1945).

The U.S. Congress passes the Marshall Plan, approving $17 billion in aid for Europe (1948).

Harry Truman is elected U.S. president (1948).

The North Atlantic Treaty – a mutual defence pact between North American and western European countries – is signed in Washington (1949).

The creation of a separate Muslim state – Pakistan – becomes the official policy of India's Muslim League (1940).

After Italian forces in North Africa are routed by the British, the German Afrika Korps commanded by General Erwin Rommel launches a successful counteroffensive (1941).

Axis forces are defeated at the Battle of El Alamein, and the Allies make landings in Morocco and Algeria (1942).

The Indian Congress confronts the British government with a "Quit India" policy, and many of its leaders are arrested and imprisoned (1942).

The first authenticated reports of the Nazis' systematic slaughter of European Jews convinces many Zionists that only by establishing their own independent state in Palestine can they enjoy peace and security (1942).

Defeat of the Axis forces in North Africa paves the way for an Allied invasion of Italy (1943).

Rioting and killings follow Muslim League calls for a separate state (1946).

India is proclaimed independent and partitioned into mainly Hindu India and predominantly Muslim Pakistan (1947).

Britain announces that it will hand over its trusteeship of Palestine to the United Nations, which announces plans for the partition of the country into Arab and Jewish areas (1947).

Jewish leaders in Palestine proclaim the state of Israel (1948).

BIBLIOGRAPHY

WORLD WAR II

Bailey, Ronald H., and the Editors of Time-Life Books, *The Air War in Europe* (World War II series). Amsterdam: Time-Life Books, 1979.

Bauer, Lt-Colonel E., *The History of World War II*. London: Orbis, 1979.

Bell, P.M.H., *The Origins of the Second World War*. London: Longman, 1986.

Bergamini, David, *Japan's Imperial Conspiracy*. London: Heinemann, 1971.

Bleuel, Hans Peter, *Strength Through Joy*. Transl. by J. Maxwell Brownjohn. London: Secker & Warburg, 1973.

Briggs, Susan, *Keep Smiling Through*. London: Weidenfeld & Nicolson/Book Club Associates, 1975.

Bullock, Alan, *Hitler: A Study in Tyranny*. Harmondsworth, Middlesex: Penguin, 1962.

Calvocoressi, Peter, and Guy Wint, *Total War*. London: Allen Lane, 1972.

Carr, Raymond, *Images of the Spanish Civil War*. London/Sydney: George Allen & Unwin, 1986.

Ciano, G.:
Ciano's Diary 1937-1938. London: Methuen, 1952.
Ciano's Diary 1939-1943. London: Heinemann, 1947.

Collier, Basil, *Japan at War*. London: Purnell Book Services/Sidgwick & Jackson, Book Club Edition, 1975.

Collier, Richard, and the Editors of Time-Life Books, *The War in the Desert* (World War II series). Amsterdam: Time-Life Books, 1977.

Davidson, Eugene, *The Making of Adolf Hitler*. London: Macdonald and Jane's, 1978.

Deighton, Len, *Blitzkrieg: From the Rise of Hitler to the Fall of Dunkirk*. London: Jonathan Cape, 1979.

Deutscher, Isaac, *The Great Purges*. Oxford/New York: Basil Blackwell, 1984.

Elson, Robert T., and the Editors of Time-Life Books, *Prelude to War* (World War II series). Amsterdam: Time-Life Books, 1977.

Fest, Joachim C., *Hitler*. London: Weidenfeld & Nicolson, 1973.

Goralski, Robert, *World War II Almanac: 1931-1945*. London: Hamish Hamilton, 1981.

Grunberger, Richard, *A Social History of the Third Reich*. Harmondsworth, Middlesex: Penguin, 1974.

Grunfeld, Frederic V., *The Hitler File: A Social History of Germany and the Nazis 1918-45*. London: Weidenfeld & Nicolson, 1974.

Hastings, Max, *Bomber Command*. London: Michael Joseph, 1979.

Hingley, Ronald, *Joseph Stalin: Man and Legend*. London: Hutchinson, 1974.

Hyde, H. Montgomery, *Stalin: The History of a Dictator*. London: Rupert Hart-Davis, 1971.

Irving, David, *The War Path: Hitler's Germany 1933-1939*. London: Michael Joseph, 1978.

Jackson, W.G.F., *The Battle for Italy*. London: Batsford, 1967.

Jones, R.V., *Most Secret War*. London: Hamish Hamilton, 1978.

Kee, Robert, *We'll Meet Again*. London/Melbourne: J. M. Dent, 1984.

Keegan, John, *Six Armies in Normandy*. London: Jonathan Cape, 1982.

Kurzman, Dan, *Day of the Bomb*. London: Weidenfeld & Nicolson, 1986.

Lewin, Ronald, *Rommel as Military Commander*. London/Princeton, New Jersey: Batsford/Van Nostrand Reinhold, 1968.

Liddell Hart, B.H., *The Other Side of the Hill*. London: Cassell, 1948.

Lowe, C.J., and F. Marzari, *Italian Foreign Policy 1870-1940*. London: Routledge, 1975.

Ludwig, E., *Talks with Mussolini*. London: G. Allen & Unwin, 1932.

Macintyre, Donald, *The Battle of the Atlantic*. London: Batsford, 1961.

Mack Smith, D.:
Mussolini. London: Weidenfeld & Nicolson, 1982.
Mussolini's Roman Empire. London: Longman, 1976.

Matanle, Ivor, *The Hitler Years: A Photographic Documentary*. Leicester: Galley Press, 1984.

Middlebrook, Martin:
Convoy. London: Allen Lane, 1976.
The Nuremberg Raid 30-31 March 1944. London: Allen Lane, 1973.

Milward, Alan S., *War, Economy and Society 1939-1945*. London: Allen Lane, 1977.

Mrázková, Daniela, and Vladimír Remeš, eds., *The Russian War: 1941-1945*. London: Jonathan Cape, 1978.

O'Neill, Robert John, *The German Army and the Nazi Party 1933-1939*. London: Cassell, 1966.

Pryce-Jones, David, *Paris in The Third Reich*. London: Collins, 1981.

Rauschning, Hermann, *Hitler Speaks*. London: Thornton Butterworth, 1939.

Read, Anthony, and David Fisher, *The Deadly Embrace: Hitler, Stalin and the* Nazi-Soviet Pact 1939-1941. London: Michael Joseph, 1988.

Reynolds, Clark G., *The Fast Carriers: The Forging of an Air Navy*. New York: McGraw-Hill, 1968.

Rutherford, Ward, *Hitler's Propaganda Machine*. London: Bison Books, 1978.

Seaton, Albert, *The Fall of Fortress Europe 1943-1945*. London: Batsford, 1981.

Shaw, John, and the Editors of Time-Life Books, *Red Army Resurgent* (World War II series). Amsterdam: Time-Life Books, 1971.

Shirer, William L., *The Rise and Fall of the Third Reich*. London: Secker & Warburg, 1960.

Simons, Gerald, and the Editors of Time-Life Books, *Victory in Europe* (World War II series). Amsterdam: Time-Life Books, 1982.

Steinberg, Rafael, and the Editors of Time-Life Books:
Island Fighting (World War II series). Amsterdam: Time-Life Books, 1978.
Return to the Philippines (World War II series). Alexandria, Virginia: Time-Life Books, 1979.

Taylor, A.J.P., *The War Lords*. London: Hamish Hamilton, 1977.

Toland, John, *Hitler: The Pictorial Documentary of His Life*. London: Hutchinson, 1979.

Trevor-Roper, Hugh, *The Last Days of Hitler*. London: Macmillan, 1947.

Werth, Alexander, *Russia at War*. London: Hamish Hamilton, 1946.

Willmott, H.P., *June 1944*. Poole, Dorset: Blandford, 1984.

Wiskemann, Elizabeth, *Fascism in Italy: Its Development and Influence*. London/New York: Macmillan/St. Martin's Press, 1969.

Zhukov, Georgy K., *The Memoirs of Marshal Zhukov.* London: Jonathan Cape, 1971.
Zich, Arthur, and the Editors of Time-Life Books, *The Rising Sun* (World War II series). Amsterdam: Time-Life Books, 1977.
Ziemke, Earl F., and the Editors of Time-Life Books, *The Soviet Juggernaut* (World War II series). Amsterdam: Time-Life Books, 1980.

INDIA
Brown, J.M.:
Gandhi's Rise to Power: Indian Politics 1915-1922. Cambridge: Cambridge University Press, 1972.
Gandhi and Civil Disobedience: The Mahatma in Indian Politics 1928-1934. Cambridge: Cambridge University Press, 1977.
Modern India: The Origins of an Asian Democracy. Oxford: Oxford University Press, 1985.
Collins, Larry, and Dominique Lapierre, *Freedom at Midnight.* London: Collins, 1975.
Copley, Antony, *Gandhi: against the tide.* Oxford: Basil Blackwell, 1987.
Edwardes, Michael, *The Last Years of British India.* London: Cassell, 1963.
Fischer, Louis, *The Life of Mahatma Gandhi.* London: Grafton, 1982.
Golant, William, *The Long Afternoon: British India 1601-1947.* London: Hamish Hamilton, 1975.
Gopal, Ram, *How India Struggled for Freedom.* Bombay: The Book Centre (Private) Ltd., distributed in London by Frederick Muller, 1967.
Hardy, Peter, *The Muslims of British India.* Cambridge: Cambridge University Press, 1972.
Nehru, Jawahir-lal, *The Discovery of India.* London: Meridian Books, 1946.
Pandey, Bishwa N., *The Break-up of British India.* London/New York: Macmillan/St. Martin's Press, 1969.
Payne, Robert, *The Life and Death of Mahatma Gandhi.* London: The Bodley Head, 1969.
Spear, P., *A History of India, Vol. II.* London: Pelican, 1965, revised 1979.

CHINA
Fairbank, John King, *The Great Chinese Revolution 1800-1985.* New York: Harper & Row, 1986.
Fairbank, John King, and Denis Twitchett, general eds., *The Cambridge History of China,* Vols. 12 and 13. Cambridge: Cambridge University Press, 1983 and 1986.
Fitzgerald, C.P., *The Birth of Communist China.* London: Penguin, 1964.
Guillermaz, Jacques, *A History of the Chinese Communist Party 1921-1949.* London: Methuen, 1968.
Griffith, Samuel, *The Chinese People's Liberation Army.* London: Weidenfeld & Nicolson, 1968.
Han Suyin, *The Morning Deluge.* London: Jonathan Cape, 1972.
Harrison, James Pinckney, *The Long March to Power.* London: Macmillan, 1973.
Liu, F.F., *A Military History of Modern China, 1924-1949.* Princeton, New Jersey: Princeton University Press, 1956.
O'Neill, Hugh B., *Companion to Chinese History.* New York/Oxford: Facts on File Publications, 1987.
Payne, Pierre Stephen Robert, *Mao Tse-tung.* New York/Oxford: Weybright & Talley, 1969.
Rodzinski, Witold, *The Walled Kingdom.* London: Fontana Press, 1984.
Salisbury, Harrison E.:
China: 100 Years of Revolution. London: André Deutsch, 1983.
The Long March: The Untold Story. London: Macmillan, 1985.
Snow, Edgar:
Scorched Earth. London: Victor Gollancz, 1941.
Red Star Over China. London: Victor Gollancz, 1968.
Wilson, Dick, *The Long March 1935.* London: Hamish Hamilton, 1971.

GENERAL
The American Heritage History of the 20's and 30's by the Editors of *American Heritage* magazine. New York: American Heritage Publishing Co., 1970.
Beales, H.L., and R. S. Lambert, *Memoirs of the Unemployed.* London: Victor Gollancz, 1934.
Bullock, Alan, ed., *The Twentieth Century.* London: Thames and Hudson, 1971.
Byers, Anthony, *Centenary of Service: A History of Electricity in the Home.* London: The Electricity Council, 1981.
Dimbleby, David, and David Reynolds, *An Ocean Apart.* London/Sydney/Auckland/Toronto: BBC Books/Hodder & Stoughton, 1988.
Forty, Adrian, *Objects of Desire: Design and Society 1750-1980.* London: Thames and Hudson, 1986.
Galbraith, John Kenneth, *The Great Crash 1929.* London: Hamish Hamilton, 1955.
Gordon, Bob, *Early Electrical Appliances.* Aylesbury, Buckinghamshire: Shire Publications, 1984.
Mitchell, Broadus, *Depression Decade: From New Era through New Deal 1929-1941,* Vol. IX of *The Economic History of the United States.* New York: Holt, Rinehart and Winston, 1966.
Sontag, Raymond J., *A Broken World, 1919-1939.* New York: Harper & Row, 1971.
Sparke, Penny, *Electrical Appliances.* London/Sydney: Unwin Hyman, 1987.
Taylor, A.J.P., and J. M. Roberts, eds., *History of the 20th Century.* London: Purnell, 1968.

ACKNOWLEDGEMENTS

The following materials have been reprinted with the kind permission of the publishers: Page 52: "Hitler always faces me . . . " in *Ciano's Diary, 1939-43,* by G. Ciano, London: Heinemann, 1947. Page 152 and page 154: "Night marching is wonderful . . ." and "The army watched breathlessly . . ." in *The Great Road: The Life and Times of Chu Teh,* by Agnes Smedley, New York: Monthly Review Press, 1956.
The editors wish to thank the following individuals and institutions for their valuable assistance in the preparation of this volume:
England: Cambridge – Dr. Orlando Figes, Trinity College; Mike Kerrigan; Dr. David Reynolds, Christ's College. Cumbria – Carolyn Johnson, Holker Hall. Dorking, Surrey – Jon Kimche. London – Diana Condell and Ray Allen, Department of Exhibits and Firearms, Imperial War Museum; Dr. Ray Earwicker, Assistant Secretary, Trades Union Congress; Judith Heaton; Kate Poole; Dr. Penny Spark, Senior Lecturer, Department of Cultural History, Royal College of Art; Deborah Thompson; Gerald L. Wells, Curator, Vintage Wireless Museum; David Woodcock, Curator, Department of Engineering, Science Museum. Tonbridge, Kent – John Norris, Curator, and Cyril Botterill, Museum Assistant, Milne Museum (South Eastern Electricity Board). Wimborne, Dorset – John Batchelor.
France: Paris – François Avril, Curateur, Département des Manuscrits, Bibliothèque Nationale; Jeannette Chalufour, Archives Tallandier; Michel Fleury, Président de la IV section de l'École pratique des haute études; Serge-Antoine Legrand, Maisons-Alfort.
Japan: Tokyo – Mieko Ikeda.
U.S.A.: Washington – Larry Sherer.

The index for this volume was prepared by Ann Marangos.

INDEX

Numerals in italics indicate an illustration of the subject mentioned.

D

E

F

G

H

I

J

K

L

M

N

O

P

PICTURE CREDITS

The sources for the illustrations that appear in this book are listed below. Credits from left to right are separated by semi-colons; from top to bottom they are separated by dashes.

Cover: The Hulton-Deutsch Collection, London; Popperfoto, London; Ullstein Bilderdienst, West Berlin. **2, 3:** Maps by Gray and Stuart, London. **9:** John Frost Newspapers, New Barnet, Herts. **10, 11:** Bilderdienst Süddeutscher Verlag, Munich; Library of Congress, Washington D.C. (2) **12, 13:** The Hulton-Deutsch Collection, London; Chicago Historical Society, Chicago, DN C 8769. **14:** The Hulton-Deutsch Collection, London. **16, 17:** Maps by Alan Hollingbery. **18:** Alfred Eisenstaedt for *LIFE.* **19, 20:** Farabolafoto, Milan. **22:** Trustees of the Imperial War Museum, London. **23:** Derek Bayes, London/Trustees of the Imperial War Museum, London. **24, 25:** Presseillustrationen Heinrich R. Hoffmann, Munich. **26:** Trustees of the Imperial War Museum, London. **27:** Derek Bayes, London/ Trustees of the Imperial War Museum, London. **28:** Alfred Eisenstaedt for *LIFE.* **29:** Popperfoto, London. **30, 31:** Derek Bayes, London/Trustees of the Imperial War Museum, London. **34, 35:** Presseillustrationen Heinrich R. Hoffmann, Munich; Trustees of the Imperial War Museum, London. **36, 37:** Wiener Library, London (2) – The Hulton-Deutsch Collection, London. **38:** The Hulton-Deutsch Collection, London. **39:** UPI/ Bettmann Newsphotos, New York. **41:** Photo Oronoz, Madrid/Archivo Historico Militar, Madrid. **42:** The Hulton-Deutsch Collection, London. **43:** Czechoslovak News Agency (CTK), Prague. **44:** Popperfoto, London. **45:** Low cartoon/Solo Agency, London, courtesy of the Cartoon Study Centre, University of Kent at Canterbury. **46:** Colorific, London. **47:** Robert Hunt Library, London. **49:** Popperfoto, London. **50:** Trustees of the Imperial War Museum, London. **53, 54:** David King Collection, London. **55:** David King Collection, London; Novosti Press Agency, London. **56-57:** David King Collection, London. **58, 59:** David King Collection, London; Popperfoto, London. **60:** Dmitri Baltermants/Magnum, London. **62, 63:** Maps by Alan Hollingbery. **64:** The Hulton-Deutsch Collection, London. **66:** Robert Hunt Library, London. **67:** Clem Albers/National Archives, Washington D.C., No. 210-G2-A6. **68:** Giancarlo Costa, Milan. **69:** Popperfoto, London. **70:** Map by Alan Hollingbery – Novosti Press Agency, London. **72, 73:** Sovfoto, New York; The Hulton-Deutsch Collection, London; Peter Fischer, courtesy of Lotte Fischer, Cologne; Popperfoto, London. **74:** Popperfoto, London. **76, 77:** Trustees of the Imperial War Museum, London; Diagram based on "Convoy. The Battle for Convoys, SC. 122 and HX. 229" by Martin Middlebrook, Allen Lane, 1976. **78, 79:** Novosti, Rome. **80, 81:** Art by Roger Stewart; U.S. Army Photo. **82:** The Hulton-Deutsch Collection, London/ Bettmann Archive, New York. **83:** Trustees of the Imperial War Museum, London. **84:** Robert Capa/Magnum, London. **85:** The Hulton-Deutsch Collection, London/Bettmann Archive, New York. **86, 87:** Popperfoto, London. **89:** Trustees of the Imperial War Museum, London. **90, 91:** Tass from Sovfoto, New York. **93:** USAF Photographic Collection, National Air and Space Museum, Smithsonian Institute, Washington D.C. – Map by Alan Hollingbery. **94:** Topham Picture Library, London. **95:** Al Freni for *LIFE,* © Time Inc. **96:** Derek Bayes, London/ Trustees of the Imperial War Museum, London – The Hulton-Deutsch Collection, London (2). **98:** The Hulton-Deutsch Collection, London. **99:** The Hulton-Deutsch Collection, London/Bettmann Archive, New York. **100:** Alfred Eisenstaedt for *LIFE,* © Time Inc. **101:** Henri Cartier-Bresson/Magnum, London. **103:** David Douglas Duncan for *LIFE.* **105:** Britain/Israel Public Affairs Centre, London. **106:** The Associated Press, London. **108:** Map by Alan Hollingbery. **110:** Weidenfeld & Nicolson Ltd., London. **112:** The Hulton-Deutsch Collection, London. **113:** National Gandhi Museum, New Delhi. **115:** AP/Wide World Photos, New York. **116-119:** Margaret Bourke-White for *LIFE.* **120:** Topham Picture Library, London. **122, 123:** The Associated Press, London. **124, 125:** Henri Cartier-Bresson/Magnum, London. **127:** Hunnar Stronachs Limited, Bombay. **129:** The Electricity Council, London. **130:** Copied by Larry Sherer, Baltimore, Maryland/ National Archives, Washington D.C., No. 33-S-4849C – T.V. Radiocorriere, Rome – Courtesy of Vintage Wireless Museum, West Dulwich, London; Culver Pictures, New York. **131:** Ullstein Bilderdienst, West Berlin – Culver Pictures, New York – Erich Lessing, Vienna/City of Vienna Library – Reproduced by permission of *Punch,* London; Derek Bayes, London/Milne Museum, Tonbridge, Kent. **132:** Photo Mayo, Tyne and Wear, courtesy of Zanussi Collection/Holker Hall, Cumbria – AEG, Frankfurt – Derek Bayes, London/Milne Museum, Tonbridge, Kent (2). **133:** Derek Bayes, London/Milne Museum, Tonbridge, Kent; Culver Pictures, New York – Erich Lessing, Vienna/City of Vienna Library – Derek Bayes, London/Milne Museum, Tonbridge, Kent. **134:** Xinhua News Agency, London. **136:** Map by Alan Hollingbery. **137:** Camera Press Limited, London. **138:** Roger-Viollet, Paris. **140:** From *Half the World* by Arnold Toynbee, Thames & Hudson Ltd., London, 1973. **141:** Popperfoto, London. **142, 143:** Mainichi Shimbun, Tokyo. **144:** Map by Alan Hollingbery; Eastfoto, New York. **146, 147:** Wu Yinxian/Magnum, London, except upper middle, Popperfoto, London. **149:** Ullstein Bilderdienst, West Berlin. **150:** Robert Capa/Magnum Photos, London. **153:**National Archives, Washington D.C., No. 11-SC-231265. **154:** Jack Wilkes for *LIFE,* © Time Inc. **157:** Associated Press, London. **158, 159:** Henri Cartier-Bresson/Magnum, London. **161:** Jim Burke for *LIFE.* **163:** Magnum, London. **165:** Map by Alan Hollingbery. **167:** Henri Ries, July 1948/Bildarchiv Preussischer Kulturbesitz, West Berlin.

Typeset by A.J. Latham Limited, Dunstable, Bedfordshire.
Printed and bound by Brepols S.A. - Turnhout, Belgium.
Colour separations by Fotolitomec, S.N.C., Milan, Italy.